BUSINESS

UNDERSTANDING

AND AGILITY

SUPPORTED BY

ASSISTED INTELLIGENCE

MICHAEL H. BRACKETT

115 Linda Vista
Sedona, AZ 86336 USA
https://www.TechnicsPub.com

Cover design by Lorena Molinari

First Printing 2021

Copyright © 2021 by Michael H. Brackett

ISBN, print ed.	9781634629744
ISBN, Kindle ed.	9781634629751
ISBN, ePub ed.	9781634629768
ISBN, PDF ed.	9781634629775

Library of Congress Control Number: 2021946173

Dedicated to all the professionals that want to make a real difference!

CONTENTS AT A GLANCE

CONTENTS

FIGURES

PREFACE

Most public and private sector organizations are facing a huge, and rapidly increasing, disparity in their business data and processes. That disparity results in decreased business understanding, which increases uncertainty about the organization's business. Any increase in uncertainty about the organization's business decreases the organization's agility and increases the probability of a less than successful business operation.

Increasing business understanding decreases uncertainty, increases agility, and increases the probability of a successful business operation. Increasing business understanding requires an overarching construct for business understanding and agility, with an underlying foundation of theories, concepts, principles, and techniques to create and maintain that construct. It also requires a formal business culture oriented toward thorough business understanding and agility.

I started on a professional venture over 60 years ago, building simulation models for timber stands and water resources. I encountered many problems understanding the data and the algorithms – processes – used in the simulations. That lack of understanding increased uncertainty and resulted in poor simulations. I decided to tackle those problems and develop formal data and processes for simulations. That decision led to a long professional venture improving both data resource management and processes resource management that lead toward a thorough business understanding.

I could have titled the book *Business Architecture*, but many books, articles, and presentations contain the word *architecture*, which gets into the current turmoil of an undefined and confusing term with little chance of resolution. That term has many different concepts, strategies for development, and formats for presentation, often depending on the orientation and agenda of the promotor.

Architecture books don't sell well today. The reason is that an architecture is the means to an end objective, not the end objective itself. The end objective is the acquisition, storage, retrieval, and use of a thorough business understanding for agile business operation. The means to that end objective is the creation and maintenance of an overarching construct with an underlying foundation of theories, concepts, principles, and techniques.

I could have titled the book *Business Decisions*, or *Successful Business Operation*, or a variety of other titles, but those titles don't get to the heart of the problem – thorough business understanding. *Business understanding* must be in the title. However, business understanding must lead an organization in some direction, other than understanding for understanding's sake. That direction is the ability for an organization to be agile in an increasingly dynamic business environment.

It's the agility resulting from a thorough understanding that leads to business success. Therefore, the title is ***Business Understanding and Agility***. The theme is to create and maintain a single, formal, comprehensive, overarching construct for an organization to thoroughly understand its business, so it can be agile to readily adapt to changes, and be successful.

You probably noticed the subtitle ***Supported by Assisted Intelligence*** and wondered what that meant. Did I mean artificial intelligence?

Well, yes and no. Artificial intelligence today covers a wide range of topics from decision support systems, to robotics and diagnostics, to learning machines, to machines taking over the world and destroying mankind. I want to avoid those perceptions, but I also want to emphasize that computers can be brought to bear on the task of thoroughly understanding and organization's business so it can be agile and successful.

The theories, concepts, principles, and techniques for creating and maintaining a thorough business understanding are well-established. The intelligence to use those theories, concepts, principles, and techniques is readily available. The problem is that most public and private sector organizations today are not using that intelligence, for whatever reason – and I've heard many reasons. The result is rampant disparity in the business understanding, with impacts, often severe, on the organization's business.

I use *assisted intelligence* to emphasize the intelligence that already exists today to provide automated support for the creation and maintenance of a thorough business understanding. Organizations don't need to wait for evolving artificial intelligence technology. Organizations don't need to wait for another organization to develop artificial intelligence technology which they can purchase. Most organization can use assisted intelligence, today, within their own organization, based on their own goals, objectives, and policies.

An organization's business understanding is contained in its data resource and processes resource. Those two resources are the starting point for a formal overarching construct to thoroughly understand an organization's business and allow the organization to be agile and successful in its business operation.

From 2011 through 2016, I wrote a series of six books in the Data Resource Simplexity series.[1] The first three books are oriented toward Data

---

[1] Refer to the Bibliography for books in the Data Resource Simplexity series.

Resource Architecture and the last three books are oriented toward Data Resource Understanding. The Data Resource Simplexity series of books describes the theories, concept, principles, and techniques for thoroughly understanding and managing an organization's data resource, integrating disparate data into a single organization-wide data resource of comparate data, and documenting that data resource so the organization at large can thoroughly understand its data and use those data to support the business.

Over the years, I collected a plethora of miscellaneous notes containing ideas, thoughts, comments, complaints, suggestions, and criticisms about data and processes resource management. Those notes were about how data and processes could be formally managed, if an organization were to do it right from the beginning, and keep doing it right. Those notes were in addition to the material I published in the Data Resource Simplexity series of books.

I needed a way to present these miscellaneous notes, in an organized form, to get the message across that data and processes could be formally managed, and their management could be integrated to directly support an organization's business. I decided to present the material through a group of professionals that meet at an international conference, and begin complaining about the sad state of data and processes management in most organizations. The complaints evolve into a series of discussions where the professionals present their separate thoughts.

From 2106 through 2018, I wrote a series of three speculative business fiction books that describe how data and processes could be managed as a single, combined, critical resource of an organization. [2] The material is based on existing business fact, is speculative business fiction today, but could become future business fact with minimal effort and huge benefits.

The series begins with an understanding of the business niche where an organization operates, and progresses through a formal Business Cycle, a formal Data Resource Cycle, and a formal Processes Resource Cycle. The series progresses through formal data resource management, formal processes resource management, and the integration of data and processes as a single, combined, critical resource that provides a thorough business understanding.

The feedback I received from that series of books was distinctly bimodal. The feedback was either *Spot-on*, or *Who the H do you think you are?* Very few comments fell between those two extremes.

I refined the material and prepared a series of e-learning classes for Data & Processes Resource Management that described the problems with traditional data and processes management, and the formal management of data and processes for an organization. The feedback I received from that

---

[2] Refer to Bibliography for the Speculative Business Fiction books.

series was again bimodal, the same as the feedback from the Speculative Business Fiction books.

I felt I had a fresh and enlightening message, but wasn't sure how to present the details of that message. After pondering the situation and various alternatives, I decided to refine the material again and write another technical book. The book would be oriented toward the formal management of data and processes as a single, combined, critical resource of the organization that contains the organization's thorough business understanding leading to business agility and success.

Business Understanding and Agility is about establishing a business understanding culture consisting of an overarching construct for thorough business understanding with an underlying foundation of theories, concepts, principles, and techniques for using that business understanding to be agile and successfully operate the business.

I wondered if a thorough business understanding culture is a conclusion or a beginning. I, and many of my professional friends, believe it is both a conclusion and a beginning. It's the conclusion of an *illusion* that the current physical data and processes manipulation approaches can ever achieve thorough business understanding and agility. It's the beginning of a *reality* that an overarching construct supported by proper concepts, principles, and techniques are mandatory for achieving thorough business understanding, agility, and successful business operation.

Business Understanding and Agility is for executives, business and technical managers, business professionals, and technical data and processes staff. It begins with the current problems, proceeds through understanding an organization's business niche, documenting that understanding within a formal construct of architectures and models, using assisted intelligence. Formal terms are comprehensively defined and consistently used throughout the book.

The material may be provocative and controversial, may not represent current hype, may not be industry standard, may be contrary to mainstream practice, may be contrary to the agenda, may be contrary to the establishment, and may be disturbing and threatening to some data management professionals and processes management professionals.

However, the material produces a high-quality data and processes resource, with understandable data and processes, that supports an organization's business activities. It is enlightening and enthusing to business professionals, and may be enlightening and enthusing to data management professionals and processes management professionals.

I hope you find ***Business Understanding and Agility*** interesting, informative, and thought-provoking. Be ready to reset your view of business understanding and agility in light of new revelations.

Michael Brackett
Olympia, Washington
October, 2021

ACKNOWLEDGEMENTS

Acknowledging all the people that contributed thoughts, ideas, feedbacks, and criticisms that lead to the current book would be lengthy and nearly impossible to complete. Instead, I'll acknowledge all those people, over many years, from public and private sector organizations, that showed an interest in promoting and supporting new approaches to business understanding and agility, or that criticized those approaches for a variety of reasons. Input from both groups led to a new concept of business understanding supporting an organization's enduring agility to be successful in its business endeavors.

ABOUT THE AUTHOR

Mr. Brackett retired from the State of Washington in June, 1996, where he was the State's Data Resource Coordinator. He was responsible for developing the State's common data architecture that spans multiple jurisdictions, such as state agencies, local jurisdictions, Native American tribes, public utilities, and Federal agencies, and includes multiple disciplines, such as water resource, growth management, and criminal justice. He is the founder of Data Resource Design and Remodeling and is a Consulting Data Architect specializing in developing integrated data resources.

Mr. Brackett has been in the data management field for 60 years, during which time he developed many innovative concepts and techniques for designing applications and managing data resources. He is the originator of the Common Data Architecture concept, the Data Resource Management Framework, the data naming taxonomy and data naming vocabulary, the Five-Tier Five-Schema concept, the data rule concept, the Business Intelligence Value Chain, the data resource data concept, the architecture-driven data model concept, and many new techniques for understanding and integrating disparate data. He has evolved to a recognized thought leader, a visionary thought leader, and is now considered a legend in data resource management.

Mr. Brackett has written fifteen technical books on application design, data design, and common data architectures. He has written numerous articles and developed a series of e-learning classes. He is a well-known international author, speaker, and consultant on data resource management topics.

Mr. Brackett has a BS in Forestry (Forest Management) and a MS in Forestry (Botany) from the University of Washington, and a MS in Soils (Geology) from Washington State University. He is a charter member and a lifetime member of DAMA-PS, the Seattle Chapter of DAMA International established in 1985. He saw the formation of DAMA National in 1986 and DAMA International in 1988. He served as Vice President of Conferences for DAMA International; as the President of DAMA International from 2000 through 2003; and as Past President of DAMA International for 2004 and 2005. He was the founder and the first President of the DAMA International Foundation, an organization established for developing a formal data management profession. He was the Production Editor for the first DAMA-DMBOK released in April, 2009.

Mr. Brackett received DAMA International's Lifetime Achievement

Award in 2006 for his work in data resource management, the second person in the history of DAMA International to receive that award. Mr. Brackett presented the first Lifetime Achievement Award to John Zachman in 2003. He taught Data Design and Modeling in the Data Resource Management Certificate Program at the University of Washington, and has been a member of the adjunct faculty at Washington State University and The Evergreen State College. He is listed in *Who's Who in the West*, *Who's Who in Education*, and *International Who's Who*.

Mr. Brackett is retired and enjoys a variety of activities, including back country hiking, cross-country skiing, snowshoeing, biking, kayaking, dancing, and writing. He lives in Olympia, Washington.

Chapter 1
BASIC PROBLEMS AND NEEDS

The identification of problems drives problem resolution.

An organization's business understanding is contained in its data resource and processes resource. Those two resources are used to thoroughly understand and successfully operate the organization's business. Any problems with the use of those resources to understand and operate the business impact the chances for successful business operation.

Albert Einstein said if he had only an hour to solve a world problem, he would spend 55 minutes understanding and defining the problem, and then five minutes solving the problem. Any problems with the organization's business success must begin by identifying problems with the organization's data resource and processes resource. Those problems can then be tackled and resolved to improve an organization's agility and chances of success.

The Basic Problems and Needs Chapter describes the problems with the organization's data resource and processes resource, and the needs to resolve those problems. The chapter begins by describing the approach to identifying problems and needs, and progresses through the identification of basic data resource problems and needs, and basic processes resource problems and needs. The chapter theme is that understanding the current situation is the first step to identifying problems, and identifying problems is the first step to solving those problems.

THE APPROACH

The current situation in most public and private sector organizations is the disparate nature of their data resource and processes resource. The disparity in data and processes is high, and is rapidly increasing. Since the organization's business understanding is contained in the disparate data resource and processes resource, that's where problems should be identified.

However, some people believe that identifying business operation problems is a better approach than identifying data resource and processes resource problems. The reasoning is that people who operate the business have the business understanding. They should know the business problems, and should be able to document those problems.

The resolution of these two approaches lies in defining the extent of an organization's data resource and processes resource. The data resource and processes resource are far more than just data and processes in electronic form, far more than computer instructions, and far more than electronic information systems. The data resource and processes resource are the sum total of all data and processes at the organization's disposal, whether manual or automated, wherever stored and however retrieved, including the human resource.

The complete, comprehensive, organization-wide, persistent business understanding is contained in this expanded scope of the data resource and processes resource. You will see the reason for this expanded scope as the problems and their solutions are presented in the coming chapters.

Many of the notes I collected over the years about the data resource and the processes resource began with business operation problems and were traced back to data and processes problems. Many of my professional friends and associates believe the best approach is to start is with the data resource and processes resource problems. Other professional friends and associates believe that starting with business operation problems will eventually produce the same result, but will likely take longer to track those problems back to the data resource and processes resource.

Most business operation problems are essentially symptomatic problems of a deeper problem with the data resource and processes resource. Therefore, resolving most business operation problems begins with identifying the data resource and processes resource problems, and the needs to resolve those problems. Focusing on the data resource and processes resource problems will likely resolve the majority of business operation problems.

Definitions

Identifying the data resource and processes resource problems and needs begins with a few comprehensive definitions. Many of the definitions appear in previous books, articles, and e-learning classes. A few definitions have slight refinements over earlier definitions, but that's the nature of comprehensive definitions – they evolve as our understanding evolves.

The following definitions pertain to understanding, uncertainty, and agility.

Thorough means detailed, exhaustive, meticulous, comprehensive, and complete. The problem is that *thorough business understanding* has no formal, comprehensive, discipline-wide, agreed-to definition. The term has a variety of different definitions, that are seldom comprehensive, often overlap, and frequently conflict.

Understanding is a mental grasp; comprehension; the power of comprehending; the capacity to apprehend general relations of particulars; the power to make experience intelligible by applying concepts and categories.

Understand is to grasp the reasonableness of something; to grasp the meaning of; to have thorough or technical acquaintance with or expertness in the practice of; to be thoroughly familiar with the character and propensities of to accept as fact or truth or regard as plausible, to interpret in one of a number of possible ways; to achieve a grasp of the nature, significance, or explanation of something; to believe or infer something to be the case.

Uncertainty is the quality or state of being uncertain; something that is uncertain.

Uncertain is indefinite; indeterminate; not certain to occur; not reliable; not known beyond doubt; not having certain knowledge; not clearly identified or defined; not constant.

Agility is the quality or state of being agile.

Agile is able to move quickly and easily, able to think and understand quickly, energetic, flexible, adaptable, iterative, and evolving.

Business agility is the state of an organization being agile in its business understanding and operation.

The following definitions pertain to identifying the problems and the needs to resolve those problems.

A *problem* is a source of perplexity, distress, or vexation; a difficult situation disrupting or impacting the organization's business.

A *symptom* is subjective evidence of a disturbance or disorder; something that indicates the existence of something else.

A *manifestation* is the act, process, or instance of making evident or certain by showing or displaying.

A *symptomatic problem* is a symptom or manifestation of a deeper problem, at a point in time or over a period of time, and may be persistent or sporadic. Resolving a symptomatic problem only allows other symptomatic problems to surface.

A *specific problem* is a situation identified within an organization resulting in one or more symptomatic problems that impact the organization's business. It's an indication of a deeper basic problem. Resolving a specific problem only allows other specific problems to surface.

A *common problem* is a specific problem that is widespread across many organizations.

A *basic problem* is an elemental problem causing one or more specific problems in one or more organizations. Resolving a basic problem, resolves associated specific problems and their associated symptomatic problems.

A *need* is something requisite, desirable, or useful; something wanted or necessary for well-being of the business. When achieved, it will resolve one or more associated problems.

A *specific need* is a need that when achieved resolves one or more specific problems.

A ***common need*** is a need that when achieved resolves one or more associated common problems.

A ***basic need*** is a need that when achieved resolves one or more basic problems.

Sequence

Problem identification begins with identifying symptomatic problems, and progresses through specific problems, to common problems, to basic problems. When the basic problems have been identified, basic needs are identified that resolve the basic problems. Problem resolution proceeds in the reverse direction. Resolving basic problems resolves common problems, which resolves specific problems, which resolves symptomatic problems. Looking at resolution another way, meeting basic needs, meets common needs, which meets specific needs.

The sequence is summarized below and has been used for many years to identify problems and needs in a variety of public and private sector organizations.

- Identify the symptomatic problems.
- Identify the specific problems causing those symptomatic problems.
- Identify the common problems across many organizations.
- Identify the basic problems causing the common problems.
- Identify the basic needs that resolve the basic problems.
- Resolving basic problems resolves common problems.
- Resolving common problems resolves specific problems.
- Resolving specific problems resolves symptomatic problems.

The sequence of identifying problems and meeting needs emphasizes that problems can only be solved when those problems are thoroughly understood.

A Typical Scenario

I frequently use a scenario at conferences and with clients to clarify the problems with data. I ask:

How many attendees work for an organization that provides goods and/or services to citizens or customers?
Nearly every hand goes up.

How many attendees rely on the data resource to support their business?
Nearly every hand stays up.

How many attendees stake the success of their business on the data resource?

Again, nearly every hand confidently stays up.

How many attendees know all the data their organization has available, the meaning of those data, and the quality of those data?
Nearly every hand goes down.

Uh, Oh! What just happened?

Nearly every organization has data and stakes their business success on those data, yet the organization at large doesn't know all the data that are available, the meaning of those data, or the quality of those data!

Really?

BASIC DATA PROBLEMS

The basic problem and need identification sequence describe above has been used for many years to identify data resource problems across many public and private sector organizations. The symptomatic problems and specific problems with the data resource are not listed, because those lists would be extensive, and you are likely aware, or acutely aware, of many of the symptomatic problems. The common data resource problems are listed in Appendix A. The basic data resource problems are described below.

Definitions

The term *state* will be used in a variety of different contexts and definitions through the book. *State* is the condition or stage of physical being characterized by definite properties or features.

Disparate means essentially not alike; fundamentally distinct or different in kind, quality, or character; low quality, defective, discordant, ambiguous, and heterogenous; poorly understood, and cannot be readily integrated to support an organization's activities. *Disparity* is the noun form of disparate

A *disparate data resource* is substantially composed of disparate data that are dis-integrated and not subject-oriented. It is a state of disarray, in which the low quality does not, and cannot, adequately support an organization's business information demand.

The *business information demand* is an organization's continuously increasing, constantly changing, need for current, accurate, integrated information, often on short notice or very short notice, to support its business activities.

The business information demand is not being met in most public and private sector organizations today. The current data resource in most public and private sector organizations is not supplying all the quality information needed to provide a thorough understanding of the business to fully support an organization's business activities. The result is an impact on the organization's business understanding, operation, agility, and chance of business success.

Traditional typically means an established or customary pattern of thought, action, or behavior.

Traditional data management (**TDM**) is the way data are typically managed in most organizations today. It is seldom based on established theories, concepts, principles, and techniques, and leads to a disparate data resource that does not support the organization's current or future business information demand.

Traditional data management is characterized by four basic problems: lexical challenge, style-driven substance, bad hype, and technology-driven disparity. These basic problems lead to a disparate data resource that seldom provides a thorough understanding for an organization to successfully operate its business. The four basic problems with traditional data management are described below.

Lexical Challenge

The first basic data problem is a lexical challenge. The ***lexical challenge*** is the creation of words and terms, often with no definitions, minimal definitions, unclear definitions, incorrect definitions, multiple definitions, and conflicting definitions; which have a non-denotative meaning, with many connotative meanings that fit a wide variety of situations; are often used interchangeably and inappropriately; often create confusing synonyms and homonyms; are misused, abused, and corrupted; and are defined and redefined to the point they are worn out and meaningless, then are discarded without regard for their real meaning or impact on an organization's activities. New words and terms are created, and the cycle continues.

For some reason, people can't formally define and consistently use terms that are relevant to data resource management. They can't consult the dictionary for established roots, prefixes, and suffixes. They can't build on the shoulders of others. They take existing terms, mush them into new terms, provide weak definitions, and promote those terms as a new approach to data resource management. That's unprofessional! A formal data resource management profession cannot be built on unprofessional terms.

Here are a few examples of the lexical challenge in traditional data management today.

Data lake is a prominent term. Have you ever seen a data lake? A depression in the ground, full of data, floating around, a few boats with propellers churning the data, with temperature gradients and waves, currents flowing according to the laws of fluid mechanics, where data are squirted in and sucked out as necessary.

Maybe that's what is meant by *data in motion*. Sounds like the old federated data, which didn't work.

I haven't seen a data lake. Well, maybe I have, in some organizations. A mass of data, in a pool of databases, swirling around the organization, with people frantically churning the data trying to find, understand, and use appropriate data to support business activities.

Data governance is another prominent term. *Governance* means government. *Government* is the act or process of governing; the authoritative direction or control of something. *Data governance* would mean the governing of data, the authoritative direction and control of data. Laws, rule, and regulations are established. If data don't follow them, they are punished, fined, or imprisoned. Better yet, they are simply deleted.

Sounds a lot like the old data administration, which didn't work. Data cannot be governed any more than data can be administered. Only people that manage and use data can be governed or administered.

Blockchain is the technology at the heart of bitcoin and other virtual currencies. It's an open, distributed ledger that records transactions efficiently and in a verifiable and permanent way. It uses blocks that are linked using cryptography, where each block contains a cryptographic hash, a timestamp, and transaction data, usually represented as a Merkle Tree.

Blockchain proponents say it's a new way to manage all data, which is not true. It's only another way that data can be processed and used. The management of data as an organization resource remains the same. It does not require rethinking data resource management. Data are still normalized within a single organization-wide data architecture and denormalized as necessary for specific processing.

The *democratization of data* recently appeared as a new way to manage data. *Democratization* is to make democratic; favoring democracy; social equality. *Democratic* is relating to or favoring democracy. *Democracy* is government by the people; rule of the majority. *Bureaucratization* is to make bureaucratic; favoring bureaucracy. *Bureaucratic* is a body of non-elected officials making administrative policy. *Bureaucracy* is to make bureaucratic.

Data are not intelligent. *Intelligent* is having a high degree of intelligence and mental capacity; revealing or reflecting good thought and judgement; the ability to learn, understand, and reason. Therefore, data cannot be democratic or bureaucratic, and cannot be intelligent. Data cannot administer or govern themselves.

Data administration didn't work. Data governance didn't work. What's the chance that the democratization of data will work?

Unstructured data is another prominent term. *Unstructured* means without structure; an amorphous mess. *Unstructured data* would be data that

7

have no structure and are an amorphous mess. Most unstructured data are actually structured in a very complex manner that many people don't understand, or want to understand, hence the term *unstructured. Complex structured data* is more appropriate.

The unprofessional terminology goes on, and on, and on, ad nauseum. For example, *mining* is tearing up the ground, taking what is needed, and discarding the rest. *Data mining* would be tearing up the data, taking what is needed, and discarding the rest. Data taken is not available for others. *Data vault* would be locking the data away in a secure vault where no one can use those data, unless they have access to that vault. *Data exploration* would be more appropriate.

I could list more inappropriate terms I've heard over the years, and you could probably list many terms I haven't encountered. The terms keep coming, and when they don't work, they are discarded, and new terms are promoted hoping they will work.

Style-Driven Substance

The second basic data problem is style-driven substance. *Style* is the manner of accomplishment, the way that something is performed or accomplished; the action, method, or technique to accomplish an end result. *Substance* is the end result; the product; the essence of some action, method, or technique.

Style-driven substance is a traditional management situation, characterized by a lexical challenge, bad hype, and technology-driven disparity, leading to a disparate data resource and a disparate processes resource that are poorly understood and fail to fully support an organization's activities.[1]

Style-driven substance emphasizes style over substance. A person typically does something the way they want to do it from their perspective, not the way they should do it from the organization's perspective. Their personal style is more important than a consistent result—the substance—which typically leads to disparity that compromises an organization's business success.

Bad Hype

The third basic data problem is bad hype. *Hype* is to promote or publicize extravagantly, to put on or to deceive, to inspire people for or against some purpose. Hype is driven by personal and organizational agendas, which can be good or bad, depending on a person's perspective. Hype seldom includes comprehensive definitions that provide any thorough understanding of the

---

[1] Some definitions include the processes resource, which is described in the next section.

purpose.

Bad hype is hype that avoids any formality in order to achieve the results intended by the hype promoter. It usually ignores future needs in favor of current needs desired by the hype promoter. Bad hype is fueled by the lexical challenge and supports style-driven substance.

Technology-Driven Disparity

The fourth basic data problem is technology-driven disparity. ***Technology-driven disparity*** is the use of technology to drive the development of disparate data or disparate processes without any regard for formal theories, concepts, principles, or techniques, or any formal data resource or processes resource development. It usually considers current needs without any consideration for future needs.

Traditional data management has evolved to technology-driven disparity, which is very similar to the radar-assisted collisions situation when radar was first installed on ships. Technology is used to accomplish a task according to style-driven substance.

Data management today is a data manipulation industry, not a formal data resource management program. A good analogy is health care, which today is largely an illness treatment industry, not a formal health management program. The result of technology-driven disparity is high disparity and low business understanding.

Impacts of Basic Data Problems

The four basic data problems are interrelated. Each basic data problem feeds or supports the other basic data problems. An organization at large, which is a collection of people, can get caught in an ongoing cycle of the four basic data problems that leads to a disparate data resource. The impacts of a disparate data resource are decreased business understanding, increased business uncertainty, decreased quality, and increased disparity, which lead to less that effective and efficient business operation, limited agility, and reduced chance of business success.

BASIC DATA NEEDS

Resolution of the basic data problems begins by establishing basic data needs and implementing those needs to build formal data resource management and a comparate data resource. The common data needs are listed in Appendix A. The basic data needs that resolve the basic data problems are described below.

Definitions

Comparate is the opposite *disparate*. ***Comparate*** means fundamentally

9

similar in kind, quality, and character; without defect; concordant; homogeneous; nearly flawless; nearly perfect; high quality, easily understood, and readily integrated to support the organization's activities. *Comparity* is the noun form of comparate.

A *comparate data resource* is composed of comparate data that adequately support the current and future business information demand. The data are easily identified and understood, readily accessed and shared, and utilized to their fullest potential. It is an integrated, subject oriented, business-driven resource that is the official record of reference for the organization's business.

Data resource management (DRM) is the formal management of all data at the organization's disposal, including both manual and automated data, as a critical resource of the organization, based on established theories, concepts, principles, and techniques, leading to a comparate data resource, that fully supports the organization's current and future business information demand.

Data resource management is characterized by lexical richness, substance-driven style, good hype, and technology-assisted comparity leading to a comparate data resource that provides a thorough understanding for an organization to successfully operate its business. These four basic needs for data resource management are described below.

Lexical Richness

The first basic data need is lexical richness. *Lexical richness* is the opposite of the *lexical challenge*. **Lexical richness** is the creation of words and terms, with comprehensive, denotative definitions that have no connotative meanings; that are complete, clear, correct, meaningful, and consistently used; and are persistent over time.

Professionals need to move from the lexical challenge to lexical richness. They need to create formal terms, relevant to data resource management, following established roots, prefixes, and suffixes, and comprehensively define those terms.

However, many people don't want the formality of lexical richness. They claim the discipline is already lexically rich, and refer to a plethora of existing definitions as proof. Let's be clear! Traditional data management does have numerous terms. However, those terms are not comprehensively defined, consistently used, or persistent over time. Therefore, traditional data management is lexically challenged.

Many people claim that comprehensive definitions are way too restrictive, meaning those definitions don't allow people the latitude to do their own thing their own agenda. These people are simply saying that comprehensive definitions limit style-driven substance.

People are using bad hype against establishing formal data resource management, rather than using good hype to promote formal data resource management. The obstacle to overcome is to encourage people to develop a full set of formal terms, with comprehensive definitions, that are persistent over time, and are consistently use those terms to manage the organization's data resource.

Substance-Driven Style

The second basic data need is substance-driven style. *Substance-driven style* is the opposite of *style-driven substance*. **Substance-driven style** is a formal management situation, characterized by lexical richness, good hype, and technology-assisted comparity, leading to a comparate data resource and comparate processes resource that are thoroughly understood and fully support an organization's activities.

Substance-driven style emphasizes substance over style. A person does something the way it should be done to ensure comparity of the organization's data resource. A consistent result for the organization is more important than a person's style, and leads to a comparate data resource.

Good Hype

The third basic data need is good hype. *Good hype* is the opposite of *bad hype*. **Good hype** is hype that supports formality to achieve the results intended by the promoter. It does not compromise formality for quick results. It recognizes future needs as well as current needs. Good hype is supported by lexical richness and supports substance-driven style.

Technology-Assisted Comparity

The fourth basic data need is technology-assisted comparity. *Technology-assisted comparity* is the opposite of *technology-driven disparity*. **Technology-assisted comparity** is the use of technology to assist the formal development of comparate data and processes resources, rather than drive the development of disparate data and disparate processes resources. It's a major feature of substance-driven style that directly supports the cognitive processes of data and processes resource management.

Technology-assisted comparity uses technology to assist comparity, rather than to drive disparity. It's similar to how radar is used to avoid collisions between ships, after people learned how to use radar. The details of technology-assisted comparity are described in the Assisted Intelligence Chapter.

Benefits of Basic Data Needs

The four basic data needs are interrelated and support each other. The benefits of implementing the basic data needs are the creation of formal data resource management, which leads to a comparate data resource, that increases business understanding, decreases uncertainty, decreases disparity, increases quality, increases agility, ensures better business operation, and increases the chance of business success.

BASIC PROCESSES PROBLEMS

I suspect if I use the same scenario with processes that I use with data, I'd get very similar results. The symptomatic problems and specific problems with the processes resource that I've gathered over the years would be extensive, and you are likely aware, or acutely aware, of many of the problems. The common processes resource problems are listed in Appendix B. The basic processes resource problems are described below.

Definitions

Processes disparity is the disparity across all the processes that an organization uses to manage its business activities.

A *disparate processes resource* is substantially composed of disparate processes that that are dis-integrated. It is a state of disarray, in which the low quality does not, and cannot, adequately support an organization's business information demand.

Indications are that the processes resource in organizations is far more disparate than the data resource. When I started into data resource integration a number of years ago, I looked at processes to determine how processes could be temporarily adjusted while the data resource was integrated. That's when I discovered that processes were far more disparate than data.

That discovery led to a concern about whether data disparity or processes disparity should be tackled first. After many discussions, the decision was made to tackle the least disparate resource first. The sequence was data resource integration, followed by processes resource integration.

Traditional processes management (**TPM**) is the way processes are typically managed in most organizations today. It is seldom based on established theories, concepts, principles, and techniques, and leads to a disparate processes resource that does not support the organization's current or future business information demand.

Traditional processes management is characterized by the same basic problems that characterize traditional data management. Traditional processes management is also characterized by inappropriate business decisions, inadequate business rules, unacceptable design and development, informal data and processes names, and incomplete processes documentation. These five basic processes problems are described below.

Inappropriate Business Decisions

The first basic processes problem is inappropriate business decisions. Business decisions are often made during development and implementation and included in processes. Many of these business decisions are made by developers and do not originate from business professionals. Business professionals are not aware of, nor have reviewed, approved, or substantiated, all business decisions included in processes.

Inadequate Business Rules

The second basic processes problem is inadequate business rules. Business rules are scattered in a wide variety of places throughout the data resource and the processes resource. Some rules are linked with the data as data integrity rules, and some are linked with the processes as process logic and decision rules. Rules are not consistent across all processes. or data,.

Business rules may be located in the design specifications or in the developed process and databases. They may conflict, overlap, and be redundant, and their form may be difficult to understand. Many business rules are difficult to locate and review, because they are not located in a single repository.

Unacceptable Design and Development

The third basic processes problem is unacceptable design and development. Many processes are developed and implemented without any formal design based on business needs. Many process development efforts jump from high-level concepts directly to development and implementation. Many processes have flawed logic, resulting from a lack of formal processes integrity rules.

Processes are seldom developed within a single processes architecture. They cannot be understood and managed within a common context, resulting in competing processes, conflicting processes, overlapping processes, and redundant processes.

Many processes are tightly coupled to their own databases. Many of those databases have redundant data that originate from one source, requiring bridges to be maintained between databases, which require additional processes. Many workflows of individual processes through an organization are vague, out of sequence, and difficult to understand.

Informal Data and Processes Names

The fourth basic processes problem is informal data and processes names. Processes management terms are inconsistent and poorly defined. Processes seldom have formal names or abbreviated names. The names of processes are not consistent across all processes and across all processes models. Processes seldom follow any formal naming, or name abbreviation standard or technique.

Processes often use informal and inconsistently abbreviated data names that are inconsistent within and across processes. The data names are often not the same as the data names in databases. Working data names within processes are seldom formally named or comprehensively defined. Data names in purchased applications are often generic without comprehensive definitions, seldom follow an organization's data names, and are seldom cross-referenced to the organization's data names.

Incomplete Processes Documentation

The fifth basic processes problem is incomplete processes documentation. Manual and automated processes are not well documented, internally or externally. The details of many processes are known only by a few people, and understanding is often passed from person to person. But people are transient and understanding can be lost.

Design specifications and system generation specifications are often lost or discarded after implementation, intentionally or unintentionally. Design enhancements and change histories are seldom documented or kept up to date. Documentation that is maintained is seldom maintained in one location, that is readily accessible, and easily understood by both business professionals and developers.

Business decisions are often contained in processes, are difficult to locate, and are difficult to understand. They are seldom formally documented in one place where they can be reviewed by business professionals.

Business rules are often contained in both processes and data, are difficult to locate, and are difficult to understand. They are seldom formally documented in one place where they can be reviewed by business professionals.

Impact of Basic Processes Problems

The five basic processes problems are interrelated. Each basic processes problem feeds and supports the other basic processes problems. An organization can get caught in an ongoing cycle of basic processes problems that leads to a disparate processes resource. The impacts of a disparate processes resource, similar to the impacts of a disparate data resource, are decreased business understanding, increased business uncertainty, decreased quality, increased disparity, which lead to less than effective and efficient business operation, limited agility, and reduced chance of business success.

BASIC PROCESSES NEEDS

Resolution of the basic processes problems begins by establishing basic processes needs, and implementing those needs to build formal processes resource management and a comparate processes resource. The common processes needs are listed in Appendix B. The basic processes needs that resolve the basic processes problems are described below.

Definitions

A *comparate processes resource* is composed of comparate processes that adequately support the current and future business information demand. The processes are easily identified and understood, readily accessed and shared, and utilized to their fullest potential. It's an integrated, business-driven resource that is the official record of reference for the organization's business.

Processes resource management (**PRM**) is the formal management of all processes at the organization's disposal, including both manual and automated processes, as a critical resource of the organization, based on established theories, concepts, principles, and techniques, leading to a comparate processes resource, that fully supports the organization's current and future business information demand.

Processes resource management is characterized by appropriate business decisions, adequate business rules, acceptable design and development, formal data and processes names, and complete processes documentation leading to a comparate processes resource that provides a thorough understanding for an organization to successfully operate its business. These five basic needs for processes resource management are described below.

Appropriate Business Decisions

The first basic processes need is appropriate business decisions. Business decisions must come from the business professionals. Ideally, business decisions are included in the processes design that is approved by business professionals. However, if situations are encountered during development and implementation that require changed or new business decisions, those decisions must also come from the business professionals or be approved by business professionals before implementation.

Adequate Business Rules

The second basic processes need is adequate business rules. Business rules need to be linked with the data as data integrity rules, or with the processes as processes integrity rules, as appropriate. However, business rules also need to be readily accessible by business professionals, and be in a form that is understandable to business professionals, to ensure the business rules are consistent across all data and processes.

Business rules are not the same as business requirements. Business requirements are specific business needs that processes must meet. Business rules may be included with business requirements, but must be designated as rules about the business.

Acceptable Design and Development

The third basic processes need is acceptable design and development. Processes design must be oriented toward the business and must be readily understood by business professionals. Processes must be designed and managed within a single organization-wide processes architecture, and their data must be designed and managed within a single organization-wide data architecture.

Processes design and development must follow a formal design and development cycle that applies to all manual and automated processes. Processes design and development must include process logic and decisions, and business workflow through the organization.

Formal Data and Processes Names

The fourth basic processes need is formal data and processes names. All processes must have formal processes names and data names with comprehensive definitions, including working data within processes. Any processes or data name abbreviations must follow a formal name abbreviation scheme. Data names must be used consistently within and across processes and databases. Processes and data names in purchased applications must be cross-referenced to the organization's data names.

Complete Processes Documentation

The fifth basic processes need is complete processes documentation. All manual and automated processes must be documented, both internally and externally. Design specifications, system generation specifications, and all design change histories must be documented, readily available, and easily understood by business professionals and developers.

Business decisions must be documented, linked to their use in processes, readily available, and easily understood by business professionals and developers. Business rules must be documented, linked to their use in processes and data, readily available, and easily understood by business professionals and developers.

Benefits of Basic Processes Needs

The five basic processes needs are interrelated and support each other. The benefits of implementing the basic processes needs are the creation of formal processes resource management, which leads to a comparate processes resource that increases business understanding, decreases uncertainty, decreases disparity, increases quality, increases agility, ensures better business operation, and increases the chance of business success.

SUMMARY

Identifying basic problems and basic needs for data and processes follows a specific sequence from symptomatic problems, to specific problems, to common problems, to basic problems, to basic needs that resolve those basic problems. Meeting the basic needs resolves the basic problems, which resolves the common problems, which resolves the specific problems, which resolves the symptomatic problems. That sequence was followed to identify the basic data problems and needs, and the basic processes problems and needs.

The basic problems with traditional data management are a lexical challenge, style-driven substance, bad hype, and technology-driven disparity. The impacts of those basic problems are a disparate data resource that decreases business understanding, increases uncertainty, decreases quality, and increases disparity, which impacts business operation, limits agility, and reduces the chance of business success.

The basic needs for data resource management are lexical richness, substance-driven style, good hype, and technology-assisted comparity. The benefits of implementing those basic data needs are formal data resource management and a comparate data resource that increases business understanding, decreases uncertainty, decreases disparity, increases quality, increases agility, ensues better business operation, and increases the chance of business success.

The basic problems with traditional processes management are inappropriate business decisions, inadequate business rules, unacceptable design and development, informal data and processes names, and incomplete processes documentation. The impacts of these basic problems are a disparate processes resource with the same impacts as traditional data management.

The basic needs for processes resource management are appropriate business decisions, adequate business rules, acceptable design and development, formal data and processes names, and complete processes documentation. The benefits of these basic needs are formal processes resource management and a comparate processes resource with the same benefits as the comparate data resource.

Formal definitions were provided for identifying problems and needs, for traditional data management and data resource management, and for traditional processes management and processes resource management.

QUESTIONS

The following questions are provided as a review of the Basic Problems and Needs Chapter, and to stimulate thought about the basic problems and basic needs for data and processes.

1. What is the sequence for identifying problems and needs?
2. What is the difference between disparity and comparity?
3. What is the business information demand?
4. Why is the business information demand not being met?
5. What is traditional data management?
6. What is a disparate data resource?
7. What are the basic problems with traditional data management?
8. What are the impacts of the basic data problems?
9. What is data resource management?
10. What is a comparate data resource?
11. What are the basic data needs for data resource management?
12. What are the benefits of meeting the basic data needs?
13. What is traditional processes management?
14. What is a disparate processes resource?
15. What are the basic problems with traditional processes management?
16. What are the impacts of the basic processes problems?
17. What is processes resource management?
18. What is a comparate processes resource?
19. What are the basic needs for processes resource management?
20. What are the benefits of meeting the basic processes needs?

Chapter 2
FUNDAMENTAL PROBLEMS AND NEEDS

Manage data and processes as a single, combined, critical resource.

The Basic Problems and Needs Chapter described the basic problems with the data resource and processes resource in most organizations today, and the basic needs to resolve those problems. The basic problems are about the separate data resource and processes resource, and about the separate traditional data management and traditional processes management. The basic needs apply to the separate data resource and processes resource, and to the separate data resource management and processes resource management. Meeting the basic needs resolves the basic problems with each of the two resources.

Describing basic problems and basic needs for data and for processes is a great first step to understanding an organizations business. But the problems are much deeper than the two sets of basic problems. Deeper fundamental problems exist across the data resource and the processes resource, and across data resource management and processes resource management. Those fundamental problems must be identified and resolved before an organization can fully understand its business.

The Fundamental Problems and Needs Chapter describes the fundamental problems across data and processes, and the fundamental needs to resolve those fundamental problems. The chapter continues Einstein's approach to understanding the problems before resolving those problems. Only by identifying and resolving the fundamental problems across the two resources can an organization take its business understanding to a higher level. The chapter theme is identifying the fundamental problems across the data resource and processes resource, resolving those fundamental problems, and evolving to an overarching construct for business understanding and agility within a Business Understanding Vision.

FUNDAMENTAL PROBLEMS

On close examination, the basic data problems also apply to processes, and the basic processes problems also apply to data. Processes are characterized by a lexical challenge, style-driven substance, bad hype, and technology-driven, the same as data. Only the details are different. Data are characterized by inappropriate business decisions, inadequate business rules, unacceptable design and development, informal data and processes names, and incomplete processes documentation, the same as processes. Only the details are different.

The impacts of the basic data problems are similar for processes, and the impact of basic processes problems are similar for data. The benefits of the basic data needs are similar for processes, and the benefits of basic processes needs are similar for data. These similarities are not surprising, when you think about it. The same traditional attitudes and management styles apply to developing data and to developing processes.

Looking at the basic problems historically, everything has changed, yet nothing has changed. Business has changed and technology has changed, yet disparity and lack of business understanding continue to increase. New approaches and techniques keep appearing, yet organizations are no better than they were a decade ago. In fact, many organizations are worse than they were a decade ago with the increasing disparity.

Meeting the basic needs for data and processes resolves the basic problems as defined, but doesn't resolve all the problems. Meeting the basic needs surfaces fundamental problems across both data and processes. The data and processes disparity continues to increase and the level of business understanding and agility continues to decrease. The fundamental problems must be identified and resolved to achieve thorough business understanding.

Definitions

A *fundamental problem* is a major problem that is the cause or origin of one or more basic problems. It's a deeper or root cause of basic problems.

A fundamental problem in the current context is a problem across both the data resource and the processes resource, and across both data resource management and processes resource management.

The fundamental problems are that data and processes are separate resources, data and processes are not considered a critical resource, data and processes management is not integrated, and there is no common vision for thorough business understanding. Each of these fundamental problems is described below.

Data and Processes Are Separate Resources

The first fundamental problem is that data and processes are separate resources. Most public and private sector organizations still manage a data resource separate from the processes resource. Even if each of those two resources are formally managed and integrated within their respective single organization-wide architectures, they are still considered separate resources.

Organization structures, professional conferences, books, articles, presentations, professional organizations, and so on, are largely oriented toward the data people or the processes people. Integration between data and processes is often done on-the-fly and usually during development and implementation. That operational integration is often done with the existing disparate data and processes resources, usually resulting in greater disparity.

Data and Processes Not Critical Resources

The second fundamental problem is that data and processes are usually not considered critical resources. Sometimes data are considered a critical resource. Sometimes information is considered a critical resource, but the distinction between data and information is not always clear or specified. Seldom are processes considered a critical resource.

A disparate resource cannot be considered a critical resource. Disparity and criticality are direct opposites. When a resource is not considered a critical resource, the management of that resource tends to be less formal. The result is a resource that does not fully support an organization's business.

Data and Processes Management Not Integrated

The third fundamental problem is that data management and processes management are not integrated. The situation exists with traditional data management and traditional processes management. It also exists with formal data resource management and processes resource management. A change from traditional data management to data resource management, and from traditional processes management to processes resource management does not guarantee, or even encourage, the two managements be integrated. The data people and the processes people manage their own domains.

Many apparent data problems are the result of processes management problems. Many apparent processes problems are the result of data management problems. The mismanagement of one resource results in mismanagement of the other resource. One major aspect of mismanagement is the use of data and processes names. Other major disconnects include business decisions, business rules, and so on.

No Vision for Thorough Business Understanding

The fourth fundamental problem is lack of a vision for thorough business understanding. No formal vision exists for combining data and processes as a critical resource, for combining the management of data and processes, or for the use of a combined data resource to provide a thorough business understanding.

Lack of a formal vision promotes people doing their own thing – style-driven substance – which is the cause of many basic problems. It allows people to keep presenting something new for fame and glory, rather than building on the shoulders of other. It promotes a lack of formality that is unprofessional and detrimental to the organization.

Impact of Fundamental Problems

The impacts of the fundamental problems are the same as the impacts of the basic data problems and basic processes problems: increased disparity, decreased business understanding, increased business uncertainty, decreased quality, and decreased agility, which lead to less than effective and efficient business operation, and reduced chance of business success. The similar impacts are not surprising, because fundamental problems across data and processes still exist, even when the separate basic problems are resolved.

FUNDAMENTAL NEEDS

The fundamental problems across data and processes must be resolved by establishing fundamental needs. A *fundamental need* is a need that when achieved resolves one or more fundamental problems.

The fundamental needs are to unite the data and processes resources, consider data and processes a critical resource, integrate data and processes resource management, and establish a Business Understanding Vision. Each of these fundamental needs is described below.

Unite Data and Processes Resources

The first fundamental need is to unite the data resource and the processes resource into a single interdependent data and processes resource for the organization. This fundamental need has two components to combine the data and processes resources, and to build a single organization-wide data architecture and a single organization-wide processes architecture. Each of these components is described below.

Combine Data and Processes Resources

The first component of unite data and processes resources is to combine the data resource and the processes resource into a single data and processes resource, while maintaining the architecture independence of each resource.

The rationale for combining the data resource and processes into a single data and processes resource is fourfold. First, data are useless without processes. Data are facts that cannot be captured, transmitted, stored, retrieved, changed, displayed, analyzed, and so on, without processes. Second, processes are decisions and actions that cannot operate without data. Third, processes are data that provide instructions to people and/or machines. Processes can be created, stored, retrieved, transmitted, displayed, changed, and so on, like any other data. Fourth, the business information demand requires information, and that information requires both data and processes.

The data resource and processes resource are *dependent*, because neither resource can exist without the other. The two resources are *independent*, because the architecture of one resource architecture does not drive the other resource architecture. The two resources *interact* operationally to support the business information demand. Therefore, the data resource and the processes resource are interdependent.

Data–processes interdependence is the situation in which data are dependent on processes and processes are dependent on data, but the architecture of one resource does not drive the architecture of the other resource.

Since the data resource and the processes resource are interdependent, they can be combined into a single data and processes resource.

The ***data and processes resource*** (**DPR**) is a combined data resource and processes resource that is an interdependent, critical resource of the organization. It is the combined record of reference for the organization. It provides an interdependent business understanding resource that is greater than the sum of the separate resources.

Object-Oriented

The object-oriented paradigm of yesteryear promised to be a driving force to combine data and processes. It provided an excellent opportunity for joint data and processes management. However, object-oriented deteriorated into (often bitter) arguments. Did data drive processes, or did processes drive data? The answer was *neither* and *both*, because data and processes are interdependent.

The problem was that personalities got in the way and people became polarized. Object-oriented became the data faction versus the processes faction. The data faction said they needed data to be in a form to (fill in the blank). The processes faction said they needed processes to be in a form to (fill in the blank). Neither faction understood the total picture. People had to know whether data drove processes, or whether processes drove data. They couldn't get their act together, which resulted in a stalemate.

Object-oriented eventually failed and evolved into GUIs (graphical user interfaces). GUIs, not surprisingly, require both data and processes to prepare and display the interfaces. People failed to recognize that data and processes must work together – they are interdependent.

In retrospect, object-oriented was right about the interdependence of data and processes, and had the potential to bring data and processes together. But object-oriented was wrong about determining data-driven processes versus processes-driven data. It failed due to personal agendas and arguments. An

23

excellent opportunity was missed, which impacted many organizations.

The object-oriented situation was only a symptom of a more fundamental problem much deeper than object-oriented. That problem was the separate management of the data resource and the processes resource. Even today, there is a strong resistance to combining data and processes management.

Single Organization-Wide Architectures

The second component of unite data and processes resources is to build a single organization-wide data architecture for the data resource, and a single organization-wide processes architecture for the processes resource. Disparate data are formally integrated within the single organization-wide data architecture, and disparate processes are formally integrated within the single organization-wide processes architecture.

A *single organization-wide architecture* is a formally developed proper architecture, spanning the entire organization, which includes all related components, either data components or processes components, available to the organization, from within or without, in any form, that the organization needs to conduct business.

Proper means marked by suitability, rightness, or appropriateness; in a thorough manner; complete and correct; organized, coordinated, and appropriate.

Proper architecture is an architecture that is complete, correct, organized, coordinated, and appropriate for fully supporting the organization's business. It minimizes disparity, maximizes understanding, and promotes comparity. It's the result of the formal development of organization-wide architectures.

The *single organization-wide data architecture* is one, formally developed, proper data architecture, spanning the entire organization, which includes all data available to an organization, from within or without, in any form, that the organization needs to conduct business.

The *single organization-wide processes architecture* is one, formally developed, proper processes architecture, spanning the entire organization, which includes all processes available to the organization, from within or without, in any form, that the organization needs to conduct business.

Note use of the word *The* rather than *A* in the two definitions. The word *The* means *only one* architecture for data and *only one* architecture for processes, where *A* could mean one of many architectures for data and for processes. The emphasis is on one single architecture for data and one single architecture for processes across the entire organization.

Formal resource integration is the permanent integration of the data resource within a single organization-wide data architecture, or integration of the processes resource within a single organization-wide processes architecture. It is not an operational integration that temporarily integrates data or processes for a specific purpose.

The details for formal data resource integration are described in the Data Resource Simplexity series of books, including interim processes changes that need to be made while the data resource is integrated. I'm not aware of any detailed approach for formal processes resource integration, but an approach could be developed based on the details for formal data resource integration.

The typical sequence for data resource integration is to begin with the data resource, then continue with the processes resource. The reason for this sequence is that processes typically have greater disparity than data. Integrating the least disparate resource first makes integration of the most disparate resource easier. When the data resource and processes resource are integrated within their respective organization-wide architectures, combining the two resources becomes much easier.

Consider Data and Processes a Critical Resource

The second fundamental need is to consider the combined data and processes resource as a critical resource for understanding and operating the organization's business. The traditional critical resources have been: data and/or information, human resource, and finances; data and/or information, human resource, finances, and real property; and a variety of other groupings.

Contemporary typically means modern, state of the art, cutting edge, leading edge, innovative, and so on.

Since data are a critical resource, and data and processes are interdependent, then processes are also a critical resource. Therefore, the contemporary critical resources are: the interdependent data and processes resource, the human resource, financial resource, real property, and offerings that include products and services.

A question often asked is, "Why offerings?" The answer is that many executives consider offerings a critical resource. Many offerings can be unique and are often proprietary. Therefore, offerings need to be included as a critical resource of the organization.

Another question often asked is, "Are data an asset?" The answer is twofold. First, senior managers deal with assets and liabilities. In most cases, senior managers consider data a liability, not an asset. Second, financial executives say data are an asset only when they are listed on the chart of accounts or general ledger. Data are not listed on the chart of accounts or general ledger for any organization I've encountered. Therefore, data are generally not considered to be an asset.

The best approach is to formally manage data as a critical resource, so that senior managers consider data an asset, and financial executives include data as an asset on the chart of accounts or general ledger.

A related question is, "Are processes an asset?" The answer is the same as for data. The best approach with processes, the same as for data, is to formally manage processes as a critical resource, so that senior managers consider processes an asset, and financial executives include processes as an asset on the chart of accounts or general ledger.

The question could be asked, "Is the combined data and processes resource an asset?" The answer is definitely "Yes," and the prognosis is excellent, if an organization proceeds with implementation of the fundamental needs so that senior managers consider the combined resource as an asset, and financial executives include the combined resource as an asset on the general ledger or chart of accounts.

Integrate Data and Processes Resource Management

The third fundamental need is to integrate data resource management and processes resource management into data and processes resource management to manage the interdependent data and processes resource as a single, critical resource of the organization. This fundamental need has two components: data and processes resource management, and a data and processes resource culture. Each of these components is described below.

Data and Processes Resource Management

The first component of integrate data and processes resource management is to combine data resource management and processes resource management into the formal management of interdependent resources within their respective organization-wide architectures. The result ensures that data management problems do not cause processes resource problems, and processes management problems do not cause data resource problems.

Data and processes resource management (**DPRM**) is the formal management of all data and processes the organization has available, as a critical resource, based on established theories, concepts, principles, and techniques, leading to a comparate resource that fully supports the current and future business information demand.

For those that have been around for a while, the organization unit name before *Information Technology* was *Data Processing*. In many respects, that former name was the correct name. Data were being processed by processes to meet the business information demand. Something was lost moving from *data processing* to *information technology*.

Data and Processes Resource Culture

The second component of integrate data and processes resource management is to support data and processes resource management with a data and processes resource culture. The culture is often ignored in today's technology-driven environment. A formal culture needs to be established to support data and processes resource management.

Data and processes resource culture (**DPRC**) is an organizational culture that supports formal data and processes resource management. It includes lexical richness, good hype, substance-driven style, and technology-assisted comparity, as well as other cultural aspects that promote thorough business understanding and successful business operation.

Establish Business Understanding Vision

The fourth fundamental need is to establish a Business Understanding Vision. The ***Business Understanding Vision*** is an overarching construct for business understanding and agility, supported by an underlying foundation of theories, concepts, principles, and techniques to create and maintain that construct.

The remainder of this book is about developing and maintaining the overarching construct for business understanding and agility.

The underlying theories, concepts, principles, and techniques for formal data resource management are not covered in the current book. Their inclusion would take too much space and would detract from the main theme of establishing an overarching construct for business understanding and agility. The Data Resource Simplexity series of books contains the details of the theories, concepts, principles, and techniques for data resource management. They are well stated and are as sound today as when they were published.

To the best of my knowledge, an equivalent set of theories, concepts, principles, and techniques for formal processes resource management has not been developed. However, with a little thought and time, and the data resource theories, concepts, principles, and techniques as a pattern, an equivalent set of theories, concepts, principles, and techniques could be developed for formal processes resource management.

Benefits of Fundamental Needs

The benefits of meeting the fundamental needs include all the benefits of the meeting the basic needs: increased business understanding, decreased uncertainty, decreased disparity, increased quality, and increased agility, which ensure better business operation, and increases the chance of business success. The benefits also include a combined data and processes resource within single organization-wide architectures, treating that resource as a critical resource, combined data and processes management with a supporting culture, and a solid vision of an overarching construct for business understanding and agility, supported by a foundation of theories, concepts, principles, and techniques to create and maintain that overarching construct.

The benefits provide a sound and simple approach to thoroughly understanding an organization's business – the key component to a successful business. Albert Einstein said that everything should be as simple as possible, and no simpler. Data and processes resource management and a supporting culture for documenting an organization's business understanding is as simple as possible. It may be very detailed, but it is simple, and there is elegance in simplicity.

Today's problems exist because what we have been doing is too non-simple and too non-elegant. Organizations are making things more difficult than they need to be, and are suffering the results. An organization has the opportunity to fulfill its potential, or to squander it, based on how they manage their business understanding.

DATA AND PROCESSES RESOURCE MANAGEMENT

Formally managing an organization's business understanding begins with fundamental definitions, data resource definitions, and processes resource definitions related to data and processes resource management.

Fundamental Definitions

The following definitions are fundamental to data and processes resource management.

Organization includes any public sector, quasi-public sector, or private sector group, conducting some form of activity, whether for profit or not for profit, regardless of size, for however long it has operated or intends to operate.

A *citizen* is a person that develops a relationship with a public-sector organization. A *customer* is a person that develops a relationship with a private sector organization.

Caution—do not confuse *citizen* and *customer,* and don't use *consumer* to include both *citizen* and *customer*. Citizens and customers are different entities that have different relationships with public and private sector organizations.

Citizen relationship management is the relationship between citizens and public-sector organizations. *Customer relationship management* is the relationship between customers and private sector organizations.

The terms *logical* and *physical* are no longer used for managing data and processes. All efforts from identifying business needs to implementation and operation are preformed logically and result in a physical product. For example, a *logical model* follows a logical process and produces a physical result. Also, a *physical model* follows a logical process and produces a physical product. Therefore, *logical* and *physical* have no meaning, in spite of their common use.

The proper terms are *business* and *implementation*. *Business* replaces *logical*, because the result is used to understand the business and define business needs. Similarly, *implementation* replaces *physical*, because the result of business needs is implemented to operate the business.

Data Resource Definitions

The following definitions pertain to data resource management.

Data are individual facts, combined facts, or calculated facts that are out of context, have no meaning, and are difficult to understand. The term *data* is plural.

Datum is the singular form of data representing one fact.

If the term *data* were singular, then only one data exists. If only one data exists, why do organizations have so many problems managing it?

For those that still believe *data* is singular, here's the Data-datum Challenge. Provide a minimum three sentence comprehensive and denotative definition of *data* as singular, beginning with "Data is …" Then provide a word meaning data in the plural, recognizing that *data* has not been designated an irregular noun.

Data are named with a noun or adjective-noun combination. Examples of datum names are Employee, Retired Employee, River, Vehicle, Vehicle Collision, and so on. Each datum has a comprehensive, denotative definition.

Raw data are data that are out of context, have no meaning, and are difficult to understand.

Raw datum is an individual datum that is out of context, has no meaning, and is difficult to understand.

Data in context are data that have meaning and can be readily understood. They are raw data wrapped with meaning.

Datum in context is an individual datum that has meaning and can be readily understood. It is a raw datum wrapped with meaning.

Data resource is the total collection of all data available to the organization, from within or without the organization, however, whenever, and wherever those data are stored and retrieved.

Datum resource is not a valid term. It would be a resource of only one datum.

Data management is a traditional term representing the management of data, usually not as a critical resource and not formal.

Information is a set of data in context, with relevance to one or more people at a point in time or for a period of time. Information is more than data in context – it must have relevance and a time frame.

Data are the raw material and information is the product. Data are pervasive over time, but information is convenience for one or more people at a point in time or for a period of time.

For those that still believe information is the plural form of data, here's the Information Definition Challenge. If *information* is the plural of data, how do you distinguish between information that is relevant and timely and information that is not relevant and timely?

Non-information is a set of data in context that is not relevant or timely to the recipient. It is often called out-formation, because it is out of relevance and the time frame for a recipient.

General information is a set of data in context that *could be* relevant to one or more people at a point in time or for a period of time.

Specific information is a set of data in context that *is* relevant to one or more people at a point in time or for a period of time

Information management is coordinating the need for information across the organization to ensure adequate support for the current and future business information demand. It should not be confused with data resource management that provides the raw material to produce information.

Business information management is the formal management of general information and specific information to support an organization's business information demand.

Information resource is not a valid term, because the timeliness and relevance of an individual or group of individuals cannot be managed as a resource.

Information resource management is not a valid term, because the timeliness and relevance of an individual or group of individuals cannot be managed as a resource.

Knowledge is cognizance, cognition, the fact or condition of knowing something with familiarity gained through experience or association. It is information that has been retained with an understanding about the significance of that information.

Tacit knowledge, also known as *implicit knowledge*, is the knowledge that a person retains in their mind. It's relatively hard to transfer to others and to disseminate widely.

Explicit knowledge, also known as *formal knowledge*, is knowledge that has been codified and stored in various media, and is held for mankind. It is readily transferable to other media and capable of being disseminated.

Organizational knowledge is information that is of significance to the organization, is combined with experience and understanding, and is retained. It is information in context with respect to understanding that is meaningful to the business.

Knowledge management is the management of an environment that encourages people to generate tacit knowledge, render it into explicit knowledge, and feed it back to the organization.

The Data–Information–Knowledge Cycle

The *Data–Information–Knowledge Cycle* is a cycle from data, to data in context, to relevant information (specific or general), to knowledge, and back to data when that information or knowledge is stored. The Data–Information–Knowledge Cycle is shown in Figure 2.1

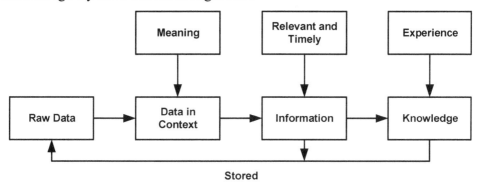

Figure 2.1. The Data–Information–Knowledge Cycle.

Starting on the left, Raw Data are combined with Meaning to become Data in Context. When Relevant and Timely are added, Data in Context become Information. When Information is combined with Experience, it becomes Knowledge. When stored, Information and Knowledge become Raw Data, and the cycle continues.

For example, when a person doesn't have knowledge about a topic, raw data can be obtained from another person or other source, put in context, which, if relevant and timely, become information. When the person retains that information, and possibly combines it with experience, it becomes knowledge. When the person documents and stores that knowledge, it becomes raw data.

A good example is a library with volumes of data, but little information. A person visits the library, looks at the data, provides meaning to those data, and determines those data are relevant and timely. Those data then become information to that person.

Another good example is Goethe's *Faust* in German. The text is only raw data. The reader must know German to apply meaning to those raw data, and must have an interest at a point in time, for *Faust* to become information.

Processes Resource Definitions

The following definitions pertain to the processes resource.

Methodology is derived from *methodo* and *ology* meaning *method study* or the *study of methods*.

Method is a procedure or process for attaining a goal; a way, technique, or process for doing something; a body of skills or techniques; a discipline that deals with principles and techniques.

Traditional processes management focusses on methodology rather than on method. We have been studying methods way too long. We need to quit studying methods and develop formal methods for managing data and processes as a critical resource.

A *process* is a specific grouping of one or more sets of actions and decisions defining the logic that responds to an event. Conversely, a specific grouping of one or more sets of actions and decisions uniquely defines a process. Two or more processes cannot have the same specific grouping of sets of actions and decisions.

Processes is the plural form of process.

A *manual process* is a process performed manually by people, such as employees of an organization, or citizens or customers of the organization.

An *automated process* is a process performed by computers, or other mechanical or electronic devices, with minimal or no involvement of people.

Processes are named with a verb-noun combination. Examples of process names are Calculate Interest, Issue Business License, Schedule Surgery, Post Job Opening, and so on. Each process has a comprehensive, denotative definition.

Raw processes are processes that are out of context, have no meaning, and are difficult to understand.

Raw process is a process that is out of context, has no meaning, and is difficult to understand.

Process in context is an individual process that has meaning and can be readily understood. A raw process wrapped with meaning.

Processes in context are processes that have meaning and can be readily understood. They are raw processes wrapped with meaning.

Process management is the management of a single business process the organization uses to support its business activities.

Processes management is a traditional term representing the management of processes, usually not as a critical resource and not formal.

Processes resource is the total collection of all processes available to the organization, from within or without the organization, however, whenever, and wherever those processes are stored and retrieved.

Process resource is not a valid term. It would be a resource of only one process.

Business and Non-business Realms

So far, the definitions have been oriented toward the business realm. The *business realm* is the sphere or extent of business activities which organizations manage. It includes all business activities, such as finance, human resource, manufacturing, medical procedures, marketing, scientific research, education, information, and so on, over which an organization has control.

Business data are any data currently being used, will be used, or might be used that *are relevant* to the organization's business.

Business processes are any processes currently being used, will be used, or might be used that *are relevant* to an organization's business

The *non-business realm* is the sphere or extent of activities which organizations cannot manage. It includes physical, chemical, biological, and radiological activities, and the combinations of those activities, over which an organization has no control.

Non-business data are any data used, created, or managed by non-business processes.

Non-business processes are any processes in the non-business realm.

One good example of the non-business realm is the human genetic code. The business process is documenting and unlocking the genetic code. The non-business processes are how the genetic code regulates the human body.

Another good example is understanding how the brain functions. The business process is understanding the brain function. The non-business process is how the brain actually functions.

SUMMARY

Meeting the basic needs for data and processes resolved many basic problems with data and with processes. It was a great first step. However, it surfaced fundamental problems across data and processes. Those fundamental problems had to be identified and resolved.

The sequence presented in Chapter 1 is enhanced to include the following two items:

- Identify the fundamental problems to resolve the basic problems.
- Identify the fundamental needs to resolve the fundamental problems.
- Resolving fundamental problems resolves basic problems.

The fundamental problems are that data and processes are separate resources, data and processes are not a critical resource, data and processes management is not integrated, and there is no vision for business understanding. The fundamental needs to resolve those fundamental problems are to unite the data and processes resources, consider data and processes a critical resource, integrate data and processes resource management, and establish a Business Understanding Vision.

Unite the data and processes resources includes two components for combining the data and processes resources, and building a single organization-wide data architecture and a single organization-wide processes architecture. Data-processes interdependence, and the data and processes resource were defined for combining the data and processes resources. The single organization-wide data architecture is used to integrate the data resource and the single organization-wide processes architecture is used to integrate the processes resource.

The data and processes resource is considered a critical resource, along with the human resource, financial resource, real property, and offerings. That critical resource is formally managed so that senior managers consider it an asset and financial executives include it on the chart of accounts or general ledger.

Integrate data and processes includes two components for data and processes resource management and a supporting data and processes resource culture. Data and processes resource management, and data and processes resource culture were defined.

Establish a Business Understanding Vision is an overarching construct for business understanding and agility, supported by an underlying foundation of theories, concepts, principles, and techniques to create and maintain that overarching construct.

The benefits of meeting the fundamental needs are increased business understanding, decreased uncertainty, decreased disparity, increased quality, and increased agility which ensure better business operation, and increases the chance of business success.

Additional basic definitions, data resource definitions, and processes resource definitions were provided. The Data-Information-Knowledge Cycle was defined, and both the business realm and non-business realm were defined. These definitions provide a foundation for meeting the fundamental needs and providing a thorough business understanding so organizations can be successful.

QUESTIONS

The following questions are provided as a review of the Fundamental Problems and Needs Chapter, and to stimulate thought about fundamental problems and needs.

1. What are the fundamental problems with data and processes?
2. How are the fundamental problems different from the basic problems?
3. What are the fundamental needs for data and processes?

4. What is data-processes interdependence?
5. What is the data and processes resource?
6. What is a single organization-wide architecture?
7. How is formal integration used to create single organization-wide architectures?
8. What are the contemporary critical resources for an organization?
9. Can the data and processes resource be considered an asset?
10. Why do data management and processes management need to be integrated?
11. Why is a supporting data and processes resource culture needed?
12. How are the components of a Business Understanding Vision related?
13. What are the benefits of meeting the fundamental needs?
14. Why is a distinction made between *citizen* and *customer*?
15. Why are the terms *logical* and *physical* changed to *business* and *implementation*?
16. What is the difference between data and information?
17. What is the Data-Information-Knowledge Cycle?
18. What is the difference between methodology and method?
19. What is the difference between the business realm and the non-business realm?
20. Why must the fundamental needs for data and processes be met?

Chapter 3
BUSINESS UNDERSTANDING

Business understanding drives the organization's business.

The Fundamental Problems and Needs Chapter described the fundamental problems across the data resource and the processes resource, and the fundamental needs to resolve those problems. The Business Understanding Vision was presented for an overarching construct for business understanding and agility.

The Business Understanding Chapter describes the overall business environment, an organization's business niche within that business environment, and the Business Understanding Sequence. The Business Niche Cycle, with its Understand Phase and Operate Phase, supports the organization's business. The Data Resource Cycle, and Processes Resource Cycle are combined into a Business Cycle with Organization as the focus.

The business functions and drivers are described, and business-driven, data-driven, and processes-driven are defined. The chapter theme is how a business understanding is gained from a cohesive Business Cycle and why an organization must fully understand its business to be agile and successful.

BUSINESS ENVIRONMENT

The business environment is viewed from an ecological perspective, where organisms have a specific niche based on cognitive and sensory powers, current surroundings, and previous experiences that are unique to those organisms and affect their behavior. The ecological perspective is self-centered, where different organisms have different ecological niches, even though they share the same environment.

Change *organism* to *organization*, which is a collection of organisms, and qualify *environment* to be *business environment*.

The ***business environment*** is the total of all business activities, everywhere, including commercial, industrial, scientific, environmental, education, and so on; that involves goods, services, research, and so on; conducted by large or small organizations, or individuals; whether for profit or not for profit.

The term *business world* should be avoided, because it is restrictive to the Earth. The term *business universe* should be avoided, because it's oriented to space and astronomy. The term *business climate* is acceptable and goes well with *business environment*.

The ***business niche*** is a subset of the business environment where an organization chooses to operate its business.

The business niche is composed of individual business niche objects, which can be a person, place, thing, or concept; business niche events; and business niche relationships that are of interest to the organization. It's a collection of organizations with similar business interests.

The overall business environment and the organization's business niche within that overall business environment are shown in Figure 3.1. The large oval represents the overall business environment, and the smaller oval represents the organization's business niche within the overall business environment.

Figure 3.1. The business environment and business niche.

BUSINESS NICHE CYCLE

An organization interacts with its business niche in two ways, as shown in Figure 3.2. An organization understands the business niche, shown by the arrow on the right from the business niche to the organization, and it operates in that business niche according to that understanding, shown by the arrow on the left from the organization to the business niche.

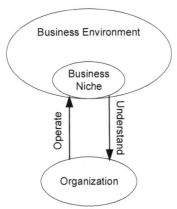

Figure 3.2. Organization interactions with its business niche.

The organization, its business niche, and the two interactions between the organization and its business niche form the Business Niche Cycle, shown in

Figure 3.3. The two interactions between the Organization and its Business Niche become an Understand Phase and an Operate Phase.

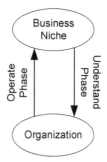

Figure 3.3. The Business Niche Cycle.

The **Business Niche Cycle** is a cycle between the organization and its business niche. The organization understands its business niche, and operates in that business niche according to the understanding gained, and the organization's goals and objectives.

The **Business Niche Understand Phase** is a phase of the Business Niche Cycle. An organization regularly observes its business niche to gain insight about the business niche, to confirm or adjust its business niche within the overall business environment, and to adjust its business activities to successfully operate in that business niche.

The Business Niche Understand Phase requires observation of the business niche to observe, analyze, and evaluate the business niche. An organization's successful business depends on routine observation of its business niche. The business niche details are described in the Business Niche Chapter, and business niche observation is described in the Business Nice Observation Chapter.

The **Business Niche Operate Phase** is a phase of the Business Niche Cycle. An organization retrieves business processes, and stores and retrieves data as necessary to conduct its business activities.

A **business moment** is a point in space-time, or the span of space-time, an organization conducts its business activities. It's a snapshot of business activities at a point in space-time or over a span of space-time.

Space-time is combined location and time. Location is useless without time, and time is useless without location. Space-time must include both location and time.

A **point in space-time** is a single location in space and a single point in time. A **span of space-time** is either an area of space at a point in time, a period of time at a point in space, or both an area of space and a period of time.

Theoretical physicists believe that space and time do not exist. The space and time that organizations know are only objectified facts that people agree to use. Organizations place events in time, rather than work with linear time.

BUSINESS UNDERSTANDING SEQUENCE

The organization's business understanding occurs at five different levels, from understanding the business environment to understanding the data and processes necessary to support business operations. The *Business Understanding Sequence* is a series of five levels of an organization's understanding from business environment understanding, to business niche understanding, to preliminary data and preliminary processes understanding, to data and processes architecture understanding, to data and processes understanding.

The Business Understanding Sequence is shown in Figure 3.4. Each of the five levels of business understanding is described below.

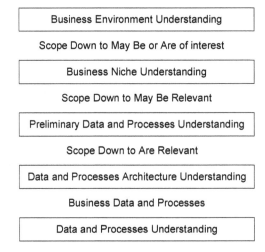

Figure 3.4. Business Understanding Sequence.

Business environment understanding is the organization's first level of understanding about the multitude and complexity of the interacting components in the business environment.

The business environment has far too many interacting components for an organization to fully comprehend and understand, and most of those components are not of interest to the organization. The business environment is scoped down to the business niche where an organization operates. The business niche is smaller and has fewer interacting components that could be of interest to the organization, and that the organization can comprehend and understand.

Business niche understanding is the organization's second level of understanding about its business niche within the business environment, that contains a smaller set of interacting components which *may be of interest* or *are of interest* to the organization.

May be of interest means the initial identification of components in the organization's business niche contain data and processes that could possibly be of interest to the organization.

Are of interest means additional understanding of components in the organization's business niche contain data and processes that are definitely of interest to the organization.

Many business niche components contain data and processes that *may be of interest* to the organization. These components are scoped down to data and processes that *are of interest* to the organization, and are further scoped down to preliminary data and processes. The scoping process is described in more detail in the Business Niche Chapter and the Business Niche Observation Chapter.

Preliminary data and processes understanding is the organization's third level of understanding about the preliminary data and processes that *may be relevant* to the organization.

May be relevant means that data and processes identified in the organization's business niche could possibly be relevant to the organization's business operation.

The preliminary data and preliminary processes that *may be relevant* to the organization feed the Data Resource Cycle and the Processes Resource Cycle. The Data Resource Cycle and Processes Resource Cycle are described in detail in the Data Resource Chapter and the Processes Resource Chapter.

Data and processes architecture understanding is the organization's fourth level of understanding about the data and processes that *are relevant* to the organization.

Are relevant means that data and processes have been determined to be relevant to the organization's business operation.

The data and processes that *are relevant* to the organization enhance the single organization-wide data resource architecture and the single organization-wide processes resource architecture.

Data and processes understanding is the organization's fifth level of understanding about the data that populate the data resource architecture and the processes that populate the processes resource architecture to operate the business.

The single organization-wide data resource architecture is populated with business data – the facts – necessary to operate the business. The single organization-wide processes resource architecture is populated with business processes – the decisions and actions – necessary to operate the business.

DATA RESOURCE AND PROCESSES RESOURCE CYCLES

The Understand Phase of the Business Niche Cycle drives both the Data Resource Cycle and the Processes Resource Cycle. The Business Niche Understand Phase is shown in Figure 3.5.

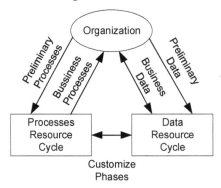

Figure 3.5. Business Niche Understand Phase.

The Processes Resource Cycle on the lower left uses preliminary processes to build business processes that are used to support the organization's business. The Data Resource Cycle on the lower right uses preliminary data to build business data that are stored and retrieved to support the organization's business. The two cycles interact during their Customize Phases. The Customize Phases of each cycle interact to ensure that the data and processes work together. The Data Resource Cycle and Processes Resource Cycle are described in in the next two chapters on the Data Resource and the Processes Resource.

BUSINESS CYCLE

The Business Niche Cycle, Processes Resource Cycle, and Data Resource Cycle overlap to form the Business Cycle, shown in Figure 3.6.

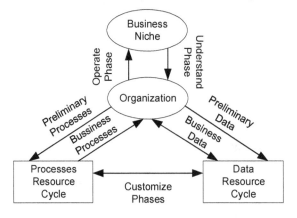

Figure 3.6. The Business Cycle.

The Business Niche Cycle between the business niche and the organization is shown at the top, the Processes Resource Cycle is shown on the lower left, and the Data Resource Cycle is shown on the lower right. The Business Cycle shows the importance of formally managing the data and processes resource with formal data and processes resource management.

The *Business Cycle* is an integration of the Business Niche Cycle, the Data Resource Cycle, and the Processes Resource Cycle with Organization as the focus. The organization understands its business niche, determines the data and processes needed to operate in that business niche, and operates its business according to those data and processes.

BUSINESS FUNCTIONS AND DRIVERS

The Understand Phase and the Operate Phase of the Business Niche Cycle represent two basic business functions to understand the business and to operate the business. The *Understand Business Function* is oriented toward thoroughly understanding the organization's business during the Business Niche Understand Phase. The *Operate Business Function* is oriented toward successfully operating the organization's agile business during the Business Niche Operate Phase.

These two basic business functions are interconnected. An organization needs to thoroughly understand the business to be agile and successfully operate the business. An organization also needs to know the intended business to thoroughly understand that business. Thorough business understanding depends on knowing the intended business, and successful business operation depends on thorough business understanding. The *business function association* is the interconnected relationship between the Understand Business Function and the Operate Business Function.

These two interconnected business functions lead to a question about what drives the Business Cycle. The Business Cycle is business-driven, and it is data-driven, and it is processes-driven. In the Business Niche Cycle, the intended operation drives understanding, and understanding drives operation. In the Data Resource Cycle, understanding drives data resource development, and the data resource supports drives operation. In the Processes Resource Cycle, understanding drives processes resource development, and the processes resource drives business operation.

An organization's goals, objectives, policies, and so on, become the organization's motivation for how it wants to do business. That motivation drives the Business Cycle. Motivation will be explained in more detail in the Business Understanding Framework Chapter.

Business-driven means the organization's motivation drives the understanding of its business niche, which is documented in the data and processes resource. The organization's operation in its business niche is supported by the data and processes resource. The **Business-Driven Motto** is the combined data and processes resource is of the business, by the business, and for the business. Development of the combined data and processes resource is driven by the business.

The **Business-Driven Rationale** is the degree to which an organization understands their business and develops a comparate data and processes resource equals the degree to which the organization is agile and successful in that business

Data-driven means the data drive the organization's business. Many business decisions and actions are based on data values. A comparate data resource provides the quality data for making decisions and taking actions.

Processes-driven means processes drive the organization's business. A process makes decisions and takes actions, which often triggers other processes. A comparate processes resource provides the quality decisions and actions.

The Business Niche Cycle, Data Resource Cycle, and Processes Resource Cycle come together to form the Business Cycle. Motivation drives understanding, understanding drives data and processes resource development, data drive processes, and processes drive business operation. An organization must fully comprehend the Business Cycle to be agile and successful.

Astronaut John Young said, "Anyone who sits on top of the largest hydrogen-oxygen fueled system in the world, knowing they're going to light the bottom, and doesn't get a little worried, does not fully understand the situation."

An organization that launches a business, stakes their time, effort, and reputation on that business, and isn't a little worried about the success of that business, does not fully comprehend the gravity of the situation. That organization needs to fully understand the Business Cycle.

SUMMARY

Meeting the fundamental needs begins with a thorough business understanding. The organization defines its business niche within the overall business environment. The organization interacts with its business niche through the Understand Phase and the Operate Phase of the Business Niche Cycle.

The Business Understanding Sequence consists of five levels of understanding for the business environment, the organization's business niche, the preliminary data and processes, the data and processes architectures, and the business data and processes populating those architectures that support business operation.

The Business Niche Cycle, Data Resource Cycle, and Processes Resource Cycle overlap with Organization as the focus to form the Business Cycle. The Understand Phase and the Operate Phase of the Business Niche Cycle represent two interconnected business functions to understand the business and to operate the business. An organization needs to understand the business to be agile and successfully operate the business, and it needs to know the intended business operations to understand the business.

Business-driven means the organization's motivation drives business understanding. Data-driven means the data values drive the business decisions and actions in processes. Processes-driven means processes drive the organization's business, and can trigger other processes. An organization must fully comprehend the Business Cycle to be agile and successful in its business operations.

QUESTIONS

The following questions are provided as a review of the Business Understanding Chapter, and to stimulate thought about a thorough business understanding.

1. What is the business environment?
2. What is the difference between the business environment and an organization's business niche?
3. What is the Business Niche Cycle?
4. What are the two phases of the Business Niche Cycle?
5. What do the two phases of the Business Niche Cycle accomplish?
6. What are the levels of the Business Understanding Sequence?
7. Why is the Business Understanding Sequence necessary?
8. What is the Business Cycle?
9. What is the focus of the Business Cycle?
10. How are the Business Niche Cycle, the Data Resource Cycle, and the Processes Resource Cycle related?
11. What are the two major business functions of an organization?
12. How are the two major business functions of an organization interconnected?
13. What is business-driven?
14. What is the Business-Driven Motto?
15. What is the rationale for being business-driven?
16. What is the impact of not being business-driven?
17. What is the motivation for business-driven?
18. What is data-driven?
19. What is processes-driven?

20. Why must an organization fully comprehend the Business Cycle to be agile and successful?

Chapter 4
DATA RESOURCE

A comparate data resource is crucial for business understanding.

The Business Understanding Chapter described the need for a thorough business understanding, and the Business Understanding Sequence with five levels of understanding from the business environment to the data resource and processes resource that jointly support business operation. The Business Niche Cycle, Data Resource Cycle, Processes Resource Cycle, Business Cycle, and two interconnected business functions were described.

The Data Resource Chapter describes the Data Resource Cycle with its four phases to build and maintain a comparate data resource of facts to provide understanding about the business; data resource documentation to provide understanding about the data resource; Data Resource Laws and Rules, violations of those laws and rules, and the impacts of those violations. The chapter theme is how an organization continues to build and maintain a thorough business understanding with the data resource.

DATA RESOURCE CYCLE

The fourth level of the Business Understanding Sequence is data and processes architecture understanding, and the fifth level is data and processes understanding. The Data Resource Cycle supports both the fourth and fifth levels of the Business Understanding Sequence for the data resource. Each phase and state of the Data Resource Cycle is described, the relationship between the Data Resource Cycle and the Five-Schema Concept is described, and an overview of data resource documentation to understand the data resource is presented.

The ***Data Resource Cycle*** is a cycle of data resource design, development, and management that begins with an organization's understanding of the business niche where it operates, progresses through formal design and development of a comparate data resource based on that understanding, and to use of the data resource to support the organization's agility and successful operation in their business niche.

The Data Resource Cycle is shown in Figure 4.1. The cycle begins with the organization understanding its business niche, and flows clockwise to the organization storing and retrieving data to operate in its business niche. The cycle consists of four states and four phases. The states are shown as nodes and the phases are shown as arcs between those nodes.

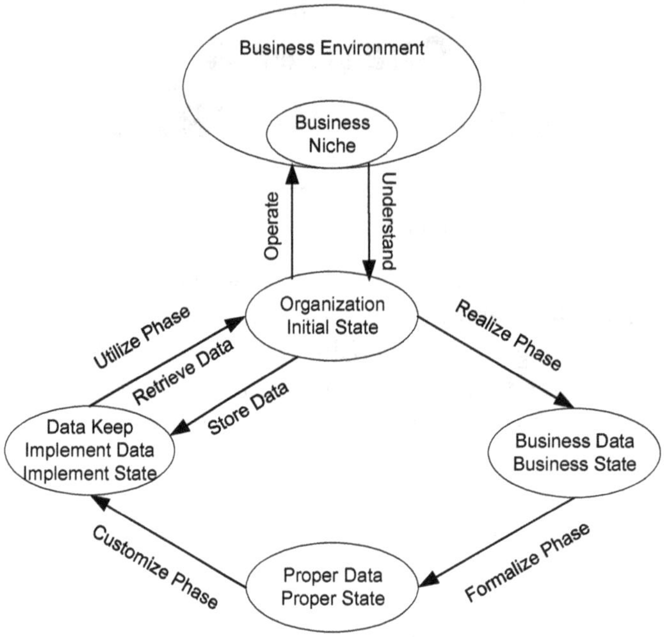

Figure 4.1. The Data Resource Cycle.

The **Data Resource Method** is the formal discipline for managing data as a critical resource of the organization. It's the study of objects, events, rules, relationships, and empirical values in the business niche where an organization operates, within a single organization-wide data architecture, expressed in a variety of different models depending on the scope, audience, and the understanding needed to reduce uncertainty, increase agility, and successfully operate the business. It's the discovery, understanding, and documentation of an organization's internal perception of the external business niche that is pervasive in all disciplines.

An *objective* is something toward which effort is directed; an aim or end of an action; a goal.

The **Data Resource Method Objective** is to get the right data, to the right people, in the right place, at the right time, in the right form, at the right cost, so they can make the right decisions, and take the right actions.

The operative term in that objective is *the right data*. If business professionals had the right data, knew they had the right data, knew the quality of those data, and thoroughly understood those data, then they would have far fewer problems understanding and managing the organization's business. Not having the right data, understanding those data, and knowing they are the right data, is where data resource management fails – big time!

Getting data to the right people, in the right place, at the right time, in the right form, at the right cost are simply technology issues that are relatively easy to managed. That's making sure data are readily available when and where needed.

Making the right decisions and taking the right actions are part of the decision-making process, not part of data resource management. The right data help decision makers make more informed decisions, but they do not help decision makers make better decisions! Better decisions are part of the decision-making process. Both data resource management and IT frequently fail to recognize the difference between more informed decisions and better decisions.

The emphasis of the objective is *the right data.* Business professionals need to find the right data, thoroughly understanding those data, and know those data are high quality. The current meta-data fiasco is preventing business professionals from getting the right data, which is seriously impacting the business.

Initial State

An organization's observation of its business niche identifies preliminary data, which become the initial state for the Data Resource Cycle. The Initial State is shown in the oval for Organization Initial State. Observation of the business niche and identification of preliminary data that form the initial state are described in more detail in the Business Niche Observation Chapter.

The ***Data Resource Initial State*** represents the preliminary data that *may be relevant* to the organization. It is intermediate between the Consensus Phase of the Business Niche Observation Cycle and the Data Resource Realize Phase.

Preliminary data are any data the organization identifies during observation of its business niche that *may be relevant* to the organization's business.

Realize Phase

The ***Data Resource Realize Phase*** is the first phase of the Data Resource Cycle. Preliminary data that *may be relevant* to the organization are reviewed and business data that *are relevant* to the organization are identified. The Data Resource Realize Phase leads to the Data Resource Business State.

The ***Data Resource Business State*** represents business data that *are relevant* to the organization. It is intermediate between the Data Resource Realize Phase and the Data Resource Formalize Phase.

Note the distinction between preliminary data that *may be relevant*, and business data that *are relevant*. The distinction will become clear as observation of the organization's business niche is described.

Formalize Phase

The ***Data Resource Formalize Phase*** is the second phase of the Data Resource Cycle. Business data are formally normalized to proper data within the single organization-wide data architecture for a common and thorough understanding of the data resource. The Data Resource Realize Phase leads to the Data Resource Proper State.

The ***Data Resource Proper State*** represents proper data within the single organization-wide data architecture. It is intermediate between the Data Resource Formalize Phase and the Data Resource Customize Phase.

Proper data are business data that have been formally normalized within the single organization-wide data architecture.

Normalize has many textual and mathematical definitions. However, a simple textual definition clarifies normalize for data and processes resource management. ***Normalize*** is to put something into a normal or standard form for an intended purpose.

Data normalization normalizes data into a single organization-wide data architecture, to achieve and maintain data resource comparity and understanding, with minimum energy.

Customize Phase

The ***Data Resource Customize Phase*** is the third phase of the Data Resource Cycle. Proper data are formally denormalized to implement data, without compromising those proper data, so the operating environment operates efficiently. The Data Resource Customize Phase leads to the Data Resource Implement State.

Denormalize has many textual and mathematical definitions. However, a simple textual definition clarifies denormalize for data and processes management. ***Denormalize*** is taking something out of normal or standard form for a specific purpose.

Data denormalization takes data out of their normal form in the single organization-wide data architecture for a special purpose. The normalized form in the single organization-wide data architecture is not altered in any way.

The ***Data Resource Implement State*** represents implement data that have been formally denormalized from proper data.

Implement data are proper data that have been formally denormalized for optimum operational performance, without compromising the proper data. They are the design for a data keep.

A ***data keep*** is any location, real or virtual, within or without the organization, where data in any form, electronic or manual, are stored and can be retrieved. Design of a data keep is usually based on the implement data.

The term *data keep* is used to prevent any connotative meanings for commonly used terms, such as database, data store, data vault, data warehouse, filing cabinet, library, desk drawer, disk, file, repository, cloud, and so on. It also represents human resource storage, as described earlier. It represents any form of data, such as text, books, magazines, presentations, documents, images, and so on.

In a broad sense, a data keep can include the human resource of an organization. However, the human resource is transient, while other data keeps are more persistent.

Utilize Phase

The *Data Resource Utilize Phase* is the fourth phase of the Data Resource Cycle. Operational data are stored in a data keep, and retrieved to support the organization's business.

Operational data provide an understanding of the organization's business that supports day-to-day business operations and operational decision making. They are the contents of a data keep according to the implement data.

Implement data are the design for a data keep—the fourth level of the Business Understanding Sequence, and *operational data* are the contents of a data keep – the fifth level of the Business Understanding Sequence. Implement data typically do not provide the design for human resource data storage.

The Five-Schema Concept

The Five-Schema Concept is part of the Five-Tier Five-Schema Concept described in the Data Resource Simplexity series of books. The Data Resource Cycle has a direct relationship to the Five-Schema Concept. That relationship is described in Appendix C.

Data Resource Documentation

The single organization-wide data architecture provides a thorough understanding of the organization's data resource – the fourth level in the Business Understanding Sequence. Operational data provide a thorough understanding of the organization's business – the fifth level in the Business Understanding Sequence. Data resource data provide an understanding of both the data architecture and the operational data. Both levels of understanding are necessary for an organization to conduct its business activities.

The term *data catalogue* has been used for many years and could be very useful. However, a simple catalogue of data is not enough to thoroughly understand an organization's data resource. An organization needs a complete and comprehensive guide to its entire data resource. The Data Resource Guide described in the Data Resource Simplexity series of books meets that need.

Data resource data are any data necessary for thoroughly understanding, formally managing, and fully utilizing the organization's data resource to support the organization's current and future business information demand. Data resource data include formal data names, denotative data definitions, proper data structures, and precise data integrity rules.

The Data Resource Cycle with the phases as nodes and the states as arcs between the nodes is shown in Figure 4.2. The cycle flows clockwise, the same as the Data Resource Cycle in Figure 4.1. Each phase of the Data Resource Cycle connects with the data resource data to store, retrieve, or reference those data resource data as necessary to understand and utilize the data resource.

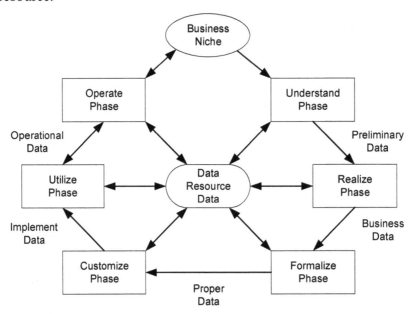

Figure 4.2. Data resource data.

Data Resource Data replace the traditional *meta-data*, which is usually defined as *data about the data*. However, that definition leads to an infinite regress problem.

The infinite regress problem is characterized by the story about a scientist giving a public lecture describing how the moon orbits the Earth, the Earth orbits the sun, the sun orbits the Milky Way Galaxy, and so on. A lady in the audience stands up and says, "That's rubbish. The world is flat and is supported on the back of a giant turtle." The scientist asks the lady where the giant turtle is standing. The lady replies, "You are very clever, young man, but you can't fool me. It's turtles all the way down."

The same is true for early theories of the human brain. People thought a little man, a homunculus, was inside a person's brain making all the decisions. But what's inside the brain of the homunculus? Well, another smaller homunculus, and so on – all the way down.

Meta-data have the same infinite regress problem. What defines the meta-data? What defines the data defining the meta-data? What defines those data? The situation is data defining data – all the way down.

Data resource data are self-defining, which resolves the infinite regress problem. Self-defining data resource data resolve the whole meta-data fiasco and focus on understanding the organization's data resource architecture and contents. Data resource data are part of the organization's data resource, and are formally managed the same as any other data in the organization's data resource. Data resource data are described in detail in the Data Resource Simplexity series of books.

DATA RESOURCE LAWS AND RULES

Data Resource Laws and Rules guide formal data resource management. Violations of those laws and rules create many of the common, basic, and fundamental problems described earlier.

Data Resource Laws

Data Resource Laws support formal data resource management in the creation and maintenance of an organization's comparate data resource.

A *law* is a binding custom or practice, a rule of conduct or action prescribed or commonly recognized as formally binding or enforced.

Data Resource Laws are laws that guide formal data resource management, and ensure integrity and quality of the organization's data resource.

The data resource laws are patterned after the three laws of robots, from *Robots of Dawn* by Isaac Asimov. The data resource laws may not have meaning or seem relevant now, but their meaning and relevance will become clear in the next several chapters. The term *formal design techniques* in the descriptions includes the theories, concepts, principles, and techniques that support formal data resource management.

First Data Resource Law: Identification of business data from preliminary data must be based on the organization's need for business data, whether currently needed or might be needed. Specifically, any person involved in the identification of business data from preliminary data must not disregard the organization's need, whether currently needed or might be needed, nor through inaction, allow any data currently needed or might be needed to be disregarded.

Second Data Resource Law: Normalization of the business data to proper data within the single organization-wide data architecture must be based on formal design techniques, as long as the First Data Resource Law is not violated. Specifically, any person involved in normalization of business data to proper data within the single organization-wide data architecture must not disregard the formal design techniques, nor through inaction, allow the formal design techniques to be disregarded, as long as the First Data Resource Law is not violated.

Third Data Resource Law: Denormalization of the proper data to implement data must be based on formal design techniques, as long as the First Data Resource Law and Second Data Resource Law are not violated. Specifically, any person involved in denormalization of the proper data to implement data must not disregard the formal design techniques, nor through inaction, allow the formal design techniques to be disregarded, as long as the First Data Resource Law and the Second Data Resource Law are not violated.

Data Resource Rules

The Data Resource Laws are supported by a set of Data Resource Rules.

A *rule* is an authoritative, prescribed direction for conduct, or a usual, customary, or generalized course of action or behavior; a statement that describes what is true in most or all cases; a standard method or procedure for solving problems.

Data Resource Rules are rules that guide formal data resource management, and ensure the integrity and quality of the organization's data resource. They support the Data Resource Laws.

The Data Resource Rules are:

1. Design and development of the organization's data resource must be business-driven, and must be designed to be readily adjusted to meet changing business needs in a dynamic business niche.
2. The organization's data resource must be developed for the long-term business needs, as well as the current business needs.
3. The organization's data resource must be designed and developed within the single organization-wide data architecture.
4. The single organization-wide data architecture must be independent of any processes architecture and any hardware / system software architecture.
5. All data in the organization's data resource must have formal data names and formal data name abbreviations that are meaningful to anyone in the organization.
6. All data in the organization's data resource must have comprehensive

and denotative definitions that are well understood by anyone in the organization.

7. The proper data must be developed for understanding by the business, based on business needs.

8. The proper data integrity rules must be developed by the business, based on business needs.

9. The implement data must be formally developed from the proper data, without compromising the proper data.

10. The implement data edits must be formally developed from the proper data integrity rules, without compromising the proper data integrity rules.

11. Complete and understandable documentation about the organization's data resource must be readily available, and understandable, to anyone in the organization.

12. The organization's data resource management culture must be cohesive and integrated throughout the organization.

Data Resource Law and Rule Violations

The Data Resource Laws and Data Resource Rules are often violated. A violation occurs when the formal route through the Data Resource Cycle is bypassed. The Data Resource Cycle states, phases, formal transitions, and violations are shown in the state transition diagrams in Figure 4.3.

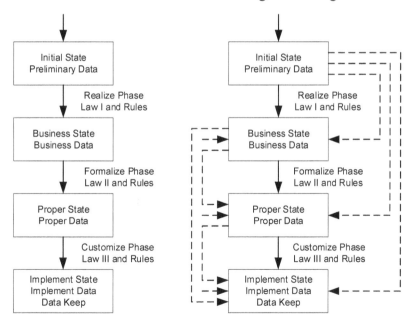

Figure 4.3. Data Resource Law and Rule violations.

The diagram on the left shows the formal transitions through the Data Resource Cycle, represented by solid lines. The formal transitions are:

- Formal transition into the Initial State.
- Formal transition between the Initial State and the Business State, following the First Data Resource Law and appropriate Rules.
- Formal transition between the Business State and the Proper State, following the Second Data Resource Law and appropriate Rules.
- Formal transition between the Proper State and the Implement State, following the Third Data Resource Law and appropriate Rules.

The diagram on the right shows the four formal transitions, plus the nine possible informal transitions, represented by dashed lines. Three informal transitions on the left directly enter the Business Sate, the Proper State, and the Implement State, ignoring Data Resource Laws and Rules.

Three additional informal transitions on the left jump from the Business State to the Proper State, from the Business State to the Implement State, and from the Proper State to the Implement State, ignoring Data Resource Laws and Rules.

Three informal transitions on the right jump from the Initial State to the Business State, from the Initial State to the Proper State, and from the Initial State to the Implement State, ignoring Data Resource Laws and Rules.

Bypassing the First Data Resource Law and appropriate Data Resource Rules results in loss of an organization's understanding about the business niche where it operates, and in loss of consensus about the data needed to successfully operate the business.

Bypassing the Second Data Resource Law and appropriate Data Resource Rules results in loss of formal data normalization techniques, including names, definitions, structure, and integrity, and in loss of data understanding within the single organization-wide data architecture.

Bypassing the Third Data Resource Law and appropriate Data Resource Rules results in loss of formal data denormalization techniques, including names, definitions, structure, and edits.

The impacts of the violations are the common problems, basic problems, and fundamental problems described earlier. Initial violations create a cascade of additional violations. An organization cannot recover from the damage caused by a violation in a later phase of the Data Resource Cycle. The damage has been done!

SUMMARY

The Data Resource Cycle supports the fourth level of the Business Understanding Sequence by providing understanding of the data resource architecture. It also sets the stage for the fifth level of the Business

Understanding Sequence that provides understanding of the operational data that populate the data resource architecture. The Data Resource Cycle aligns with the Data Resource Method and Data Resource Method Objective.

The Data Resource Cycle starts with an Initial State containing preliminary data that *may be relevant* to the organization. The Realize Phase reviews those preliminary data and identifies business data that *are relevant* to the organization. The Formalize Phase normalizes those business data to proper data within the organization-wide data architecture. The Customize Phase denormalizes the proper data to implement data which are the design for a non-human resource data keep. The Utilize Phase stores operational data and retrieves operational data as necessary to support the organization's business.

The data resource is documented with data resource data that provide an understanding of the data resource. Each phase of the Data Resource Cycle interacts with the data resource data to enhance and maintain that data resource understanding. Data resource data are self-defining and replace the traditional meta-data that create an infinite regress problem.

Three Data Resource Laws and twelve associated Data Resource Rules support formal data resource management, and creation and maintenance of an organization's comparate data resource. Violations of the Data Resource Laws and Rules, which are violations of the formal Data Resource Cycle, result in a cascade of common problems, basic problems, and fundamental problems found in most organizations today. The damage has been done, and recovery from these problems, if possible, is difficult and costly.

QUESTIONS

The following questions are provided as a review of the Data Resource Chapter, and to stimulate thought about formal data resource management and the Data Resource Cycle.

1. How does the organization interact with its business niche?
2. What is the Data Resource Cycle?
3. What is the Data Resource Method?
4. What is the Data Resource Method Objective?
5. What is the initial state for the Data Resource Cycle?
6. What does the Data Resource Realize Phase accomplish?
7. What is the difference between preliminary data and business data?
8. What does the Data Resource Formalize Phase accomplish?
9. What is the difference between proper data and business data?
10. What does the Data Resource Customize Phase accomplish?
11. What is the difference between implement data and proper data?
12. What does the Data Resource Utilize Phase accomplish?

13. What is the difference between operational data and implement data?
14. How is the organization's data resource understanding documented?
15. What is the difference between data resource data and traditional meta-data?
16. What are the Data Resource Laws?
17. What are the Data Resource Rules?
18. What are the formal transitions through the Data Resource Cycle?
19. What are the informal transitions through the Data Resource Cycle?
20. How do the informal transitions through the Data Resource Cycle impact the organization?

Chapter 5
PROCESSES RESOURCE

A comparate processes resource is crucial for business understanding.

The Data Resource Chapter described formal data resource management to build and maintain a comparate data resource of facts that provide understanding about the business, which is the first part of combined data and processes resource management. The second part of combined data and processes resource management is formal processes resource management to build and maintain a comparate processes resource of decisions and actions that provide additional understanding about the business, and to build and maintain an understanding of the processes resource.

The Processes Resource Chapter describes the Processes Resource Cycle with its four phases to build and maintain a comparate processes resource of decisions and actions that provide understanding about the business, including a link between the Data Resource Customize Phase and the Processes Resource Customize Phase; processes resource documentation to provide understanding of the processes resource; and Processes Resource Laws and Rules, violations of those laws and rules, and the impacts of those violations. The chapter theme is how an organization continues to build and maintain a thorough business understanding with the processes resource.

PROCESSES RESOURCE CYCLE

The fourth level of the Business Understanding Sequence is data and processes architecture understanding, and the fifth level is data and processes understanding. The Processes Resource Cycle supports both the fourth and fifth levels of the Business Understanding Sequence for the processes resource. Each phase and state of the Processes Resource Cycle is described. An overview of the processes resource documentation to understand the data resource is presented. The link between the Data Resource Cycle and the Processes Resource Cycle Customize Phases is described.

The *Processes Resource Cycle* is a cycle of processes resource design, development, and management that begins with an organization's understanding of the business niche where it operates, progresses through formal design and development of a processes resource based on that understanding, to use of the processes resource to support the organization's agility and successful operation in their business niche.

The Processes Resource Cycle is shown in Figure 5.1. The cycle begins with the organization understanding its business niche, and flows counter-clockwise to the organization retrieving processes to operate in its business niche. The cycle consists of four states and four phases. The states are shown as nodes and the phases are arcs between those nodes. The reason for the diagram flowing counter-clockwise will become obvious.

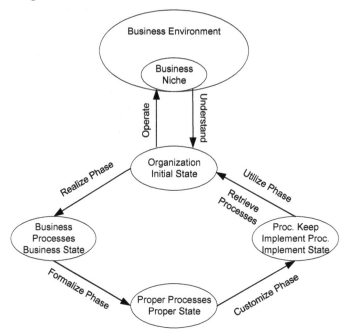

Figure 5.1. The Processes Resource Cycle.

The ***Processes Resource Method*** is the formal discipline for managing processes as a critical resource of the organization. It's the study of the objects, events, rules, relationships, and processes in the business niche where an organization operates, within a single organization-wide processes architecture, expressed in a variety of different models, depending on the scope, audience, and understanding needed to reduce uncertainty, and successfully operate the business. It's the discovery, understanding, and documentation of an organization's internal perception of the external business niche that is pervasive in all disciplines.

The ***Processes Resource Method Objective*** is the right processes, used by the right people, in the right place, at the right time, in the right form, at the right cost, so they can make the right decisions, and take the right actions.

The operative term in that objective is *the right processes*, meaning people thoroughly understand the processes and use them appropriately. Not thoroughly understanding processes and using them appropriately is where processes resource management fails – big time!

The right processes are determined from formal processes names and denotative definitions. All processes must be formally named and comprehensively defined, and those names and definitions must be readily available to anyone in the organization. The process logic needs to be complete and correct. People need to thoroughly understand processes, to make sure they use the right processes.

Used by the right people means the people or organization units authorized to use or initiate processes can access those processes, while others cannot. That's an authorization process.

In the right place means where the processes are performed. Some processes must be performed in a specific location, such as a lab or by a computer. Other processes can be performed in many different locations, such as crime scene investigations.

At the right time means within the appropriate time window allowed for the process. Some processes are very time-critical, and others are less time-critical. At the right time also means in the right sequence, or the right time interval.

The right form is the way in which the process is performed. Processes could be performed many different ways, and the right form for a particular situation is important.

The cost of performing a process is important. The cost may be prohibitive, and the process should not be performed. The process may need to be performed regardless of the cost. If cost is important, evaluation of the cost and whether to continue should be part of the process, or a supporting process.

The right decisions and right actions are part of the decision-making process, as explained earlier for data. Decisions can be made by decision makers, or by automated processes. Automated processes are developed and approved by decision-makers, so the decision makers ultimately control the decision-making process.

Initial State

An organization's understanding of its business niche identifies preliminary processes, which become the initial state for the Processes Resource Cycle. The Initial State is shown in the oval for Organization Initial State. Observation of the business niche and identification of preliminary processes are descried in more detail in the Business Niche Observation Chapter.

The *Processes Resource Initial State* represents the preliminary processes that *may be relevant* to the organization. It is intermediate between the Consensus Phase of the Business Niche Observation Cycle and the

Processes Resource Realize Phase.

Preliminary processes are any processes the organization identifies during observation of its business niche that *may be relevant* to the organization's business.

Realize Phase

The *Processes Resource Realize Phase* is the first phase of the Processes Resource Cycle. Preliminary processes that *may be relevant* to the organization are reviewed and business processes that *are relevant* to the organization are identified. The Processes Resource Realize Phase leads to the Processes Resource Business State.

The *Processes Resource Business State* represents business processes that are relevant to the organization. It is intermediate between the Processes Resource Realize Phase and the Processes Resource Formalize Phase.

Note the distinction between preliminary processes that *may be relevant*, and business processes that *are relevant*. The distinction will become clear as observation of the organization's business niche is described.

Formalize Phase

The *Processes Resource Formalize Phase* is the second phase of the Processes Resource Cycle. Business Processes are formally normalized to proper processes within the single organization-wide processes architecture for a common and thorough understanding of the processes resource. The Processes Resource Realize Phase leads to the Processes Resource Proper State.

The *Processes Resource Proper State* represents proper processes within the single organization-wide processes architecture. It is intermediate between the Processes Resource Formalize Phase and the Processes Resource Customize Phase.

Proper processes are business processes that have been formally normalized within the single organization-wide processes architecture.

Processes normalization normalizes processes into a single organization-wide processes architecture, to achieve and maintain processes resource comparity and understanding, with minimum energy.

Customize Phase

The *Processes Resource Customize Phase* is the third phase of the Processes Resource Cycle. Proper processes are formally denormalized to implement processes, without compromising those proper processes, so the operating environment operates efficiently. The Processes Resource Customize Phase lads to the Processes Resource Implement State.

Processes denormalization takes processes out of their normal form in the single organization-wide processes architecture for a special purpose. The normalized form in the single organization wide processes architecture is not altered in any way.

The *Processes Resource Implement State* represents implement processes that have been formally denormalized from proper processes.

Operational processes are proper processes that have been formally denormalized for optimum operational performance, without compromising the proper processes. They provide an understanding of the organization's business that supports day-to-day business operations.

Unlike data, when processes have been developed and tested in the Processes Resource Customize Phase and are ready for implementation, they are stored in a processes keep and are ready for retrieval and use to support the organization's business.

The *processes keep* is any location, real or virtual, within or without the organization, where operational processes in any form, electronic or manual, are stored and can be retrieved.

The term *processes keep* is used to prevent any connotative meanings for commonly used terms for locations where processes are stored.

In a broad sense, a processes keep can include the human resource of an organization. However, the human resource is transient, while other processes keeps are more persistent.

Utilize Phase

The *Processes Resource Utilize Phase* is the fourth phase of the Processes Resource Cycle. Operational Processes are retrieved from the processes keep and initiated to support the organization's business.

Processes Resource Documentation

The single organization-wide processes architecture provides a thorough understanding of the organization's processes resource – the fourth level in the Business Understanding Sequence. Operational processes provide a thorough understanding of the organization's processes – the fifth level in the Business Understanding Sequence. Processes resource data provide an understanding of both the processes architecture and the operational processes. Both levels of understanding are necessary for an organization to conduct its business activities.

Processes resource data are any data necessary for thoroughly understanding, formally managing, and fully utilizing the organization's processes to fully support the organization's current and future business information demand.

Processes resource data replaces the often-used *meta-process*, which is typically defined as the *data about processes*. *Meta-process* is a term intended to be parallel to *meta-data*. However, *meta-process* literally means *processes about processes*. It does not mean *data about processes*. Therefore, the term *processes resource data* is used, which is parallel to *data resource data*.

I'm not aware of any formal structure for processes resource data or a comprehensive Processes Resource Guide, similar to data resource data and the Data Resource Guide. However, a formal structure for processes resource data and Processes Resource Guide could be developed similar to the data resource data and Data Resource Guide described in the Data Resource Simplexity series of books. The result would help an organization formally manage its processes resource.

Processes resource data do not face an infinite regress problem like data resource data. Therefore, processes resource data do not need to be self-defining. However, the definition of processes could have its own infinite regress problem. A process could range from a simple decision or action to an information system. Documenting processes at the decision or action level is too low. Similarly, documenting processes at the information system level is too high. Process documentation lies somewhere within this range. The situation will be described in more detail in the Business Understanding Components Chapter.

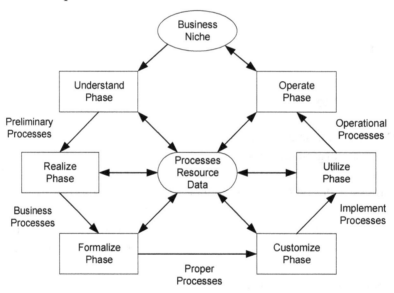

Figure 5.2. Processes resource data.

The Processes Resource Cycle with the phases as nodes and the states as arcs between the nodes is shown in Figure 5.2. The cycle flows counter-clockwise, the same as the Processes Resource Cycle in Figure 5.1. Each phase of the Processes Resource Cycle connects to the processes resource data to store, retrieve, or reference processes resource data as necessary to understand and utilize the processes resource.

Linked Customize Phases

The last two phases of the Processes Resource Cycle and the Data Resource Cycle are shown in Figure 5.3. One reason the Data Resource Cycle (on the right) flows clockwise and the Processes Resource Cycle (on the left) flows counter-clockwise is to show how the two Utilize Phases support the Operate Phase at the top of the diagram.

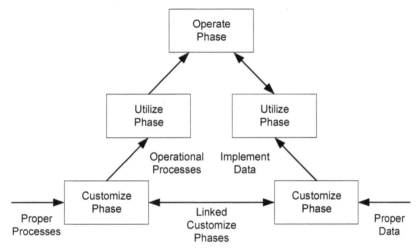

Figure 5.3. Linked Customize Phases.

The Processes Resource Cycle and Data Resource Cycle come together to form the combined, interdependent data and processes resource, supported by combined data and processes resource management, to support the organization's business. The Operate Phase retrieves operational processes from a processes keep developed in the Processes Resource Utilize Phase as necessary to support business operations. The Operate Phase also stores operational data in a data keep and retrieves operational data from a data keep developed in the Data Resource Utilize Phase as necessary to support business operations.

Remember the object-oriented arguments about whether data drove processes design, or whether processes drove data design? That issue is resolved with a link between the Processes Resource Customize Phase, on the lower left, and the Data Resource Customize Phase, on the lower right.

The Data Resource Customize Phase formally denormalizes proper data to implement data, which become the design for a data keep where operational data are stored and retrieved. The Processes Resource Customize Phase formally denormalizes proper processes to operational processes. The link between the Data Resource Customize Phase and the Processes Resource Customize Phase is where the data and the processes are denormalized as appropriate to work together for a specific purpose.

Proper data can have multiple denormalizations to implement data, and proper processes can have multiple denormalizations to operational processes for specific purposes. However, the data resource has only one set of proper data within the single organization-wide data architecture, and the processes resource has only one set of proper processes within the single organization-wide processes architectures. The denormalizations of the proper forms are for specific purposes.

PROCESSES RESOURCE LAWS AND RULES

Processes Resource Laws and Rules guide formal processes resource management. Violations of those laws and rules create many of the common, basic, and fundamental problems described earlier.

Processes Resource Laws

Processes Resource Laws support formal processes resource management in the creation and maintenance of an organization's comparate processes resource. Their structure is parallel to the Data Resource Laws.

Processes Resource Laws are laws that guide formal processes resource management, and ensure integrity and quality of the organization's processes resource.

First Processes Resource Law: Identification of the preliminary processes must be based on the organization's need for business processes, whether currently needed or might be needed. Specifically, any person involved in the identification of the business processes must not disregard the organization's need, whether currently needed or might be needed, nor through inaction allow any processes currently needed or might be needed to be disregarded.

Second Processes Resource Law: Normalization of the business processes to proper processes within the single organization-wide processes architecture must be based on formal design techniques, as long as the First Processes Resource Law is not violated. Specifically, any person involved in normalization of business processes to proper processes within the single organization-wide processes architecture must not disregard the formal design techniques, nor through inaction, allow the formal design techniques to be disregarded, as long as the First Processes Resource Law is not violated.

Third Processes Resource Law: Denormalization of the proper processes to of the operational processes must be based on formal design techniques, as long as the First Processes Resource Law and Second Processes Resource Law are not violated. Specifically, any person involved in denormalization of proper processes to operational processes must not disregard the formal design techniques, nor through inaction, allow the formal design techniques, as long as the First Processes Resource Law and the Second Processes Resource Law are not violated.

Processes Resource Rules

The Processes Resource Laws are supported by a set of Processes Resource Rules. *Processes Resource Rules* are rules that guide formal processes resource management, and ensure the integrity and quality of the organization's processes resource. They support the Processes Resource Laws.

The Processes Resource Rules are:

1. Design and development of the organization's processes resource must be business-driven, and must be designed to be readily adjusted to meet changing business needs in a dynamic business niche.
2. The organization's processes resource must be developed for the long-term business needs, as well as the current business needs.
3. The organization's processes must be designed and developed within the single organization-wide processes architecture.
4. The single organization-wide processes architecture must be independent of any data architecture and any hardware / system software architecture.
5. All processes in the organization's processes resource must have formal names and formal name abbreviations that are meaningful to anyone in the organization.
6. All processes in the organization's processes resource must have comprehensive and denotative definitions that are well understood by anyone in the organization.
7. The proper processes must be developed for understanding by the business, based on business needs.
8. An exhaustive set of processes integrity rules must be jointly developed and maintained by business professionals and technical developers.
9. The operational processes must be formally developed from the proper processes, without compromising those proper processes.
10. Every operational process must pass the processes integrity rules before it can be implemented.

11. Complete and understandable documentation about the organization's processes must be readily available, and understandable, to anyone in the organization.

12. The organization's processes resource management culture must be cohesive and integrated throughout the organization.

Processes Law and Rule Violations

The Processes Resource Laws and Processes Resource Rules are often violated. A violation occurs when the formal route through the Processes Resource Cycle is bypassed. The Processes Resource Cycle states and phases are shown in the state transition diagram in Figure 5.4.

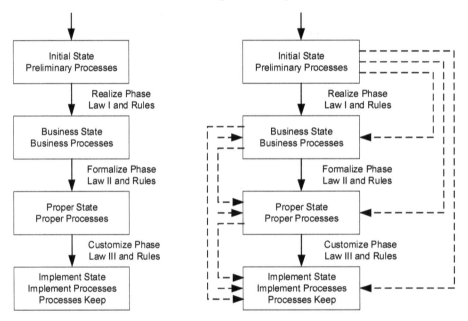

Figure 5.4. Processes laws and rules violations.

The diagram on the left shows the formal transitions through the Processes Resource Cycle, represented by solid lines. The formal transitions are:

- Formal transition into the Initial State.
- Formal transition between the Initial State and the Business State, following the First Processes Resource Law and appropriate Rules.
- Formal transition between the Business State and the Proper State, following the second Processes Resource Law and appropriate Rules.
- Formal transition between the Proper State and the Implement State, following the Third Processes Resource Law and appropriate Rules.

The diagram on the right shows the four formal transitions, plus the nine possible informal transitions, represented by dashed lines. The three informal transitions on the left directly enter the Business Sate, the Proper State, and the Implement State, ignoring Data Resource Laws and Rules.

The three additional informal transitions on the left jump from the Business State to the Proper State, from the Business State to the Implement State, and from the Proper State to the Implement State, ignoring Processes Resource Laws and Rules.

The three informal transitions on the right jump from the Initial State to the Business State, from the Initial State to the Proper State, and from the Initial State to the Implement State, ignoring Processes Resource Laws and Rules.

Bypassing the First Processes Resource Law and appropriate Processes Resource Rules results in a loss of an organization's understanding about the business niche where it operates, and in a loss of consensus about the processes needed to successfully operate the business.

Bypassing the Second Processes Resource Law and appropriate Processes Resource Rules results in a loss of formal processes normalization techniques, including names, definitions, structure, and integrity, and in loss of processes understanding within the single organization-wide processes architecture.

Bypassing the Third Processes Resource Law and appropriate Processes Resource Rules results in loss of formal processes denormalization techniques, including names, definitions, structure, and edits.

The impacts of the violations are the common problems, basic problems, and fundamental problems described earlier. Initial violations create a cascade of additional violations. An organization can't recover from the damage caused by a violation in a later state in the cycle. Like the data resource, the damage has been done!

Violations of the Data Resource Cycle and the Processes Resource Cycle are commonly referred to as brute-force development. ***Brute-force development*** is any action that bypasses or circumvents one or more phases in the formal Data Resource Cycle or Processes Resource Cycle. It's any action that jumps to a different state, or ignores the Data Resource Laws and Rules or the Processes Resource Laws and Rules.

Brute-force development ignores the big picture and future needs. It focuses on current needs in a data manipulation industry. The result is an unnecessary use of resources and an ultimate impact on the organization's business success.

SUMMARY

The Processes Resource Cycle supports the fourth level of the Business

Understanding Sequence by providing understanding of the processes resource architecture. It also sets the stage for the fifth level of the Business Understanding Sequence that provides understanding of the operational processes that populate the processes resource architecture. The Processes Resource Cycle meets the Processes Resource Method and Processes Resource Method Objective.

The Processes Resource Cycle starts with an initial state containing preliminary processes that *may be relevant*. The Realize Phase reviews those preliminary processes and identifies business processes that *are relevant*. The Formalize Phase normalizes the business processes to proper processes within an organization-wide processes architecture. The Customize Phase denormalizes the proper processes to operational processes that are stored in the processes keep. The Utilize Phase retrieves operational processes as necessary to support the organization's business.

The Data Resource Customize Phase and the Processes Resource Customize Phase interact to denormalize data and/or processes to work together for a specific purpose.

The processes resource is documented with processes resource data that provide an understanding of the processes resource. Each phase of the Business Niche Cycle and the Processes Resource Cycle interact with the processes resource data to enhance and maintain that processes resource understanding. *Processes resource data* replaces *meta-processes*, which is an incorrect term for documenting the processes resource.

Three Processes Resource Laws and twelve associated Processes Resource Rules support formal processes resource management, and creation and maintenance of an organization's comparate processes resource. Violation of the Processes Resource Laws and Rules, which are violations of the formal Processes Resource Cycle, result in a cascade of common problems, basic problems, and fundamental problems found in most organizations today. The damage has been done, and recovery from these problems, if possible, is difficult and costly.

QUESTIONS

The following questions are provided as a review of the Processes Resource Chapter, and to stimulate thought about processes resource management and the Processes Resource Cycle.

1. What is the Processes Resource Cycle?
2. What is the Processes Resource Method?
3. What is the Processes Resource Method Objective?
4. What is the initial state for the Processes Resource Cycle?
5. What does the Processes Resource Realize Phase accomplish?

6. What is the difference between preliminary processes and business processes?
7. What does the Processes Resource Phase accomplish?
8. What is the difference between proper processes and business processes?
9. What does the Processes Resource Customize Phase accomplish?
10. What is the difference between operational processes and proper processes?
11. What is the purpose of the link between the Data Resource Customize Phase and the Processes Resource Customize Phase?
12. Why are operational processes stored in a processes keep in the Customize Phase?
13. How does the Processes Resource Utilize Phase differ from the Data Resource Utilize Phase?
14. How is the organization's processes resource documented?
15. Why does processes resource data not have an infinite regress problem?
16. What are the Processes Resource Laws?
17. What are the Processes Resource Rules?
18. What are the formal transitions through the Processes Resource Cycle?
19. What are the informal transitions through the Processes Resource Cycle?
20. How do the informal transitions through the Processes Resource Cycle impact the organization?

Chapter 6
BUSINESS NICHE

Understand the business niche to observe the business niche.

The Data Resource Chapter and the Processes Resource Chapter described cycles for developing a comparate data resource and a comparate processes resource that supports an organization's business. Those two resource cycles are driven by preliminary data and preliminary processes that are identified during observation of the organization's business niche. However, before describing observation of the organization's business niche, the details of a dynamic business niche with its multitude of interacting components must be understood. Starting downstream of understanding a dynamic business niche only leads to disparity and uncertainty.

The Business Niche Chapter describes the business niche state, the dynamic nature of a business niche, the set of components in a business niche, and business niche scenarios. The chapter theme is to understand the business niche components and their interactions so an organization can observe its business niche to better understand its business.

BUSINESS NICHE STATE

The business niche consists of a complex set of objects that interact in a variety of different ways over time to form events. An *object* is a person, place, thing, or concept. An *event* is a single happening or interaction between two or more objects at a point in space-time or over a span of space-time. An event cannot happen without objects. An event has a unique set of features, and a unique set of features define an event.

Events are named with a noun-verb combination. Examples of event names are Hazardous Waste Spill, Business License Application, Volcano Eruption, Vehicle Collision, and so on. Each event has a comprehensive, denotative definition.

An *event type* is a classification of events, such as fire, flood, natural disaster, permit application, and so on.

Each event type has a denotative definition that applies to all events in that event type. A specific event inherits the event type definition, and includes a more specific comprehensive definition about the specific event.

The complex interaction of objects and events in the business niche is based on mathematics. *Mathematics* is the science of numbers and their operations, interrelations, combinations, generalizations, abstractions, configurations, and so on. It includes mathematical structures, empirical domains, and any correspondence linking those structures and domains. The correspondence is relationships and rules.

The complex interactions of objects and events in the business niche are probabilities that are supported by the First Law of Ecology. Barry Commoner established four basic and inescapable Laws of Ecology to describe the web of life on Earth. The First Law of Ecology states that everything is connected to something else. Everything is a network of relationships with interconnections and interactions, and one thing can never be done in isolation. It's all about relationships that act on one another, have surprising consequences, influence behavior, have cycles and feedback loops, with constant adjustments for stability and balance. Organisms have accumulated stress, which depends on complexity, requiring adjustment. Successful organisms resist greater stress.

An organization's web of business is equivalent to the web of life referred to in the Laws of Ecology, because an organization's business niche within the overall business environment is aligned with ecology, as described in the Business Understanding Chapter. The organization's web of business is a set of objects, events, relationships, and rules related to the organization's business, where the current state and an interacting set of probabilities result in a future state. Those evolving states become business niche states for the organization. A *business niche state* is the set of all objects, events, relationships, rules, and features in the business niche at a point in space-time.

DYNAMIC BUSINESS NICHE

An organization's business niche is not static. It's very dynamic and constantly changing, resulting in an evolving series of business niche states over time. The only thing constant in an organization's business niche is the increasing rate and magnitude of change.

The business niche is a complex set of interacting multi-threads of objects and events that happen at a point in space-time or over a span of space-time, as shown in Figure 6.1. The three dimensions of space and one dimension of time can't be represented in a two-dimensional drawing. Therefore, the three dimensions of space are shown on the vertical axis, and time is shown on the horizontal axis. An object moving up and down in the diagram is a thread moving through the three dimensions of space. An object moving horizontally to the right is a thread moving through time.

Multiple threads of objects move through space-time, coming, going, and interacting in a variety of events. A single thread in space-time is an object, such as a student, vehicle, bank account, and so on, that can be involved in a variety of events over space-time. An event can happen at a point in time, or over a span of space time.

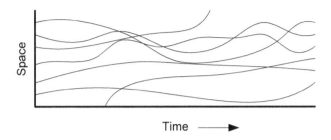

Figure 6.1. Business niche space-time.

Objects and events evolve over time, showing the dynamic nature of the organization's business niche. That dynamic nature is reflected in a series of evolving business niche states. Therefore, the business niche state at a point in space-time or over a span of space-time is important for understanding the organization's business niche. The business state will be explained further in the next chapter on Business Niche Observation.

BUSINESS NICHE COMPONENTS

The business niche contains a variety of different components. The *business niche components* are objects, events, relationships, and rules. Business niche components are described by a set of features.

Each business niche component has a state at a point in space-time or over a span of space-time, which is represented by its set of features. The business niche component states collectively determine the overall business niche state. The *Business Niche Component State* is the set of features for a business niche component at a point in space-time or over a span of space-time.

Each of the business niche components, plus features, actors, triggers, and responses is described below, with examples.

Objects

An *object* was defined earlier as a person, place, thing, or concept. A *person object* could be a driver, student, employee, criminal, pilot, patient, and so on. A *place object* could be a point, such as latitude / longitude coordinates; a line, such as a property boundary; an area, such as a state park; or a volume, such as a coal mine. A *thing object* could be a vehicle, shovel, crane, baseball, drill, and so on. A *concept object* could be a bank account, time, gravity, and so on.

Objects can be components of larger objects, such as a fuel injector is part of an engine, which is part of the power train, which is part of a vehicle.

Objects can combine and separate, like tributaries and distributaries of a river, members that join or leave a search party, multiple engine companies that fight a house fire, a vehicle that is built or salvaged for parts, and so on.

Objects have mathematical structures and empirical domains, and relationships and rules that are the correspondence linking those mathematical structures and empirical domains. Objects have a set of features defining that event.

Events

An *event* was defined earlier as a single happening or interaction between two or more objects at a point in space-time or over a span of space-time. An event cannot happen without objects.

Events can be business events, such as issue a business license, an employee retires, a house is sold, a vehicle is involved in a collision, a student enrolls in a university, a bank account is closed, a client visit, budget preparation, a fire response, and so on. Events can be natural events, such as a rain storm, volcanic eruption, wildfire, hurricane, earthquake, and so on.

An event can be as simple as checking the time, or turning on lights. An event can be very detailed, such as the investigation of a major crime, or determining the cause of a large industrial accident. An event can be short term, such as a lightning strike, or long term, such as building a hydroelectric dam.

Events have mathematical structures and empirical domains, and relationships and rules that are the correspondence linking those mathematical structures and empirical domains. Events have a set of features defining that event.

Events can trigger processes that respond to those events. Processes can resolve and/or track events.

Relationships

A *relationship* is an association, connection, bond, or tie between objects, between objects and events, between events, between features and the components they define, and between rules and the components they qualify.

A relationship is a major component of the correspondence in mathematics. It is also a major component of the First Law of Ecology that supports the web of life and the web of business.

A relationship is not the same as a relation. Relationships occur in the business niche and the organization's web of business. Relations occur in data structures and processes structures. Relationships in the business niche do not automatically become relations in data or processes structures.

An employee working for an organization is a relationship between the employee object and the organization object. A vehicle involved in a collision is a relationship between a vehicle object and the collision event. A fire event has a relationship with the 9-1-1 call event, which has a relationship to the fire department response event, and so on. Relationships have a set of features defining that relationship.

Rules

A *rule* was defined earlier as an authoritative, prescribed direction for conduct, or a usual, customary, or generalized course of action or behavior; a statement that describes what is true in most or all cases; a standard method or procedure for solving problems.

A rule is a major component of the correspondence in mathematics. It is also a major component of the First Law of Ecology that supports the web of life and the web of business.

The business niche abounds with laws, regulations, administrative codes, requirements, criteria, conditions, constraints, deadlines, and so on. Each of these becomes a rule for the organization's business. Rules have a set of features defining that rule.

Features

A *feature* is a fact about an object, event, relationship, or rule.

Typical features are size, shape, color, height, weight, age, time, duration, location, speed, direction, distance, name, and so on.

The term *condition* could be used instead of *feature*. However, *condition* has two meanings. First, *condition* could mean the status of something, such as a patient after surgery, or the weather during a vehicle collision. That meaning might be appropriate. Second, *condition* could mean the criteria that must be met, such as with a contract or an agreement. That meaning would not be appropriate. Therefore, *feature* is used rather than *condition*.

Criteria are specific details that an organization must meet, or that a citizen or customer of the organization must meet. Criteria are not conditions or features.

Each event has a set of specific features. Looking at the situation the other way around, a set of specific features uniquely defines an event. Two or more events cannot have the same set of specific features. Each object also has a set of specific features that uniquely defines that object. Each actor has a set of specific features, since an actor is an object. In addition, an actor can be a feature defining an event.

Actors

An *actor* is an object that plays a role or participates in events.

A *person* is the most prominent actor in many different events. However, more than people can be actors. Any object could be an actor, depending on the event. A *place* can be an actor. A city, meaning the city government or population, can be an actor. A zoo, meaning the animals in the zoo and zoo management, can be an actor. A *thing* can be an actor, such as an automobile involved in a collision. A magma chamber can be an actor in a volcanic eruption; a storm can be an actor in property damage; and animals can be actors in a variety of different situations.

A *concept* may or may not be an actor. Time can be an actor, such as a point in time or a period of elapsed time. A point in time can trigger an event, such as payroll at midnight on the last day of the month. A period of time can be either something must happen during the period, meaning the clock is ticking, or nothing can happen until the period is over, meaning a waiting period. Gravity can be an actor, such as a building collapse or a landslide. A bank account, location, and similar concepts, cannot be actors.

Triggers

A *trigger* is generally defined as a stimulus to initiate a process; to initiate, actuate, or set off a process. A trigger is more specifically defined for the organization's business. A ***trigger*** is the arrival of a stimulus to initiate, actuate, or set off a process. It's the arrival of an input, in any form, that initiates or could initiate a response to handle that input.

Traditionally, a trigger was defined as the arrival of an input, the demand for an output, or time. However, the demand for an output is the arrival of that demand, which is the arrival of an input. A point in time or the end of an elapsed time are also the arrival of an input. State transition diagrams show an input to a state as the only trigger for processes in that state. Therefore, all triggers are the arrival of an input, regardless of the form of that input.

An event can create one or more triggers to responses that resolve and/or track that event. A response could create triggers for additional responses, and so on, creating a chain of events, triggers, and responses. Examples of triggers are the arrival of an application for vehicle license, a 9-1-1 call, the due date for a payment, the receipt of a payment, a traffic light change, a request for proposal, and so on.

Responses

A *response* is generally defined as the act of responding; a reply or action; an activity; an answer; or an act. A response is more specifically defined for the organization's business.

A ***response*** is the act of responding; a reply, answer, action, reaction, or other act triggered by an input. It's an event responding to a trigger. A response cannot begin without an input, meaning it cannot self-start.

Examples of responses are the issuance of a vehicle license, a medic unit response, braking for a red traffic light, preparation of a proposal, and so on.

An actor can respond to an event that has happened or is happening. An actor can also respond to a pending event, to mitigate that event, but must have an input to be aware of that pending event. The actor's action is a process.

Qualified Definitions

These definitions of basic business niche components can be qualified with a prefix to represent the different levels in the Business Understanding Sequence. Specifically, *business environment* can be added to components identified within the business environment, *business niche* can be added to components identified within the organization's business niche, *preliminary* can be added to the data and processes that enter the Data Resource Cycle and Processes Resource Cycle, and *business* can be added to components in the data and processes resource used to operate the organization's business.

The results would be *business environment event*, *business niche event*, *business event*, and so on. For example, business environment events that are of interest to the organization become business niche objects, and business niche events that *are relevant* to the organization become business events.

One additional qualification could be a prefix *natural* for events like a volcano eruption, that triggers another natural event, like a mud flow. The result would be *natural event*, *natural trigger*, and so on.

Another qualification could be a prefix *internal* for components that originate within the organization, and *external* for components that originate outside the organization. The result would be *external business event*, *internal business event*, and so on.

Comprehensive definitions for each of the possible component prefixes for each of the levels in the Business Understanding Sequence is not necessary. However, an organization could develop a set of comprehensive definitions if desired.

BUSINESS NICHE SCENARIOS

The business niche is an on-going interaction of objects, events, triggers, and responses, spanning multiple organizations, and evolving through space-time. The business niche component descriptions above provided definitions and examples of the components, and briefly described a chain of events, triggers, and responses, involving multiple components over space-time.

Scenarios are an excellent way to understand the interactions between objects, events, triggers, and responses, and their evolution through space-time.

Vehicle Collision

Below is a scenario about two vehicles involved in a collision. You can see how objects, actors, events, and triggers evolve to resolve the initial vehicle collision event.

> Two vehicles collide, injuring one driver.
> A pedestrian observes the collision and calls 9-1-1.
> 9-1-1 dispatches the police.
> First police officer verifies injuries and requests a medic unit.
> Medic unit dispatched for injured driver.
> Medic unit requests fire department for extrication of patient.
> Second police officer blocks the road to prevent further collisions.
> Fire engine dispatched.
> Injured driver extricated from vehicle.
> Medic unit transports injured driver to hospital.
> Emergency room begins treatment of patient.
> Third police officer begins interviewing witnesses.
> First police officer requests two wreckers.
> Wreckers dispatched to scene.
> Wrecker personnel clear vehicles and debris.
> Police clear the scene.
> Reports filed, injured driver treated, litigation begins.
> And so on.

The objects are vehicles, drivers, 9-1-1 personnel, police, medic unit, fire engine, wreckers, and so on. The triggers are the 9-1-1 call, police dispatch, medic unit dispatch, patient arrival at emergency room, and so on. The events are vehicle collision, police response, driver extrication, driver transport to hospital, and so on. The features are collision details, driver details, patient vital signs, and so on.

Chained Events

Below is a scenario about chained events, beginning with lightning striking a tree. You can see how each event triggers one or more responses, which trigger additional events, resulting in more responses, more triggers, and so on.

> Lightning strikes a tree during a storm.
> Tree falls, hits electrical wires, and takes down a utility pole.
> Utility pole takes out fire hydrant.
> Water from the fire hydrant washes out the roadway.
> Resident calls the utility company when their power goes out.
> Power company crew is dispatched to scene.
> Power company crew sees the broken water main.
> Power company requests police to close the road.
> Power company requests the water utility to control the water.

Police dispatched.
Water utility crew dispatched.
Police arrive, close the road, and reroute traffic.
Power company crew begins cleanup and repairs.
Water utility crew arrives, turns off water, requests public works.
Water utility crew begins repairs.
Public works supervisor dispatched to assess roadway damage.
Public works supervisor calls for appropriate work crews.
Power company crew requests additional equipment and materials.
Power restored, water main restored, and roadway repaired.
And so on.

The objects are lightning, tree, electric wires, utility pole, fire hydrant, roadway, power company crew, and so on. The actors are the car when it hits the utility pole, the utility pole when it hits the fire hydrant, the water when it washes out the road, and so on. The triggers are lightning striking the tree, tree hitting electric wires, call to utility company, and so on. The features are the details of the storm, the damage, the repairs, and so on.

Driver's License

Below is a scenario about the issuance of a driver license. You can see how various actors are involved in the events and responses. The scenario could be more or less detailed as necessary.

Person requests driver license.
Person takes and passes written test.
Person takes and passes driving test.
Driver license issued.
Expiration notice sent six months before license expiration.
Driver re-examines and license renewed.
Driver stopped by troopers for erratic driving.
Field sobriety test shows driver is impaired.
Driver arrested and vehicle impounded.
Driver arraigned in court and court date set.
Driver convicted, fined, and license suspended.

The objects are driver, driver license, trooper, vehicle, wrecker, court, judge, and so on. The triggers are driver license request, license expiration date, erratic driving, and so on. The events are written driver test, driving test, license issue, traffic stop, and so on. The features are driver details, written and driving test details, traffic stop details, court details, and so on.

Students

Below is a scenario about a student attending a university. The scenario is less detailed, but you can see all the specific objects, triggers, events, and features that could be involved in a student attending a university.

Student enrolls in a university through admissions.
Student registers for classes through registrar.
Student attends class.
Student withdraws from class.
Class taught by professor.

The objects are student, admissions, registrar, class, professor, and so on. The triggers are enrollment application, class registration card, withdraw request, and so on. The events are university enrollment, class registration, class attendance, instruction, withdraw, and so on. The features are student detail, university detail, enrollment detail, class detail, registration detail, professor detail, and so on.

SUMMARY

The details of a business niche must be understood before the business niche can be observed to understand the organization's business. The business niche is set of interacting components based on mathematics and on the laws of ecology describing the web of life. The business niche is dynamic and constantly changing as the components interact. The business nice state is the state of interacting components at a point in space-time or over a span of space-time.

The business niche components are objects, events, actors, features, relationships, rules, triggers, and responses. Each of these components was described, including examples and scenarios that show how the components interact to form the organization's web of business.

QUESTIONS

The following questions are provided as a review of the Business Niche Chapter, and to stimulate thought about understanding the details of a dynamic business niche.

1. What is the dynamic nature of a business niche?
2. What is a business niche state?
3. How is mathematics involved in understanding the business niche?
4. How is the First Law of Ecology involved in understanding the business niche?
5. What are the business niche components?
6. What are the possible qualifications to the basic business component

names?
7. What are objects?
8. What are events?
9. How are objects and events related?
10. Which objects can be actors?
11. What is space-time?
12. How is space-time involved in understanding the business niche?
13. What are features?
14. What are relationships?
15. What's the difference between a relationship and a relation?
16. What are rules?
17. What is a trigger?
18. How are triggers related to state transitions?
19. What are responses?
20. Why do the business niche details need to be understood before the business niche can be observed?

Chapter 7
BUSINESS NICHE OBSERVATION

Observe the business niche to understand the business.

The Business Niche Chapter described the dynamic nature of the business niche with interacting multi-threads of objects and events, the concept of space-time, the business niche state at a point in space-time, and the complex set of interacting business niche components, with examples and interaction scenarios.

The Business Niche Observation Chapter describes both the act of business niche observation, which is the process of business niche observation, and the art of business niche observation, which is the character of the business niche observers and the problems that observers may encounter. The chapter theme is to understand the business niche components and identify the preliminary data and primary processes that *may be relevant* to the organization to feed the Data Resource Cycle and Processes Resource Cycle.

THE ACT OF OBSERVATION

Immanuel Kant said all our knowledge begins with observation (the senses), proceeds to understanding, and ends with reason. In the current context, observation is the act, observer is the senses, the observer's perceptions are the understanding gained, and reason is the organization's choice how it wants to do business in their business niche. That reason is in the form of the organization's data and processes resource.

The act of business niche observation is the process an organization uses to observe and understand its business niche. The act of observation includes observations of the business niche, the two realities an organization faces, perceptions gained by observers during business niche observation, the relationship between understanding and uncertainty, the observation cycle with its phases and states, observation frequency, consensus frequency, and the levels of scoping.

Observations

An organization must observe its business niche to understand the business niche and its business operations in that business niche. Thoroughly understanding the organization's business niche is crucial for a business-driven organization, and business niche observation is crucial for gaining that thorough understanding. Looking at the situation the other way, business-driven begins with an organization observing and understanding its business niche.

Observation is the act of observing; an act of recognizing and noting a fact or occurrence; a judgement on or influence from what one has observed. *Observe* is to inspect or take note; to watch carefully, especially with attention to details or behavior; to come to realize or know; to take notice.

Business niche observation is the act of observing the organization's business niche, at a point in space-time or over a span of space-time, discovering components that *may be of interest* to the organization, understanding those components, and identifying data and processes that *may be relevant* to the organization. It's a snapshot of the business niche state during the observation moment.

The business niche state is only known through observation. Looking at it the other way, observations are the determination of the business niche state during the observation moments. There is no independent determination of the business niche state during the observation moment. The observations, and the resulting perceptions, are the determination of the business niche state.

When an observer makes an observation of the business niche, whether at a point in space-time or over a span of space-time, it's referred to as an observation moment. Observation moments occur during the Understand Phase of the Business Niche Cycle.

An ***observation moment*** is the point in space-time, or the span of space-time, that an observer is observing the business niche and forming perceptions about that business niche. It's a snapshot of the business niche state by an observer based on their observer state.

An *observer* is one who observes; one sent to observe but not to participate; an expert analyst or commentator in a particular field. A ***business niche observer*** is one who observes the business niche to discover business niche components that *may be of interest*, understand those components, and identify and document data and processes that *may be relevant* to the organization.

The ***observer state*** is the total makeup of the observer during the observation moment. It includes the observer's perspective, the observer's experience, the observer's physical and mental state, and all aspects of the observer during the observation moment.

The observer state includes the observer's perspective of the business, such as an executive with strategic perspective, a manager for tactical perspective; a finance officer with a profit/loss and return on investment perspective; a research and development person with product improvement perspective; and so on. It includes the observer's experience, such a new hire, or a 30-year veteran. It includes the observer's physical and mental state, such as interest, attitude, exhaustion, hunger, and so on. It includes all aspects of the observer during the observation moment.

An observer has a different observer state for each observation, and the perceptions gained from observation depend on that observer's state. Documenting the observer state at the observation moment could be important to understand the perceptions gained during observation. The observer's state should be documented to the extent possible for understanding the observer's perceptions. However, observer documentation should not interrupt, impact, compromise, or otherwise alter the observation or the perceptions gained from the observation. In most situations, the observer state at the observation moment is usually not documented, or not documented in any detail.

The Two Realities

An organization faces two different realities: an external reality of the business niche and an internal reality about their business. *External reality* is the reality contained in the business niche that is external to the organization. The business niche state at a point in space-time or over a period of space-time is the external reality. External reality is sometimes referred to as *business niche reality*.

External reality cannot be completely known or determined for two reasons. First, the size and complexity of the business niche makes it virtually impossible to comprehend or describe. No observer, or set of observers, have the capacity to completely comprehend or describe the business niche. Even if it were possible to completely comprehend and describe the complexity of the business niche, that description would be so voluminous as to be incomprehensible.

Second, no independent view of the external reality exists. No observer, or set of observers, can be independent enough, meaning unconstrained by any observer state, to provide an unbiased view of the business niche. In other words, there can be no universal observer, across an entire business niche, that has zero observer state influence.

Internal reality is the reality an organization has about its business that is internal to the organization. The internal reality is contained in the organization's combined data and processes resource. Internal reality is sometimes referred to as *organization reality*.

Ideally, the organization's internal reality reflects the external reality. However, the completeness and accuracy of the organization's internal reality is not verifiable, nor is it refutable, since the external reality is not known and cannot be determined. An organization has no independent test of internal reality, only probabilities of reality gained from observer perceptions during observation. The more observers an organization has, the more skilled those observers are, and the more observations those observers make, the better the internal reality. A false internal reality results from observer presumptions, flawed observations, and a limited set of observers and observations.

Internal reality also depends on the quality of the Data Resource Cycle and Processes Resource Cycle, and the resulting organization-wide data architecture and organization-wide processes architecture. Those architectures and their contents contain the organization's internal reality. If that internal reality is incomplete, inaccurate, or otherwise flawed, then the data and processes resource will not fully support the organizations business, and the organization faces limited success or even failure. Only time will verify the completeness and accuracy, or the falsifiability, of the organization's internal reality.

Perceptions

The result of business niche observation is perceptions about the business niche gained by observers. Observation is the act, and perceptions are the result of that act. A *perception* is a mental image; an awareness of elements gained through sensations; an interpretation in light of experience; it's intuitive, and involves cognition and comprehension.

The external reality in the business niche is being observed to determine the internal reality for an organization. Each observer has their own unique perceptions of the business niche, which is their observer reality that is intermediate between the external reality of the business niche and the internal reality of the organization.

Observer reality is the perceptions gained by an observer during business niche observation that are intermediate between the external reality in the business niche and the internal reality of the organization.

Business niche components contain raw data and processes, the meaning of which is inherent in the component, but is not readily apparent to the observer. The business niche state may contain meaning, but does not provide any meaning to the observer. The observer must provide meaning to the raw data and processes – imbue the raw data and processes with meaning – based on what is meaningful to the observer, during their observer state, at the observation moment.

The raw data and processes in the business niche components do not contain or provide any indication of interest to the organization. The observer provides interest to the organization, based on the observer state at the observation moment.

The observer's perceptions emerge from the business niche components through observation. Only through the process of emergence, which depends on the observer's state at the observation moment, does an observer gain and refine perceptions about the business niche. *Emergence* is the act of emerging; to become manifest; to come into view; to rise from obscurity.

Understanding and Uncertainty

A major theme of business-driven is understanding. Understanding is the bridge between external reality in the business niche and internal reality of the organization. Observation and the perceptions gained by the observer during observation is the driver of that understanding.

Understanding and uncertainty have a reciprocal relationship. As understanding goes up, uncertainty goes down. As understanding goes down, uncertainty goes up. Looking at the relationship another way, uncertainty is a lack of understanding, and understanding is a lack of uncertainty.

Understanding-uncertainty reciprocity is the reciprocal relation between understanding and uncertainty. As understanding goes up, uncertainty goes down, and as understanding goes down, uncertainty goes up.

Going a step further, as understanding goes up, disparity goes down and comparity goes up. As understanding goes down, disparity goes up and comparity goes down. The reciprocal is as uncertainty goes up, disparity goes up and comparity goes down. As uncertainty goes down, disparity goes down and comparity goes up.

The conclusion is that understanding is required for a comparate data and processes resource. Understanding is how well the organization believes they understand the external reality. Understanding is how well the organization believes the internal reality matches the external reality, lacking any verification or refutation.

Uncertainty begins when the observations are weak. The perceptions are weak, and the preliminary data and processes are weak. When uncertainty continues through the data resource and processes resource cycles, the resulting single organization-wide architectures are weak. Ultimately, the data and processes contained in those architectures are weak, and support for the organization's business is weak.

An organization's internal reality is only as good as it's understanding of the business niche where it operates. The understanding is only as good as the observers and their perceptions. Therefore, understanding begins with the observers and their observations of the business niche.

One basic principle about understanding is that if you don't understand something, then ignoring it will not gain understanding. Ignoring understanding is what happens with traditional data management and traditional processes management today. Understanding – the culture – is being ignored, with emphasis on getting the physical data and processes developed and implemented – the technology. Technology is overriding the culture. The result is low understanding, increased uncertainty, and large quantities of disparate data and processes that impact business success.

If an organization doesn't fully understand its business niche, then anything the organization does in the Business Cycle will likely not fully support its operation in that business niche. The better an organization understands its business niche, and documents that understanding in the data and processes resources, the greater the chance its business will be successful.

Understanding is progressive and continues to evolve through the Business Cycle. Understanding ranges from a basic understanding during the business observation, to in-depth understanding during the Data Resource and Processes Resource Cycles.

A basic understanding is necessary for the observer to gain initial perceptions and determine whether data and processes *may be of interest* to the organization. Understanding increases for data and processes that *are of interest* to the organization, and for preliminary data and processes that *may be relevant* to the organization. Understanding continues through the Data Resource Cycle and Processes Resource Cycle to data and processes that *are relevant* to the organization.

Guideline: Continually gain understanding, but only to the extent necessary for the task at hand. Gain enough understanding to complete the current state in the Business Cycle, then move ahead to the next state.

Observation Cycle

Business niche observation is done during the Understand Phase of the Business Niche Cycle. The observation follows a specific Business Niche Observation Cycle. The states in the cycle align with the levels of understanding in the Business Understanding Sequence.

The *Business Niche Observation Cycle* is a cycle of states and phases, where the organization's business niche is observed at a point in space-time or over a span of space-time. Data and processes that *may be of interest* are identified, scoped down to actual data and processes that *are of interest*, are further scoped down to data and processes that *may be relevant*, and integrated to preliminary data and processes. The preliminary data and processes feed the Data Resource Cycle and Processes Resource Cycle.

The Business Niche Observation Cycle is shown in Figure 7.1. The states are nodes and the phases are arcs between the nodes. The cycle begins with the Business Niche State, evolves through the Discover Phase to the Possibility State, through the Comprehend Phase to the Actuality State, through the Chronicle Phase to the Mental Model State, and through the

Consensus Phase to the Data Resource Initial State and Processes Resource Initial State. The phases and states of the Business Niche Observation Cycle are described below.

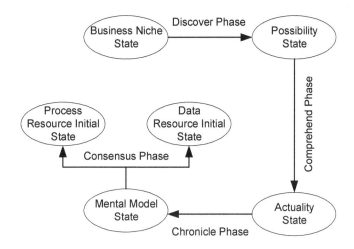

Figure 7.1. Business Niche Observation Cycle

Closely following the Business Niche Observation Cycle results in greater understanding, reduced uncertainty, and a comparate data and processes resource that supports the organization's business. Skipping any part of the Business Niche Observation Cycle reduces understanding, increases uncertainty, and leads to disparity.

Discover Phase

During the Discover Phase of the Business Niche Observation Cycle, observers observe the business niche components and discover, or realize, raw data and processes possibilities that *may be of interest* to the organization. The observer forms initial perceptions of raw data and processes based on the observer state at the observation moment. The Discover Phase aligns with the second level of the Business Understanding Sequence for business niche understanding.

The ***Discover Phase*** is the first phase of the Business Niche Observation Cycle. Observers observe the business niche and form initial perceptions of raw data and processes possibilities that *may be of interest* to the organization. The Discover Phase leads to the Possibility State.

The ***Possibility State*** represents raw data and processes possibilities that *may be of interest* to the organization. It is intermediate between the Discover Phase and the Comprehend Phase of the Business Niche Observation Cycle.

Business niche observation is a discovery process based on the business niche state and the observer state at the observation moment. The observer

91

should only discover the raw data and processes they perceive in the business niche components. The observer should not invent data and processes that are not perceived during observation.

A tendency exists for observers to invent data and processes they believe *may be of interest* to organization, based on the business niche state and their observer state at the observation moment. They insert their observer reality, rather than identify the organization's external reality.

Guideline: The observer should discover, not invent.

A tendency also exists for an observer to gain too much understanding too early in business niche observation, which could be a wasted effort. Time is spent gaining a more in-depth understanding of data and processes that *may be relevant* to the organization, only to eliminate those data and processes in a later phase.

Guideline: Only gain enough understanding to determine if the data or processes possibilities *may be of interest* to the organization.

Comprehend Phase

During the Comprehend Phase of the Business Niche Observation Cycle, an observer turns data and processes possibilities into actualities by adding understanding. The raw data and processes are wrapped with meaning to become data and processes in context that *are of interest* to the organization. That additional meaning is based on the observer state at the observation moment and refines the initial perceptions to mental visions. The Comprehend Phase aligns with the second level of the Business Understanding Sequence for business niche understanding.

The **Comprehend Phase** is the second phase of the Business Niche Observation Cycle. Observers gain understanding, add meaning to data and processes possibilities, and identify data and processes actualities that *are of interest* to the organization. Raw data and processes become data-in-context and processes-in-context, and the observer's initial perceptions become mental visions. The Comprehend Phase leads to the Actuality State.

The **Actuality State** represents data-in-context and processes-in-context actualities that *are of interest* to the organization. It is intermediate between the Comprehend Phase and the Chronicle Phase of the Business Niche Observation Cycle.

A **mental vision** is a set of refined initial perceptions of data-in-context and processes-in-context based on additional understanding gained by the observer.

Some data and processes identified in the Discovery Phase that *may be of interest* to the organization don't survive to data and processes that *are of interest* to the organization based on additional understanding.

Many actualities can exist for a possibility, and some actualities can be more complex than others. The situation is resolved with Occam's razor. *Occam's razor* states that the simplest theory is likely to be the correct theory, and the more complex theory is likely to be falsifiable. The simplest actuality is likely to be the correct actuality, and the more complex actuality is likely to be falsifiable.

Guideline: Select the simplest actuality for a possibility.

Chronicle Phase

During the Chronicle Phase of the Business Niche Observation Cycle, an observer documents their mental visions of data and processes actualities that *are of interest* as a mental model. The Chronicle Phase aligns with the second level of the Business Understanding Sequence for business niche understanding.

The *Chronicle Phase* is the third phase of the Business Niche Observation Cycle. Observers document their mental visions of data and processes actualities as a mental model. The Chronicle Phase leads to the Mental Model State.

The *Mental Model State* represents the documented mental visions of data and processes actualities as a mental model. It is intermediate between the Chronicle Phase and the Consensus Phase of the Business Niche Observation Cycle.

A *mental model* is the documentation of an observer's mental vision that evolves during the Comprehend Phase of the Business Niche Observation Cycle. It clarifies the observer's understanding, and uncertainty, about the data and processes identified during observation.

The observer's mental model is documented by some format and notation. The format and notation are arbitrary. The meaning of the mental model to the recipient is important.

Guideline: Document the mental models with a format and notation that is understandable to a wide range of recipients.

Consensus Phase

During the Consensus Phase of the Business Niche Observation Cycle, observers review the mental models from multiple observers and integrate the data and processes in context to identify preliminary data and preliminary processes that *may be relevant* to the organization. Those preliminary data and preliminary processes become are the initial states for the Data Resource Cycle and Processes Resource Cycle. The Consensus Phase aligns with the third level of the Business Understanding Sequence for preliminary data and processes understanding.

The *Consensus Phase* is the fourth phase of the Business Niche Observation Cycle. Observers integrate the data and processes actualities in multiple mental models and identify preliminary data and processes that *may be relevant* to the organization. The Comprehend Phase leads to the Data Resource Initial State and the Processes Resource Initial State.

The observers do not confirm the relevancy of data and processes during the Consensus. The Data Resource Cycle and Processes Resource Cycle determine data and processes that *are relevant* to the organization, which are used to build the organization-wide architectures. The Data Resource Cycle and Processes Resource Cycle align with the fourth level of the Business Understanding Sequence for data and processes architecture understanding.

The mental models from multiple observers can agree, overlap, conflict, and disagree. The mental models are not simply combined or merged. They are formally integrated based on an understanding of the existing data resource and processes resource architectures, as documented with the Data Resource Data and Processes Resource Data. The resulting preliminary data and preliminary processes include the understanding and uncertainty contained in the mental models.

The integration of mental models must be done by the observers, or a subset of the observers. Integration should not be done by others not involved in observation of the business niche, because they won't have the understanding gained during observation that may not be contained in the mental models.

Many data and processes actualities exist in the mental models based on the observer's initial perceptions and mental visions of the business niche. Occam's razor can be used to select the correct preliminary data and processes from a set of data and processes actualities, the same as it was used by individual observers during the Comprehend Phase to select the best actuality for a set of possibilities. The simplest preliminary data and preliminary processes are likely to be the correct preliminary data and preliminary processes, and the more complex are likely to be falsifiable.

Some data and processes possibilities that *are of interest* to the organization don't survive the integration to preliminary data and processes that *may be relevant* to the organization. Some data and processes are eliminated, some are combined, and some are revised during the integration process, based on the collective understanding of the observers.

Guideline: when you are through discovering and learning, you are through.

Observation Synopsis

Observation of the business niche progresses from the external reality of the business niche, through the observer realities of multiple observers, to an integrated consensus of those observer realities, to the Data Resource Cycle and Processes Resource Cycle that build and maintain organization wide architectures containing the internal reality for an organization. The progression is a conveyance of understanding and uncertainty from the business niche, through multiple observers, to the organization to support its operation in the business niche.

A brief synopsis of the phases and states in the Business Niche Observation Cycle is shown below.

Discover Phase:
>   Observers discover data and processes possibilities.
>   Initial perceptions of raw data and processes that *may be of interest.*
>   Leads to the Possibility State.
>   Represents the second level of Business Understanding Sequence – Business niche understanding.

Comprehend Phase:
>   Observers turn data and processes possibilities into actualities.
>   Raw data and processes become data and processes in context that *are of interest.*
>   Initial perceptions become mental visions of data and processes
>   Leads to the Actuality State.
>   Represents the second level of the Business Understanding Sequence – Business niche understanding.

Chronicle Phase:
>   Observers document mental visions as a mental model.
>   Leads to the Mental Model State.
>   Represents the second level of the Business Understanding Sequence – Business niche understanding.

Consensus Phase:
>   Observers integrate mental models
>   Identify data and processes that *may be relevant.*
>   Become preliminary data and preliminary processes.
>   Leads to the Initial States for the Data Resource Cycle and Processes Resource Cycles.
>   Represents the third level of the Business Understanding Sequence – Preliminary data and processes understanding.

Data and Processes Resource Cycles
>   Determine data and processes that *are relevant.*
>   Build organization-wide data architecture and organization-wide processes architectures.
>   Represents the fourth level of the Business Understanding Sequence – Data and processes architecture understanding.

Observation Frequency

The business niche is a complex set of interacting multi-threads of objects and events, that constantly evolves from a current state to a future state, based on probabilities according to the First Law of Ecology. Complexity is measured by the quantity of data needed to describe the business niche objects, events, relationships, rules, and their features. The more data needed to describe the business niche, the more complex the business niche.

Business niche complexity and the data needed to describe that complexity have a proportional relationship. As the business niche complexity increases, the quantity of data needed to describe that business niche increases.

Some segments of the business niche are more dynamic than others. The stock market and monetary exchange rates change very rapidly. Continental drift and the Earth's magnetic field change very slowly. Other segments of the business niche change at a more moderate rate. These changes result in the organization's internal reality becoming out of synch with the external reality. .

A *business niche segment* is a set of business niche components that are of interest to the organization, such as for business niche observation

An organization needs to routinely observe segments of the business niche to keep the internal reality in synch with the external reality. Rapidly changing business niche segments require more frequent observation, and slowly changing business niche segments require less frequent observation. Routine observations provide a more current internal reality for the organization.

The observation frequency should be set according to the dynamic nature in a business niche segment. When the observation frequency is less than the rate of business niche change, an organization falls behind. When the observation frequency matches the rate of business niche change, an organization is status quo. When the observation frequency is greater than the rate of business niche change, an organization improves.

Guideline: The business niche observation frequency should at least match the rate of change for the business niche segment of interest.

Consensus Frequency

The consensus frequency for integrating observer mental models is based on the observation frequency and the rate an organization wants to enhance their data resource and processes resource. The consensus frequency may immediately follow a set of observations, or it may follow several sets of observations. A consensus frequency more frequent than a set of observations is a wasted effort.

For example, an organization may have an urgent need to change its business, such as a major disaster. The consensus would immediately follow the business niche observations and start the Data Resource Cycle and Processes Resource Cycle to enhance the data resource and processes resource to meet an urgent need. The external reality is rapidly interpreted and used to enhance the internal reality. In other words, the observer realities are immediately integrated and used to start the Data Resource and Processes Resource Cycles.

Another example is a longer-term requirement where an organization wants to understand and evaluate the business niche, but not make any immediate business changes. The consensus would follow several sets of business niche observations, and then start the Data Resource Cycle and Processes Resource Cycle. The external reality is evaluated over a longer period of time before enhancing the internal reality. In other words, the observer realities are held and integrated after several sets of observations.

However, the observer realities could be integrated after each set of observations to form a consensus, which would increase the understanding of the observers before the next set of observations. After several sets of observations, the integrated observer realities would be used to start the Data Resource Cycle and Processes Resource Cycle.

Consensus at a point in space-time provides a current snapshot that is important to an organization. Multiple consensuses over a span of space-time provide a longitudinal history of the business niche that the organization can analyze to identify trends and patterns.

Guideline: The consensus frequency should meet the organization's need for understanding the business niche through observation and updating the organization's internal reality.

Levels of Scoping

Three levels of scoping occur from observation of the business niche to development of the organization's data and processes resource: business niche scoping, observation scoping, and data and processes scoping. Each of those levels of scoping is described below.

Business Niche Scoping

The business environment is too large and complex for an organization to comprehend, and an organization seldom has interest in the entire business environment. The multi-threads of business environment components are scoped down to components that are of interest to the organization's business and the organization can comprehend.

Business niche scoping designates an organization's business niche within the business environment, consisting of components that are of interest to the organization based on its intended business, and that the organization can comprehend.

Business niche scoping occurs between the first level of the Business Understanding Sequence for business environment understanding, and the second level of the Business Understanding Sequence for business niche understanding. The business environment is scoped down to a business niche that is of interest to the organization and the organization can comprehend.

The initial business niche designation is an approximation of the organization's business niche – *approximation* being the operative word. Successive observations, over space-time, by multiple observers, continually adjust the business niche within the business environment. Components currently in the business niche may be excluded, and components not currently in the business niche may be included.

An organization can adjust the scope of its business niche for two reasons. First, components that are of interest for the intended business can be added, and components that are no longer of interest for the intended business can be excluded. Adding components often requires looking at the business environment outside the business niche to identify components of interest.

Second, an organization can change their intended business, which changes the scope of its business niche. The organization changes their business, then observes the business niche to determine the result of the change. The observations result in adding components of interest and excluding components that are no longer of interest.

Business niche scoping is an ongoing process that constantly evaluates and adjusts the organization's business niche to ensure successful business operation.

Observation Scoping

Observation scoping identifies the extent of an observation in the organization's business niche. Observations seldom include the entire business niche and all the interacting components. Observations usually include a segment of the business niche containing components that are of interest for a specific purpose.

Observation scoping identifies the segment of the organization's business niche that will be observed during an observation or set of observations. It designates the segment of the business niche that is of interest to the organization for an observation or a set of observations.

Observation scoping occurs within the second level of the Business Understanding Sequence for business niche understanding by scoping the business niche to segments that *are relevant* to an observation or a set of observations.

For example, an organization may survey customers or citizens, monitor an active volcano, measure stream flow volume during major storms, monitor traffic flow during major holidays, and so on. Each of these represents a segment of the organization's business niche.

The organization is part of its business niche. Any observation of the organization is an observation of the organization's business niche. For example, business process reengineering, data resource integration, time-in-motion studies, business workflow analysis, and so on, require business niche observations. Terms like *internal observation* and *external observation* are often used to distinguish between observation within the organization and observation outside the organization.

Data and Processes Scoping

Data and processes scoping reduces the data and processes from those that *may be of interest* to the organization during the Discover Phase, to those that *are of interest* to the organization during the Comprehend Phase, to those that *may be relevant* to the organization during the Consensus Phase, to those that *are relevant* to the organization during the Data and Processes Resource Cycle.

Data and processes scoping reduces the scope of data and processes from those that *may be of interest*, to those that *are of interest*, to those that *may be relevant*, to those that *are relevant*, which are incorporated into the organization's data and processes resource.

Data and processes scoping begins in the second level of the Business Understanding Sequence for business niche understanding, and continues through the third level of the Business Understanding Sequence for preliminary data and preliminary processes understanding and the fourth level of the Business Understanding Sequence for data architecture understanding and processes architecture understanding. The data and processes are scoped down to those that *are relevant* to the organization, and are integrated into the data resource architecture and the processes resource architecture.

Note that the fifth level of the Business Understanding Sequence for data and processes understanding is an understanding of the data facts contained in the data resource architecture, and the processes decisions and actions contained in the processes resource architecture. It involves an understanding of data and processes, but not a scoping of the data and processes.

THE ART OF OBSERVATION

The art of business niche observation is how the observer observes the business niche, the character of the observer, and the observer's actions during business niche observation. It's the culture of business niche operation that includes the cognitive process of observers. However, the details of the cognitive process won't be described, because that's in the non-business realm. The art of observation stays in the business realm of what the observer does. The art of observation includes observer influence during observation, observer knowledge and objectivity, observer interest and experience, observer variability, and problems observers may have during observation.

Observer Influence

An observer could influence the business niche during observation. Animate objects, such as people and animals, can change when they know they are being observed. The situation is known as the Hawthorne Effect. Inanimate objects, such as volcanos, buildings, and so on, don't know they are being observed, and cannot change as a result of observation.

The business niche is a complex set of interacting multi-threads of components. The organization is part of its business niche, and the observer is usually part of the organization. Therefore, the observer is part of interacting multi-threads of components in the business niche. Any change in the observer's state is a change in the business niche.

In some situations, the observer may not be part of any organization in the business niche being observed. The observer could be observing a foreign business niche for a variety of reasons. In that situation, a change in the observer's state will not change the business niche. However, the Hawthorne Effect still exists.

An observer could be influenced by the business niche. The act of observing the business niche and forming perceptions can change the observer's state. The changed observer state could alter the perceptions gained from the current observation or from later observations. In other words, the observer's perceptions can be refined, during the current observation or during subsequent observations, based on the observer's experiences during observation.

For example, a man gets on a city bus with two unruly kids (the objects being observed). He does nothing to control the unruly kids. A passenger (the observer) boldly confronts the man about why he doesn't control his unruly kids in public. The man slowly responds that they just left the hospital where his wife had passed away. The kids don't know how to handle the loss of their mother, and he's not sure he knows how to handle the loss of his wife. The passenger immediately changes from confrontation about unruly kids to compassion for the man and his two kids (a changed observer state).

Guideline: An observer needs to be aware of observer influence on the business niche, and business niche influence on the observer.

Observer Knowledge and Objectivity

An observer must have a balance of knowledge and objectivity about the organization's data and processes resource. *Knowledge* was defined earlier.

Objectivity is generally defined as the quality or character of being objective; lack of favoritism; freedom from bias; judgement based on observable phenomena and uninfluenced by emotions or persona prejudices; the capacity to assess situations or circumstances and draw sound conclusions.

Knowledge and objectivity have a reciprocal relationship. When knowledge is up, objectivity is down, and when knowledge is down, objectivity is up. The relationship is not right or wrong, just a fact that as one goes up, the goes down. Any team, including business niche observers, needs to have both high knowledge and high objective about the subject under discussion to be successful.

Knowledge-objectivity reciprocity is the reciprocal relationship between knowledge and objectivity. When knowledge goes up, objectivity goes down, and when knowledge goes down, objectivity goes up.

The knowledge-objectivity reciprocal relationship is also known as the familiarity syndrome and as resistance to change. The *familiarity syndrome* is generally defined as the more a person knows about a topic, the less objective that person becomes about that topic. *Resistance to change* is generally defined as the situation in which the more a person knows about a topic, and the more a person has been involved with a topic, the less likely that person is to accept change related to that topic.

A person with high knowledge about a topic tends to resists change. Comments like, "We've done that for twenty years and aren't about to change now," are frequently heard from people with high knowledge and low objectivity. A person with low knowledge and high objectivity about a topic tends to make change too quickly, which could cause problems and alienate people. A person with moderate knowledge about a topic is typically more objective and more willing to accept change. That's the reason observers should have a mix of knowledge and objectivity.

The question often asked is, "How much knowledge should an observer have about the organization's data and processes?"

No knowledge of the existing single organization-wide architectures for data and processes is a detriment. The observer is likely to form perceptions quite different from the existing organization-wide architectures, which requires additional time to resolve through consensus, and through the Data Resource Cycle and the Processes Resource Cycle.

Extensive knowledge of the existing single organization-wide architectures for data and processes could be a detriment to identifying new or different data and processes. The observer could be resistant to change and fail to observe differences or enhancements that would be beneficial to the organization's data and processes.

A moderate familiarity of the single organization-wide architectures for data and processes is helpful, but not to the extent of constraining, compromising, influencing the observation, or gaining additional understanding about data and processes.

Guideline: An observer should have a moderate familiarity with the single organization-wide architectures for data and processes, but not an in-depth knowledge of those architectures.

Observer Skills and Interest

An observer should be skilled at business niche observation and be knowledgeable about the business niche components being observed. An observer should also have an interest in data, in processes, in both data and processes, or anything else the organization wants to know about the business environment. An observer must be able to provide a basic understanding about data and processes to determine the interest and relevance to the organization.

An observer's perceptions of the business niche during observation are relative to their position in the organization, and their makeup, background, knowledge, experience, etc. An observer only perceives what is meaningful based on the observer state at the observation moment. Different observers provide different levels of understanding based on their interest and experience. One observer's basic understanding could be another observer's in-depth understanding.

An observer should be free from any influence regarding observation. An observer cannot be told how to perceive the business niche. That would be influencing the observer, which is not acceptable. Similarly, an organization cannot be told how to perceive their business niche, that would be influencing the organization, which influences any observers in the organization.

Both business professional and technology professionals can be observers. However, technology professionals must present their mental model in business terms. They can gain perceptions in technical terms based on their expertise, but must present their perceptions in business terms so they can be readily understood by business professionals.

Observers continue to learn the art of observation and discovery. They gain experience with successive observations and their perceptions improve with experience. The mental models improve and the preliminary data and preliminary processes improve. The data resource and processes resource improve and the organization has a better chance of success.

Guideline: A variety of observer skills and interest is good, based on knowledge–objectivity reciprocity.

Observer Problems

Observers can face several problems during business niche observation that might impact or compromise the observer's perceptions and the formation of mental models. Observers might be unsure of the interest or relevance of data and processes, might be subject to the self-fulfilling prophecy, might have erroneous perceptions, and might confuse structures in the business niche with structures in the organization's data and processes resource.

Observer Unsure of Interest or Relevance

An observer might be unsure whether data or processes are of interest or relevance to the organization. When an observer is unsure about data or processes, the data or processes should be included. The Consensus Phase will likely eliminate any data or processes that are not of interest or relevance to the organization, or the Data Resource Cycle and Processes Resource Cycle will eliminate data or processes that are not relevant to the organization.

Guideline: When an observer is unsure about data or processes interest or relevance to the organization, those data or processes should be included.

An observer might not have enough understanding to consider data and processes to be of interest to the organization. The observer should not include these data or processes. Other observers, with a different observer state and observation moment, will likely consider those data and processes of interest to the organization and include them.

Guideline: Across all observations, by all observers, the data and processes of interest or relevance to organization will likely be included.

Self-fulfilling Prophecy

If an observer expects to perceive something during an observation of the business niche, they will likely perceive it. Since a business niche has no independent test of reality, the observer sees what they expect to see. What an observer expects to see becomes the observer's reality and influences the organization's understanding of the business niche. The situation is known as the self-fulfilling prophecy.

The *self-fulfilling prophecy* states that a preconceived perception will become the verified perception, which may not be true.

The observer typically poses a question or forms a hypothesis, then gains perceptions from observation about that question or hypothesis. If the observer expects a certain perception about a question or hypothesis, the observer will likely experience that perception. Posing a question or forming a hypothesis is acceptable, but having a preconceived perception about that question or hypothesis becomes the self-fulfilling prophecy that does not benefit the organization's business.

Guideline: Observers usually perceive what they expect to perceive. They seldom perceive what they don't expect. To perceive everything, observers should expect the unexpected.

Erroneous Perceptions

Each observer must be aware of three erroneous perceptions that can arise during their observations, and avoid those perceptions.

An *illusion* is an incorrect perception about something in business niche. It's something that exists in business niche, but was incorrectly perceived by the observer.

An *omission* is a non-perception of something in the business niche. It's something that exists in business niche, but was not perceived by the observer.

A *hallucination* is a perception of something not in the business niche. It's something that does not exist in business niche, but was perceived by the observer.

Erroneous perceptions cannot be easily identified by the observer, because no independent reality exists for comparison. The observer's perception becomes the only reality. Erroneous perceptions that do occur are usually identified and resolved through integration of the mental models during the Consensus Phase, and through the Data Resource Cycle and Processes Resource Cycle.

Guideline: Be aware of erroneous perceptions when observing the business niche and avoid those erroneous perceptions. Don't invent something that isn't there.

Structure Distinction

One mistake made by observers new to the business-driven approach is to structure the data and processes exactly like the structure of business niche objects, events, relationships, and rules. The structure of business niche components and the structure of data and processes are not necessarily the same. That critical mistake needs to be recognized and avoided.

The most common mistakes are to consider relationships in the business niche as data relations in the data resource. However, a relationship in the business niche may be either a data entity or a data relation, depending on the organization's internal reality and how the organization chooses to structure its data and processes. Similarly, an object in the business niche may become a data entity or a data relation, depending on the organization's internal reality and how the organization chooses to structure its data and processes. Similar situations occur with processes.

These structure mistakes are why business professionals must be involved in business niche observation, and in the design and development of the organization's data resource and processes resource. Business professionals are the ones who can best make the transition from the external reality of the business niche structure to the internal reality of the data resource or processes resource structure. That's a major theme of business-driven.

Technology professionals tend to design and develop the data resource and processes resource according to the structure of the business niche objects, events, relationships, and rules. They tend to portray the structure of data and processes according to the physical environment available to the organization, and not within the single organization-wide architectures. The situation is typical of the technology-driven disparity situation described earlier, that results in the all too familiar disparate data and processes.

The underlying problem is that multiple internal data resource and processes resource realities are created. These multiple, and often conflicting, internal realities result in a multiple data resource and processes resource disorder – a multiple data architecture and process architecture disorder – that is persistent in most organizations today.

Guideline: The structure of the business niche external reality must be formally adjusted to the structure of the organization's internal reality.

SUMMARY

Both the act of business niche observation and the art of business niche observation are important for understanding and operating the business. The act of observation includes multiple observers, each with an observer state at the observation moment, the external reality and internal reality that an organization faces, and the fact that the internal reality is not verifiable or refutable. Perceptions are gained by observers during observation through emergence, forming an observer reality. The observer provides understanding to reduce uncertainty and identify data and processes that are of interest or relevance to the organization.

The Business Niche Observation Cycle consists of states and phases that progress through the Discovery Phase to the Possibility State with perceptions of raw data and processes that *may be of interest*, the Comprehend Phase to the Actuality State with mental visions of data and processes-in-context that *are of interest*, the Chronicle Phase to the Mental Model State documenting the mental visions as mental models, and the Consensus Phase to the Data Resource Initial State and Processes Resource Initial State identifying data and processes that *may be relevant*.

The frequency of business niche observation should match the rate of business niche change, and the frequency of consensus should meet the organization's need to update their internal reality. Three levels of scoping from business niche scoping, to observation scoping, to data and processes scoping align with the Business Understanding Sequence.

The art of business niche observation is how the observer observes the business niche. The observer can influence the business niche, and can be influenced by the business niche, during observation. An observer must have a balance of knowledge and objectivity during observation – the knowledge-objectivity reciprocity.

An observer should be skilled at business niche observation, have a knowledge of the business niche components, and have an interest in data, processes, or anything else that *may be relevant* to the organization's business. An observer must be free from any influence during observation. Both business professionals and technology professionals can be observers, but technology professionals must present their perceptions in business terms understandable to business professionals.

Observers can face several problems during observation, such as being unsure of the interest or relevance of data or processes, the self-fulfilling prophecy, erroneous perceptions, and differences in structure of the external business niche and structure in the internal data and processes architectures. Observers must understand these problems and be able to avoid them during observation.

The Understand Phase of the Business Niche Cycle is oriented toward understanding the organization's business. The Operate Phase is oriented toward operating the organization's business. An organization needs to thoroughly understand the business to agile and successfully operate the business, and needs to know the intended business operation to thoroughly understand the business. Business niche observation is the activity that understands the business by observing, analyzing, and evaluating the external reality in the business niche to identify and understand the data facts, and the processes decisions and actions, that form the organization's internal reality and drive the organization's business.

QUESTIONS

The following questions are provided as a review of Business Niche Observation Chapter, and to stimulate thought about business niche observation.

1. What is business niche observation?
2. What is the act of business niche observation?
3. Why are the observation moment and observer state important during business niche observation?
4. What are the two realities an organization faces?
5. How does the observer reality bridge these two realities?
6. What is understanding-uncertainty reciprocity?
7. What are the states and phases of the Business Niche Observation Cycle?
8. What are the results of each phase in the Business Niche Observation Cycle?
9. What drives the observation frequency and the consensus frequency?

10. What are the levels of scoping that occur during business niche observation?
11. How do these levels of scoping relate to the levels of the Business Understanding Sequence?
12. What is the art of business niche observation?
13. How might an observer influence the business niche?
14. How might the business niche influence the observer?
15. What is knowledge-objective reciprocity?
16. What problems might an observer face during business niche observation?
17. What is the self-fulfilling prophecy?
18. What are the erroneous perceptions an observer might face?
19. Who can be involved in business niche observation?
20. Why is the structure of business niche components different from the structure of an organization's data and processes?

Chapter 8
INTERROGATIVES AND FRAMEWORKS

Interrogatives and frameworks directly assist business understanding.

The Business Niche Observation Chapter described the act of business niche observation – the process of observing the business niche – and the art of business niche observation – how the observer observes the business niche. The Interrogatives and Frameworks Chapter describes the traditional interrogatives and traditional business frameworks. The chapter theme is to understand the relationship between traditional interrogatives and business frameworks, and the problems with traditional interrogatives and business frameworks.

TRADITIONAL INTERROGATIVES

Interrogatives play a key role in understanding an organization's business. The need for interrogatives, the traditional interrogatives with their two roles for business understanding, and attempts to add an additional interrogative are described below.

The Need for Interrogatives

Business niche observation is about thoroughly understanding an organization's business. Observers pose questions or hypotheses, and seek answers to those questions and confirmation or refutation of hypotheses. Observers gain a thorough understanding through well-formed questions and hypotheses, which involves the use of interrogatives. In other words, business success depends on thorough understanding, and thorough understanding depends on well-formed questions and hypotheses, and well-formed questions and hypotheses depend on interrogatives.

Interrogatives are crucial to understanding. Everything we know, need to know, or want to know to thoroughly understand the business boils down to interrogatives. An *interrogative* is a word used to pose a question or a hypothesis, and seek an answer to the question, or a confirmation or refutation of the hypothesis.

The six traditional interrogatives appeared years ago in *The Elephant's Child*, from *Just So Stories*, by Rudyard Kipling.

I keep six honest serving-men:
    (They taught me all I knew)
Their names are What and Where and When
    and How and Why and Who;
I send them over land and sea,
    I send them east and west;
But after they have worked for me,
    I give them all a rest.

The *traditional interrogatives* are What, How, Where, When, Who, and Why.

The What interrogative represents the subject or topic under discussion. It sets the scope for discussion and understanding. Without a scope to focus the discussion, the discussion is useless and likely won't produce any meaningful understanding.

The How interrogative represents processes related to the What. It represents how the subject or topic under discussion is approached, understood, managed, accomplished, or resolved. It also represents the processes an organization uses to conduct its business activities.

The Where interrogative represents location – the space component of space-time – related to the What. Location typically consists of three parameters, with their appropriate base, for determining location in three dimensions.

The When interrogative represents time – the time component of space-time – related to the What. The flow of time in most organizations is segmented to a point in time or a span of time. Organizations can't change the flow of time, but they can define and change the specifications of a point in time and a span of time used in their business activities. As described earlier, location and time for the business realm are the objectified facts that people agree to use. Objectified time typically consists of one or more parameters, with their appropriate base, for determining a point in time or a span of time.

The Who interrogative represents people and groupings of people, such as organizations, teams, project members, committees, social groups, and so on, related to the What. Who only refers to people. Other life forms are referred to as things.

The Why interrogative is an explanation, purpose, justification, rationale, intention, goal, substantiation, vision, policy, guideline, incentive, and so on, that provide enthusiasm and motivation for a successful business. It is something that should be done, is being done, or has been done related to the What.

The *traditional primary interrogative* is What that sets the focus or scope for achieving understanding. A *traditional associate interrogative* is any of the other five traditional interrogatives – How, Where, When, Who, and Why – that support or clarify the traditional primary interrogative.

Using water purveyor as an example. The primary interrogative might be What component of water purveying, such as water distribution. Associate interrogatives might be How water is distributed, Where water is distributed, When water is distributed, Who receives the distributed water, and Why are they receiving the distributed water.

Another example is human resource understanding. The primary interrogative might be What are the human resource services, such as hiring, promoting, training, and so on. Associate interrogatives might be How are these services performed, Where are these services performed, When are these services performed, Who receives these services, and Why are they receiving these services.

Human resource understanding might continue with What training is offered, How training is offered, Where training is offered, When training is offered, Who receives training, and Why training is offered. The interrogatives could continue through the entire human resource function of an organization.

Traditional Interrogative Roles

Traditional interrogatives have two major roles for understanding the business and for identifying data and processes. Each of these roles is described below.

First Interrogative Role

The first interrogative role is to understand the elusive. Interrogatives are asked and answered as needed until a thorough understanding of the organization's business is achieved. The *first interrogative role* is an ongoing cycle of queries where the interrogatives are asked and answered as needed until a thorough understanding of the organization's business is achieved.

Queries begin with observation of the business niche, and continue through the Data Resource Cycle and the Processes Resource Cycle to development of the organization's data and processes resource. Queries lead to answers, which may lead to more queries, and so on, until an organization thoroughly understands its business niche and business activities to be agile and successfully operate in that business niche.

Queries use interrogatives in both a prospective and a retrospective mode. A thorough business understanding must include both the prospective and retrospective query modes.

The prospective mode is used for a planned response to an event, which includes What, How, Where, When, Who, and Why something should happen

111

when an event occurs and an input is received. The *prospective query mode* is the use of queries before the fact to understand and plan what should happen in response to an input from an event.

For example, understanding products might include the following prospective queries. What products are developed? How are the products developed? Why are those products developed? Where are the products manufactured? When are the products manufactured? Why are products manufactured at that location? When are products distributed? Who manufacturers the products? Where are the products distributed? Who distributes the products? Who are the customers for those products? Why are those our customers? And so on.

The answers to those queries lead to additional queries to gain a thorough understanding and evaluate alternatives. The sequence of queries, answers to those queries, and subsequent queries flow as necessary to seek a thorough understanding.

The retrospective mode is used to investigate what happened during or after an event, and includes What, How, When, Where, Who, and Why the event happened. The *retrospective query mode* is the use of queries after the fact to investigate what actually happened during an event.

For example, investigating an incident might include the following queries. What was the incident? Where did it happen? When did it happen? How did it happen? Why did it happen? Who was involved? How were they involved? And so on. The answers to those queries lead to additional queries to evaluate the incident and gain a thorough understanding about that incident.

Second Interrogative Role

The second interrogative role is to identify specific data and processes necessary for the organization to support its business activities. The *second interrogative role* is identifying specific data and processes needed to support an organization's business activities in its business niche, including detailed description, structure, and integrity.

Data are identified for the What, Where, When, Who, and Why about the organization's business. Processes are identified for the How about the organization's business. Data and processes identification begin with business niche observation and continue through the Data Resource Cycle and Processes Resource Cycle to formal development of an organization's data and processes resource.

These two interrogative roles may seem to be the same. However, the first interrogative role is oriented toward understanding events, investigating events, and so on, whether or not those events are part of the organization's business. The first interrogative role may or may not result in development or adjustment of an organization's data and processes resource.

The second interrogative role is oriented toward building and maintaining the organization's formal data and processes resource. It may depend on understanding gained from the first interrogative role. In other words, observation of the business niche may provide understanding about the complex interacting components – the first interrogative role, or may lead to new or improved data or processes in the organization's data and processes resource – the second interrogative role.

Additional Interrogative Attempts

Two major attempts have been made to add additional interrogatives. The first major attempt was to add business rules as the seventh interrogative. Business rules are certainly important in managing an organization's business, and are often ignored or treated lightly. However, no substantiation existed for business rules as a seventh interrogative, mainly because business rules didn't constitute a query.

After much thought and discussion, the determination was made that business rules could apply to each of the six interrogatives, and definitely apply to the data and processes resource. Therefore, arbitrarily adding business rules as a seventh interrogative was not considered feasible, and could possibly detract from the importance of business rules for data and processes.

The second major attempt was to add Which as the seventh interrogative. The prominent question was, "Is Which an interrogative?" Traditionally, Which was considered a variation of What, meaning *which one of many*. What identified the specific *which one of the many*. Therefore, What was the interrogative and Which was not considered to be an additional interrogative.

TRADITIONAL BUSINESS FRAMEWORKS

Frameworks provide a base for understanding. Business frameworks provide a base for understanding an organization's business. The need for business frameworks, traditional framework benefits, and traditional framework dilemmas are described below.

The Need for Business Frameworks

The Periodic Table of Elements is a framework that helps people understand chemistry, specifically electronic structure and chemical bonding. The Body Mass Index and the Heat and Humidity Chart are good examples of frameworks that help people understand body weight and heat related conditions. A *framework* is a graphical representation of a topic that helps people understand that topic.

An organization needs some type of business framework to thoroughly understand and manage its business activities. A *business framework* is a graphical representation of an organization's business that helps the organization thoroughly understand and manage its business activities.

Business frameworks help people understand an organization's business. Numerous business frameworks have been developed by various people and organizations. They have a variety of names, formats, notations, and meanings for different audiences. Some business frameworks are more detailed than others, and some are more complete than others. Some business frameworks are easy to understand, and others are more difficult to understand. The main difference between these business frameworks is content and presentation to a specific audience.

The most prominent business framework today, and the most elegant, is a two-dimensional matrix, presented by John Zachman, with the six traditional interrogatives horizontally across the top, and levels of specification detail vertically down the left side. The cells contain detail for each interrogative at each level of detail.

Three of the interrogatives were perceived as activity/architecture oriented. What represents data, How represents processes, and Where represents the platform, meaning the hardware and system software. Three of the interrogatives were perceived as behavior/culture oriented. When represents time location, Who represents people involved, and Why represents motivation.

Another prominent business framework uses triangles to represent the interrogatives. It consists of two larger triangles, each consisting of two smaller triangles on the bottom and one smaller triangle on the top, with an inverted triangle in the center.

The first larger triangle is an activity/architecture triangle that has What (data) and Where (platform) triangles on the bottom, supporting a How (processes) triangle on the top. The center inverted triangle represents information systems using the data and platform to support the processes.

The second larger triangle is a behavior/culture triangle that has Who (people) and When (time) triangles on the bottom, supporting a Why (motivation) triangle on the top. The center inverted triangle represents the organization's culture using the people and time to support the organization's motivation.

Traditional Framework Benefits

Traditional business frameworks provide many benefits. The six interrogatives are important for thorough business understanding. The three activity interrogatives emphasize architectural independence down through design. The data, processes, and platform architectures are separate for design, and are merged for development and implementation, as described earlier for the Data Resource Cycle and Processes Resource Cycle.

The three behavior interrogatives emphasize the importance of culture equal to architecture. A successful organization must include both architecture and culture to thoroughly understand its business, be agile, and successfully operate its business.

The levels of specification detail start at a higher level of abstraction and progress toward a more detailed level. Detailed specification cannot proceed without higher level specifications. That's brute-force development that leads to the disparity seen in many organizations today.

The term *conceptual* is a greatly misused and abused term that has no denotative meaning, and likely never will. The term is often used to get a general specification of the data or processes needed by the business, get the business professionals concurrence on that general specification, and then proceed to development and implement of the databases or processes. It's often an excuse for rapid, informal, independent, physical database and process development.

Traditional Framework Dilemmas

A dilemma began to evolve with traditional business frameworks based on six interrogatives. What did each of the six interrogatives really represent? The dilemma began with a How Dilemma, evolved to a What Dilemma, and became a Topic Dilemma. The basic problems with the dilemmas were identified and had to be resolved to thoroughly understand an organization's business.

The How Dilemma

In a traditional business framework, What represents data, and How represents processes related to those data. The data What is the driver and the processes How is related to the data. The How pertains to how the data are understood. It does not pertain to How those data-related processes are understood, or How any other processes are understood. The question became: Where is the How about business processes other than data-related processes?

That's the How Dilemma!

The ***How Dilemma*** is an uncertainty about whether How on a traditional business framework represents only processes related to the data What, or all processes for an organization.

The How Dilemma had to be resolved.

The What Dilemma

Attempts to resolve the How Dilemma led to a What Dilemma. The How Dilemma was only a symptom of a much deeper problem with interrogatives. Specifically, if What represents all processes, then How represents processes understanding, and if What represents all data, then How represents data understanding. The questions were: What does the What interrogative represent? Does it represent data or processes? Whichever component What represents, what about understanding for the other component?

That's the What Dilemma!

The *What Dilemma* is an uncertainty about whether What on a traditional business framework represents data or processes.

The What Dilemma had to be resolved before the How Dilemma could be resolved.

The Topic Dilemma

Attempts to resolve the What Dilemma led to a Topic Dilemma. The What Dilemma was only a symptom of an even deeper problem. Specifically, did data and processes have equal status as What with respect to How? The questions were: Were data and processes equal status with respect to What and How? Was there another driver of the business framework? Was the other driver a topic driver?

That's the Topic Dilemma!

The *Topic Dilemma* is an uncertainty about how both data and processes are understood in a traditional business framework.

That Topic Dilemma had to be resolved before the What Dilemma could be resolved.

The Basic Dilemma Problems

You see what happened! Interrogatives as queries had different meanings than interrogatives on traditional business frameworks. People had a mindset that What represented the data, and How represented the processes – with respect to information systems! Information systems was the implied topic of the business framework.

Two basic problems with traditional business frameworks led to the dilemmas. The first basic problem was not knowing what the What interrogative on a traditional business framework actually represented. That problem created a confusion about selection/designation versus description/explanation. In other words, it created confusion about the topic represented by a business framework versus the understanding of that topic.

The second basic problem with traditional business frameworks was the traditional business framework represented a single business activity – it represented information systems. What represented the data in information systems, and How represented processes in information systems. No other business activities were represented in traditional business frameworks.

That single focus for traditional business frameworks required a multitude of frameworks to cover all the topics in an organization's business.

116

This multitude of business frameworks were seldom developed, and if developed, were seldom maintained. Traditional business frameworks lacked a component for topic, and were unable to include the entire business of an organization.

Those two basic problems with traditional business frameworks had to be resolved. Resolution of the basic problems would solve the Topic Dilemma, which would resolve the What Dilemma, which would resolve the How Dilemma.

SUMMARY

Interrogatives are important for thoroughly understanding an organization's business. Observers use interrogatives to pose questions and seek answers, or pose hypotheses and seek confirmation or refutation. The six traditional interrogatives are What, How, Where, When, Who, and Why. The primary interrogative is What, and the associative interrogatives are How, Where, When, Who, and Why related to What.

Traditional interrogatives have two roles. The first role is an ongoing cycle of queries where interrogatives are used to understand the organization's business. Queries are used in a prospective mode to understand what should happen in response to an event, and in a retrospective mode to investigate what happened during an event. The second role is identifying specific data and processes an organization needs to support its business activities.

Two major attempts were made to add additional interrogatives, but the six traditional interrogatives remained as a solid base for understanding.

Frameworks are important for understanding a particular topic. Business frameworks help organization understand and manage their business activities. Numerous business frameworks have been developed, but two have been prominent for understanding an organization's business.

However, these business frameworks had problems, which became known as the How Dilemma, the What Dilemma, and the Topic Dilemma. The basic problems were not distinguishing between selection/designation and description/explanation, and the traditional business framework represented only one business activity. These basic problems had to be resolved for an organization to use a business framework to thoroughly understand its business.

QUESTIONS

The following questions are provided as a review of the Interrogatives and Frameworks Chapter, and to stimulate thought about the use of interrogatives and frameworks.

1. What is an interrogative?

2. Why are interrogatives necessary for business understanding?
3. What are the six traditional interrogatives?
4. What does each of the traditional interrogatives represent?
5. What are primary and associate interrogatives?
6. What are the interrogative roles?
7. What are the prospective and the retrospective query modes?
8. What attempts were made to add interrogatives.
9. What is a framework?
10. Why is a business framework necessary for business understanding?
11. What are the prominent traditional business frameworks?
12. What are the benefits of a business framework?
13. What is a framework dilemma?
14. What are the traditional business framework dilemmas?
15. What is the How Dilemma?
16. What is the What Dilemma?
17. What is the Topic Dilemma?
18. What are the impacts of the business framework dilemmas?
19. What is the basic problem with traditional business frameworks?
20. What will resolution of the basic problems accomplish?

Chapter 9
BUSINESS UNDERSTANDING
FRAMEWORK

A new business framework for understanding and agility.

The Interrogatives and Frameworks Chapter described traditional interrogatives and traditional business frameworks, including the basic problems with traditional business frameworks. The Business Understanding Framework Chapter describes the contemporary interrogatives and the contemporary business framework that resolve the basic problems with traditional frameworks to provide a solid foundation for an organization to thoroughly understand its business. The chapter theme is beginning to develop an overarching construct for business understand and agility.

CONTEMPORARY INTERROGATIVES

Two basic changes were made to resolve the basic problems with traditional business frameworks. The first basic change was addition of an interrogative to the traditional interrogatives to form a set of seven contemporary interrogatives. Contemporary interrogatives and a contemporary interrogative example are described below.

An Additional Interrogative

Early attempts to add a seventh interrogative included adding Which as an interrogative. There was tremendous resistance to changing the six traditional interrogatives by either removing or adding an interrogative. As a result, Which was considered to be a variation of What and was not added as a seventh interrogative.

After careful analysis of the three dilemmas with traditional business frameworks, Which came back as a seventh interrogative to identify the business activity. Which represents the selection/designation of the business activity for a business framework – it identifies the business activity. In traditional business frameworks, the business activity was implied as information systems, and multiple business frameworks were required for other business activities.

What was redefined to represent the description/explanation of a business activity – it describes the business activity identified by Which.

With What redefined to identify the business activity, there appeared to be no interrogative to represent data for a business activity. How still represented processes, but no interrogative represented the data. The addition of Which seemed to create another dilemma.

However, considering that data and processes form a single, combined, critical resource of the organization, How was redefined to represent both data and processes. The management of any business activity includes both data and processes, since data are dependent on processes and processes are dependent on data. Neither can be independent of the other.

The addition of Which allowed data and processes management to become a separate business activity the same as any other business activity in the organization, since both data and processes must be managed together. In other words, data and processes management is identified as a business activity by Which, and has its own What and How.

The addition of Which as an interrogative for business activity, and the redefinition of How to represent both data and processes related to the business activity identified by Which, provided the base for interrogative-driven business understanding.

Contemporary Interrogative Definitions

The addition of Which as an interrogative and the redefinition of How provided a set of seven contemporary interrogatives for understanding an organization's business. The *contemporary interrogatives* are Which, What, How, Where, When, Who, and Why.

Which identifies the business activity. It's the selection/designation of a business activity.

What describes the business activity identified by Which. It's the description/explanation of the business activity that sets the scope for thorough understanding.

How represents the combined data and processes related to the business activity identified by Which and described by What. It's the data and processes necessary to understand and perform the business activity.

Where represents the location(s) for the business activity identified by Which. It represents the location component of space-time using the objectified facts for location.

When represents the time(s) for the business activity identified by Which. It represents the time component of space-time using the objectified facts for time.

Who represents the people and groupings of people for the business activity identified by Which. It represents the people involved in a business activity.

Why represents the motivation or justification for the business activity identified by Which. It's the rationale or reasoning for conducting a business activity.

The *primary contemporary interrogative* is the interrogative Which that identifies the business activity and sets the scope for achieving a thorough understanding. An *associate contemporary interrogative* is any of the other six contemporary interrogatives – What, How, Where, When, Who, and Why – that support or clarify the contemporary primary interrogative Which.

Contemporary interrogatives have the same interrogative roles as the traditional interrogatives, and the same prospective and retrospective query modes as the traditional interrogatives, as described earlier.

Contemporary Interrogatory Example

Using business licensing as an example.

Which designates the business activity for business licensing.

What describes the business activity for business licensing.

How represents the data and processes involved in the business licensing.

Where represents the business license office locations, online access, and location of the business for business licensing.

When represents the timing and sequence of events for processing business license applications.

Who represents the business license applicants and the staff processing those business license applications.

Why represents the laws, regulations, and so on, pertaining to business licensing.

CONTEMPORARY BUSINESS FRAMEWORK

The second basic change to resolve the basic problems with traditional business frameworks was the addition of a third dimension to form a contemporary business framework. The addition of a third dimension, the description of the new contemporary business framework, the third role for interrogatives, the details of business activities, a clarification of terms, documenting the contemporary business framework, promoting the contemporary business framework, and use of the contemporary business framework in the non-business realm are described below.

A Third Dimension

Traditional business frameworks represented one business activity, usually information systems. They could represent other business activities, but that was seldom done. The major emphasis was on understanding and developing information systems.

The seventh interrogative Which identified a specific business activity, but the problem was where to place that seventh interrogative on the traditional business framework. Attempts to add Which to a two-dimensional business framework created a problem, because only one business activity could be identified for the two-dimensional framework. In some situations, a different business activity was identified for each level of specification detail of the two-dimensional framework, resulting in considerable confusion about what a business activity on the traditional business framework actually represented.

Adding another column to a traditional business framework would not have solved any problems, and would have created additional problems. In retrospect, it's good that a seventh interrogative was not added to the two-dimensional traditional business framework.

The contemporary business framework needed to be three-dimensional to include business activity as a third dimensions. Which was added as that third dimension to represent business activity. Multiple traditional business frameworks representing multiple business activities could now be portrayed as the third dimension on a contemporary business framework.

The contemporary business framework represents more than data and processes for information systems. It represents all business activities for an organization, and includes the data and processes for each of those business activities. It represents a complete business understanding for all public and private sector organizations.

Business Understanding Framework

The contemporary business framework needed a formal name to promote the new concept. Simply using the term *contemporary business framework* was not acceptable. With the orientation toward thorough business understanding, that contemporary business framework name became the Business Understanding Framework.

The *Business Understanding Framework* is the construct for a complete, integrated, thorough understanding of the organization's business. It's a three-dimensional framework with dimensions for business activity, framework interrogative, and specification detail.

The *Business Understanding Framework Objective* is to provide a construct for an organization to thoroughly understand all of its business activities, to whatever level of detail desired, so it can be agile and successful in its business operation.

The Business Understanding Framework is composed of framework cells. Each framework cell has qualifiers for business activity, framework interrogative, and specification level. The strategic structure for the Business Understanding Framework is shown in Figure 9.1.

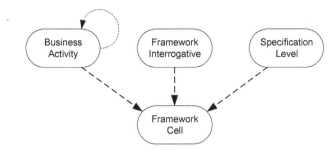

Figure 9.1. Business Understanding Framework strategic structure.

The ***business activity dimension*** of the Business Understanding Framework represents a hierarchy of the organization's business activities, from the organization at large to the most detailed business activity the organization chooses to document.

The ***framework interrogative dimension*** of the Business Understanding Framework represents the associate contemporary interrogatives used for understanding the organization's business.

Framework Interrogatives are the six associate contemporary interrogatives that qualify a Framework Cell: What, How, Where, When, Why, and Who.

The ***specification level dimension*** of the Business Understanding Framework represents the levels of specification detail from the highest abstraction to the most detailed specification.

Specification level qualifies the business framework cells. It is organization specific and can contain as many levels of specification detail as the organization needs for thorough understanding. Specification is usually linear, as shown in the diagram. However, it could be a hierarchy, which would be represented by a recursive one-to-many data relation.

Specification Level is the level of detail for the Business Understanding Framework from abstract to detailed that qualifies each Framework Cell.

Framework cells form the matrix of the Business Understanding Framework. Each framework cell is qualified by business activity, framework interrogative, and specification level.

Third Interrogative Role

Interrogatives have a role as ongoing queries to achieve understanding, and a role to identify specific data and processes needed to support business activities, as described earlier. Interrogatives now have a third role with the Business Understanding Framework.

The primary contemporary interrogative, Which, identifies the business activity in the business activity dimension of the Business Understanding Framework. The associate contemporary interrogatives, What, How, Where

When, Who, and Why, identify the columns in the Business Understanding Framework.

The *third interrogative role* is the primary contemporary interrogative identifying business activities, and the associate contemporary interrogatives identifying columns in the Business Understanding Framework.

Business Activities

The third dimension of the Business Understanding Framework is a hierarchy of business activities, from high-level abstraction representing the entire organization to the most detailed business activity an organization wants to document. Executives can view high-level business activities, managers can view mid-level business activities, and knowledge workers can view detailed business activities. The levels in the hierarchy and the business activity names are organization specific.

A *business activity* is a set of related business processes. Business activities form a hierarchy from the entire organization to the most detailed level an organization wants to document.

Business activity has a recursive relation representing the hierarchy of business activities, as shown in Figure 9.2. A business activity can include many processes, and a process can be used by many business activities. The many-to-many relation is resolved with business activity process.

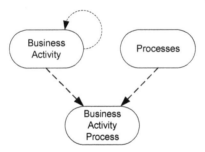

Figure 9.2. Business activity and processes strategic structure.

Organization units are not the same as business activities. Organization units form a hierarchy of responsibility and reporting relationships from high-level abstraction representing the entire organization to the most detailed organization unit an organization wants to document. The levels in the hierarchy and the organization unit names are organization specific.

An organization unit is a set of related responsibilities and reporting relationships in an organization. Organization units form a hierarchy from the entire organization to the most detailed level an organization wants to document.

Business activities and organization units have a many-to-many relationship. A business activity can be performed by many organization units, and an organization unit can perform many business activities. That many-to-many relation is resolved with business activity unit.

Business activity unit is the use of one business activity in the business activity hierarchy by one organization unit in the organization unit hierarchy.

The strategic structure for business activity and organization unit is shown in Figure 9.3. Organization unit has a recursive relation, representing the hierarchy of organization units. Business activity unit shows the use of a business activity anywhere in the business activity hierarchy by an organization unit anywhere in the organization unit hierarchy.

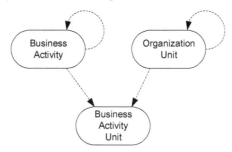

Figure 9.3. Business Activity and Organization Unit strategic structure.

Structures with a common data entity can be combined. The combined strategic structure for the Business Understanding Framework is shown in Figure 9.4.

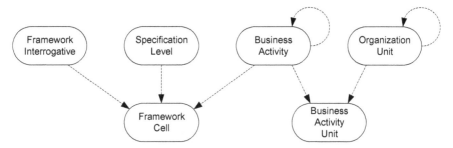

Figure 9.4. Business Understanding Framework strategic structure.

Data resource management and processes resource management are business activities that are understood and managed the same as any other business activity. Although data and processes are common across all business activities, as documented by the How interrogative, their management through the Data Resource Cycle, Processes Resource Cycle, and organization-wide architectures are business activities. Those business activities are part of the business activity hierarchy.

An organization can chose another hierarchy instead of business activity, such as a hierarchy of products, information systems, or any other subject, depending on what that organization wants to thoroughly understand. The name of that hierarchy, and the name of the resolution between that hierarchy and organization unit would be changed accordingly.

Clarification of Terms

Several terms are often confused and used interchangeably. The proper use of terms with the Business Understanding Framework are described below.

General and *specific* pertain to reasoning, not to levels of detail. *General* means a broader scope. *Specific* means a narrower scope.

Abstract and *detailed* refer to the levels of detail. *Abstract* means less detail, within the same scope. *Detailed* means more detail, within the same scope.

Complex and *simple* refer to the degree of intricacy, not levels of detail. *Complex* is very intricate. *Simple* is less intricate. *Overly complex* is more intricate than necessary for understanding. *Overly simple* is less intricate than necessary for understanding.

Complicated refers to the difficulty of understanding, not to degrees of intricacy. *More complicated* means more difficult to understand. *Less complicated* means less difficult to understand. *Overly complicated* refers to something that is more difficult to understand than necessary.

Business Understanding Framework Documentation

The Business Understanding Framework is documented with business framework data, the same as the data resource is documented as data resource data and the processes resource is documented as processes resource data. ***Business framework data*** are any data necessary for thoroughly describing and understanding the construct of an organization's Business Understanding Framework.

Business framework data can be displayed for any level of business activity, for any interrogative, for any specification level, in any format, using any notation, at any time, for any audience, the same as data resource data or processes resource data.

Business Understanding Framework Promotion

Many people have a knee-jerk reaction to adding a seventh interrogative and making the traditional business framework three-dimensional. Many people are confused by the third dimension, and the fact that the third dimension itself is a two-dimensional hierarchy for business activity that is related to another two-dimensional hierarchy for organization. A few people cannot comprehend the third dimension of the framework being two dimensional.

Albert Einstein said, "A question sometimes drives crazy; am I or others crazy?" Looking at the Business Understanding Framework from a perspective other than a person involved in its development, it's reasonable to expect some people to believe the Business Understanding Framework "sometimes drives crazy." It's a totally new concept for thoroughly understanding an organization's business.

Many people are willing to accept anything reasonable that will help them understand and operate the organization's business, once they grasp the concept. Others totally reject any change and continue to use traditional business frameworks.

Promoting the Business Understanding Framework as a totally new approach to thoroughly understanding an organization's business can be challenging. Years of mindset and resistance to change need to be overcome. Below are a few guidelines to help promote the Business Understanding Framework.

Separate the traditional framework problems and derivation of a contemporary framework from the features of the contemporary Business Understanding Framework. Focus on the features of the Business Understanding Framework and its usefulness for understanding and operating an organization's business.

Answer questions about traditional frameworks and derivation of contemporary framework only when asked. Don't dwell on the problems with the traditional business frameworks, the evolution of the Business Understanding Framework, or the details of transition to the Business Understanding Framework.

Emphasize features of the Business Understanding Framework. The Business Understanding Framework is a three-dimensional matrix that provides a construct for a complete, integrated, thorough understanding of an organization's business. It can be used as necessary to gain understanding about the organization's business. It does not have to be completed before understanding can be gained.

Identify problems the audience has understanding their business and show how the Business Understanding Framework can help them. Provide examples that are relative to the audience. Avoid examples that are not relative to the audience. Those examples might be easy for the presenter, but are difficult for the audience to relate to their business.

Start with a portion of the Business Understanding Framework that is relevant to the audience. If the audience has problems understanding organization units, start with that part of the framework. If the audience has problems with business activities, start with that part of the framework.

Another approach is to start with the basic two-dimensional framework with interrogatives and specification levels for a single business activity that is of interest to the audience. Then move to another business activity and show how the third dimension integrates business activities. Once started and some understanding is gained, it's easy to move to other parts of the Business Understanding Framework.

Guideline: Focus on what is of interest to the audience, and use the Business Understanding Framework to address that interest.

Non-Business Realm

An organization typically does not manage the non-business realm. An organization only observes and understands the non-business realm. That non-business realm understanding follows the same scenario as understanding the business realm using the Business Understanding Framework. However, the perspective needs to be broadened.

Using the human genetic code as an example. The business activity is unlocking the genetic code. The non-business activities are understanding how the genetic code works.

Which is the genetic activity being understood. What are chromosomes, genes, alleles, and so on, and their descriptions; How are the data and processes involved in the genetic activity; Where is locations in the body where data are stored and transmitted, and the processes operate; When is a relative time or sequence of processes, rather than an absolute time; Who is the amino acids, proteins, blood cells, and so on; and Why is the reason or explanation for the activity.

Another example is understanding the brain function. The business activity is understanding the brain function. The non-business activity is the brain functions, represented by Which. The other six interrogatives qualify the brain activity designated by Which.

The non-business realm can extend to physics, astronomy, chemistry, meteorology, and any other non-business realm activity an organization wants to understand.

SUMMARY

The interrogative Which was added as a seventh interrogative to identify business activity – the selection/designation. What was redefined to represent a description/explanation of business activity. How was redefined to represent the combined data and processes resource, since both data and processes must be managed as a single, combined, critical resource of the organization.

The seven contemporary interrogatives are Which, What, How, Where, When, Who, and Why. The primary contemporary interrogative is Which and the associate contemporary interrogatives are What, How, Where, When, Who, and Why.

A third dimension was added to traditional business frameworks to represent business activity, designated by Which. The three dimensions are a business activity dimension, a framework interrogative dimension, and a specification level dimension. The new three-dimensional contemporary business framework could represent all business activities in an organization, rather than a single business activity. The contemporary business framework was formally named the Business Understanding Framework.

Business activity is a two-dimensional structure representing a hierarchy of business activities. Organization unit is a separate two-dimensional structure representing a hierarchy of responsibility and reporting relationships. Business activity and organization unit have a many-to-many relationship, which is resolved with business activity unit. That enhanced structure forms the third dimension of the Business Understanding Framework.

The Business Understanding Framework is documented with business framework data, the same as the data resource is documented with data resource data, and the processes resource is documented with processes resource data. The business framework data can be displayed for any business activity, for any interrogative, for any specification level, with any format and notation, for any audience.

Successful promotion of the contemporary Business Understanding Framework follows several guidelines to ensure that the recipient can focus on what is of interest to them and their organization, rather than on the problems with traditional business frameworks and evolution to the Business Understanding Framework.

The Business Understanding Framework resolves the basic problems with traditional business frameworks, and allows an organization to thoroughly understand its business, be agile, and successfully operate the business. The Business Understanding Framework can also be used in the non-business realm to understand activities in the non-business realm, such as genetic activity, brain function, and other activities in physics, astronomy, chemistry, and so on.

QUESTIONS

The following questions are provided as a review of the Business Understanding Framework Chapter, and to stimulate thought about the Business Understanding Framework.

1. How were the basic problems with traditional business frameworks resolved?
2. How were the traditional interrogatives changed to contemporary interrogatives?
3. What do the contemporary interrogatives represent?

4. What is the primary contemporary interrogative?
5. What are the associate contemporary interrogatives?
6. What is the third interrogative role?
7. How was the traditional business framework changed to a contemporary business framework?
8. How do the contemporary interrogatives relate to the contemporary business framework?
9. What is the formal name of the contemporary business framework?
10. What are the dimensions of the Business Understanding Framework?
11. What do the dimensions of the Business Understanding Framework represent?
12. What is the structure of business activities?
13. What is the structure of organization units?
14. How do business activities relate to organization units?
15. How do business activities and organization units represent the third dimension of the Business Understanding Framework?
16. How is the Business Understanding Framework documented?
17. What are the benefits of the Business Understanding Framework?
18. How is the Business Understanding Framework used in the business realm?
19. How can the Business Understanding Framework be used in the non-business realm?
20. How can the Business Understanding Framework be promoted?

Chapter 10
ARCHITECTURES AND MODELS

Architecture and model concepts are crucial for understanding.

The Business Understanding Framework Chapter described the contemporary interrogatives and a contemporary business framework that resolve the basic problems with traditional interrogative and frameworks. The Architecture and Models Chapter describes the problems with traditional architectures and models, the resolution to those problems with contemporary architectures and models, the symmetry and perspective of architectures and models, and architecture registries. The chapter theme is to understand the problems with traditional architectures and models, and establish contemporary architectures and models that resolve those problems.

ARCHITECTURE AND MODEL PROBLEMS

Using architectures and models to understand an organization's business begins with understanding the role of architectures and models, the common architecture and model problems, the basic architecture and model problems, and the impact of those basic problems on an organization's business

Role of Architectures and Models

Architectures and models are key components for providing an in-depth understanding of every organization's business. The combined data and processes resource contains the thorough understanding about an organization's business, and that combined resource is stored according to architectures. Models are used to build those architectures and to portray portions of those architectures.

Organizations cannot be successful without formal, high-quality architectures and models. Any reduction in the quality of architectures and models impacts the quality of business understanding, agility, and success.

Common Architecture and Model Problems

Traditional architectures and models have a variety of problems that ultimately impact an organization's business. The common problems across many public and private sector organizations are listed below.

The difference between traditional architectures and models is not well understood.

Most organizations have a plethora of traditional architectures and models throughout the organization.

Traditional architectures and models have different forms, notations, and meanings that are often difficult to understand.

Multiple traditional architectures cover the same subject areas.

Multiple traditional architectures have gaps and overlaps.

Multiple traditional architectures are conflicting, redundant, and inconsistent.

Traditional architectures are often incomplete and out of date.

Traditional architectures often compete as *your-architecture* versus *my-architecture.*

Traditional architectures are usually developed independent of any organization-wide architecture.

Traditional architectures are not normalized across the organization, or even across major subject areas within an organization.

Traditional architecture versioning is difficult to manage.

Traditional model check-in and check-out procedures are complicated and confusing.

Traditional model versioning is difficult to manage.

Basic Architecture and Model Problems

The common problems with traditional architectures and models can be grouped into six basic problems.

The first basic problem is that the distinction between traditional architectures and models is unclear. One person's traditional architecture may be another person's traditional model, and visa-versa.

The second basic problem is that traditional architectures and models are difficult to understand. The format and notation vary widely across organizations and within an organization, and the format and notation are difficult to understand by anyone other than the person developing the architecture or model. In many cases, the architecture or model developer doesn't remember their own format and notation at a later date.

The third basic problem is that traditional architectures have a serious version control problem. In most cases, determining the effective date and version of a traditional architecture is difficult, if not impossible.

The fourth basic problem is that traditional models have a serious check-in / check-out and version control problem. Many organizations still check-in and check-out models, sometimes to be reviewed and sometimes to be updated. The control of that process is weak, causing confusion about the model versions and relevance.

The fifth basic problem is that traditional architectures and models are disparate across the organization. Not only is the format and notation different, but individual component names and relations are different. Many disparate architectures and models represent disparate data and processes, and disparate data and processes are represented on many disparate architectures and models.

The sixth basic problem is that the role of traditional architectures and models for understanding and operating an organization's business is not clear. Traditional architectures and models represent everything from conceptual design to physical implementation, and they are seldom labeled as to what they represent.

Impact of Architecture and Model Problems

Many people are simply throwing traditional architectures and models around, for a variety of different reasons, and eventually developing disparate databases and processes from those architectures and models. The result is the rampant, and growing, data and processes disparity seen in most public and private sector organizations today. The data disparity is often visible in most organizations, and some attempts are made to use the same data. However, the processes disparity is generally worse than data disparity, and is not quite as visible as the data disparity.

Visible disparity is the disparity in data and processes that is readily visible and obvious to the organization.

Hidden disparity is the disparity in data and processes that is not readily visible or obvious to the organization.

Traditional architectures and models often lead to brute-force development. The disparity resulting from brute-force development seriously impacts an organization's understanding and operation of its business. Business needs are not implemented or fully supported, and the business success is often compromised – all for the lack of good architectures and models.

ARCHITECTURE AND MODEL PROBLEM RESOLUTION

The basic problems with traditional architecture and models must be resolved for an organization to thoroughly understand its business, be agile, and be fully successful in its business operation. Formal, high-quality architectures and models are critical for an organization's business understanding and success. Resolution of the basic problems includes

133

understanding the distinction between architectures and models, basic architecture definitions, problems with generic architectures, and basic model definitions.

Richard Feynman's famous statement was, "What I cannot create, I do not understand." Something can only be built if it is thoroughly understood. If you don't understand it, you can't build it. The flip side is, if you understand it, you can build it. Applied to data and processes resource management, if you understand the business, you can model data and processes. If you can model data and processes, you can architect them. If you can architect them, you can build them. If you can build them, you can understand and successfully operate the business.

Architecture – Model Distinction

Architectures and models are often confused, and the terms are often used interchangeably. Two distinctions need to be made between architectures and models to begin resolving the basic problems.

First, architectures contain all descriptive, structural, and integrity detail. Architectures are stored facts that do not have any presentation format or notation. This distinction is difficult to accept at first, but will become clear as the role of architectures and models is described in more detail

Models contain a subset of detail contained in an architecture. They contain a portion of an architecture that is relevant to the recipient, at a point in time, and have a format and notation that is relevant to the recipient. The presentation format and notation only appear in models, not in the architecture.

Second, architectures are persistent over time and evolve over time. Architectures are the permanent, evolving repository – the record of reference – for the understanding about an organization's business.

Models are transient and do not evolve over time. They provide a snapshot of a portion of an architecture, at a point in time, for a recipient. Models are not changed or enhanced. Enhancements are made to architectures, and new models are prepared to portray those enhancements.

A model could contain all the components of an architecture, but the model would be quite large and difficult to comprehend, and would likely not be relevant to a recipient. However, if such a model were developed, it's still a model, because it has presentation format and notation relevant to a recipient.

Architecture Definitions

Architecture is the art, science, or profession of designing and building structures. It is the structure or structures as a whole, such as the frame, heating, plumbing, wiring, and so on, in a building. It's the style of structures and method of design and construction, such as roman or colonial architecture. It's the design of a system perceived by people, such as the architecture of the solar system.

Data architecture could be defined as *an architecture of data*, but that definition is a tautology and is neither denotative or comprehensive. A more formal definition is needed.

Data architecture is the method of the design and construction of an integrated data resource, within a single organization-wide data architecture, that is business driven, based on business niche components as perceived by the organization, and implemented into appropriate operating environments. It consists of component descriptions, structures and relations, and integrity rules that provide a consistent foundation across organizational boundaries for easily identifiable, readily available, high-quality data that support the current and future business information demand.

Datum architecture is meaningless, because an architecture can't represent a single item of data.

Processes architecture could be defined as *an architecture of processes*, but like data, that definition is a tautology. A more formal definition is needed.

Processes architecture is the method of design and construction of an integrated processes resource, within a single organization-wide processes architecture, that is business driven, based on business niche components as perceived by the organization, and implemented into appropriate operating environments. It consists of component descriptions, structures and relations, and integrity rules that provide a consistent foundation across organizational boundaries, for easily identifiable, readily available, high-quality processes that support the current and future business operations.

Process architecture is the architecture of a single process.

Business architecture is any architecture about an organization's business in the business realm.

Non-business architecture is any architecture about the non-business realm.

Proper was defined earlier. **Improper** means not proper; not in accord with fact, truth, or right procedure; incomplete or incorrect; not suited to the circumstances, design, or end.

A whole plethora of terms could be defined about architectures, but that would be unnecessary. A better approach is to define basic words, and combine those words as needed to form terms for understanding and managing an organization's data and processes resource.

For example, terms like *improper architecture, proper data architecture, improper processes architecture, business data architecture, business processes architecture, proper non-business processes architecture, improper business data architecture,* and so on, could be used to represent specific situations.

Generic Architectures

Generic architectures are often promoted as a quick way for organizations to understand their business. *Generic* means relating to, or characteristic of, a whole group or class; being or having a nonproprietary name. Synonyms for *generic* are *broad, common, universal, basic,* and *widespread.*

A *generic architecture* is an architecture that is intended to have widespread use across many different public and private sector organizations for quickly developing an architecture.

Generic can be combined with other words and terms, as described above, to form terms such as *generic data architecture* and *generic processes architecture, proper generic data architecture, improper generic processes architecture,* and so on.

Generic architectures have four basic problems. First, the attempt to fit all organizations into the same architecture is not acceptable. Each organization does business differently, and that organization's architecture must be different to represent the organizations way of doing business. Consultants and vendors often promote generic architectures, because it's easy for them to fit an organization's understanding into a generic architecture that the consultant or vendor understands. They don't have to deal with understanding a variety of different architectures unique to different organizations.

However, generic architectures are difficult for organizations, because an organization has to fit its way of understanding and doing business into an architecture that typically does not represent their business understanding and operation. It forces an organization to warp their business understanding and operation into an unfamiliar architecture.

Second, building a generic architecture for an infinite number of individual public and private sector organization's understanding of their business niche and business operation, even within the same class of business, is nearly impossible. Typically, a generic architecture is developed for a class of organizations, such as the petroleum industry, the insurance industry, education, and so on. However, even with generic architectures for a class of organizations, individual organizations have widely different business niches and widely different ways of understanding and operating their business.

If a generic architecture for a class of business were developed, the architecture would be so large that an organization would spend considerable time trying to determine how to best use that generic architecture, and much of the architecture would likely be unused. Forcing organizations into a generic architecture that does not adequately and accurately represent their business is a move toward uncertainty, confusion, and disparity.

Third, an organization does not thoroughly understand their business by simply purchasing a generic architecture and loading data and processes into that architecture. They often load disparate data and processes, and lose the opportunity to thoroughly understand their business niche and how they choose to operate in that business niche.

Fourth, a generic architecture is nearly impossible to build and maintain for multiple organizations, because no common context exists for understanding. A generic architecture has no independent test of reality for a specific organization. The only reality for an organization is the proper architecture it builds, based on observations of the business niche where it operates, and the perceptions gained from those observations.

A far better approach is for an organization is to formally develop a unique architecture that represents its specific business understanding and operation in its business niche. The organization builds a customized architecture, that they better understand, and that adequately and accurately represents their business understanding and operation. That's the best route to stopping burgeoning disparity and resolving existing disparity.

A *unique architecture* is an architecture that an organization develops based on its understanding of the business niche where it operates, and how it chooses to do business in that business niche.

Model Definitions

A *model* is a set of plans, a structural design, a miniature representation or manifestation of something, or a pattern of something to be made.

Data models can be models of either the data architecture or of data values. A *data architecture model* is a model of a data architecture that either represents a portion of an existing data architecture, or represents the development of, or enhancements to, a data architecture.

Data values often have an inherent pattern that can be modeled. A *data value model* is a model of a set of data values.

A **datum model** is meaningless, because a datum is a single data item and can't be modeled.

A *processes architecture model* is a model of the processes architecture. that either represents a portion of an existing processes architecture, or represents the development of, or enhancements to, a processes architecture.

A *process model* is a model of a single process.

A *business model* is a model of any architecture in the business realm. A *non-business model* is a model of any architecture in the non-business realm.

137

Proper and *improper* could be added to these terms, as described above for architectures, to form more specific terms for model.

CONTEMPORARY ARCHITECTURES

With the basic architecture and model definitions in place, contemporary architectures can be described in more detail, including definitions, the Architecture Trinity, chronology stamps, the construct and use of contemporary architectures, and the benefits of contemporary architectures.

Definitions

A *contemporary architecture* is a proper architecture that contains a thorough understanding about an organization's unique business in a manner that the organization can easily store and retrieve.

The *Contemporary Architecture Objective* is to develop an organization-wide, contemporary architecture that contains a thorough understanding about an organization's business and fully supports its business operation.

The Architecture Trinity

A common belief is that an architecture contains only structure, and traditional data and processes architectures typically contain only the structure of data and processes. Structure alone is not a complete architecture!

A contemporary architecture must have a trinity of components for descriptive, structural, and integrity aspects of that architecture. *Trinity* is the state of being threefold; a group of three closely related persons or things. The *Architecture Trinity* is the three components for thoroughly understanding contemporary architectures; specifically, a descriptive component, a structural component, and an integrity component.

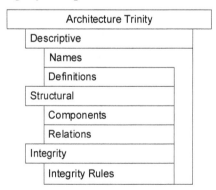

Figure 10.1. The Architecture Trinity.

The Architecture Trinity is shown in Figure 10.1. The Descriptive component consists of Names and Definitions. The descriptive names apply across all components of the Architecture Trinity, as shown by the vertical bar on the right. The Structural component consists of architecture Components and the Relations between those components. The Integrity component consists of Integrity Rules to maintain quality and designate actions for violations of the integrity rules.

An alternative Architecture Trinity is shown in Figure 10.2. The center of the triangle represents the complete contemporary architecture. The three points of the triangle represent the three components of a contemporary architecture: Descriptive, Structural, and Integrity. The three components are separate, but all three components are necessary to completely define a contemporary architecture.

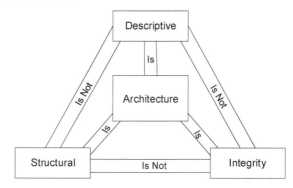

Figure 10.2. An alternative Architecture Trinity.

The three inner *Is* bands indicate the three components that comprise a complete contemporary architecture: Descriptive, Structural, and Integrity. The three outer *Is Not* bands indicate that Descriptive is not the same as Structural, which is not the same as Integrity, which is not the same as Descriptive. In other words, the three components are separate from each other, but all three contribute to an architecture. All three components of the architecture trinity are required for a thorough understanding of an organization's business.

Contemporary Architecture Construct and Use

A distinction needs to be made between building and maintaining a contemporary architecture and populating that contemporary architecture with business data and processes to understand and operate the business. Many organizations fail to make that distinction, which is a basic cultural problem leading to many of the disparity problems seen in most public and private sector organizations today.

Business data and *business processes* were defined earlier as the data and processes that *are relevant* to the organization's business. Architecture data and architecture processes are the data and processes necessary to create and maintain the contemporary architecture for containing the business understanding and operation details.

Architecture data are any data necessary to define the contemporary architecture for containing the business data and business processes, such as data resource data and processes resource data.

Architecture processes are any processes necessary to identify and define the contemporary architecture, and to develop the contemporary architecture for the business data and business processes based on those architecture processes, such as the Data Resource Cycle and Processes Resource Cycle.

The contemporary architecture contains all of the organization's data and processes. Both the architecture data and architecture processes, and the business data and business processes, are stored in the contemporary architecture. The contemporary architecture contains data and processes for both the Understand Business Function and the Operate Business Function.

Chronology Stamps

Each change to a contemporary architecture or the data contained in the contemporary architecture, whether addition, deletion, or enhancement, no matter how large or small, represents a different version. Most contemporary architectures are very dynamic due to the dynamic nature of the business niche, and both architecture data and business data change. The result is that an organization seldom knows the current version of its architecture data or business data.

The version problem is resolved with chronology stamps. A chronology stamp includes the date and time, with an accuracy acceptable to the organization for its type of business. It is placed on architecture data and business data any time those data are added, changed, or deleted, showing the effective date of those data.

A *chronology stamp* is a date-time stamp, with a level of accuracy acceptable to an organization, that is placed on architecture data and business data contained in the contemporary architecture any time those data are added, changed, or deleted.

An organization could define subject areas within its contemporary architecture. The most prominent subject areas are the five critical resources for an organization: data and processes resource, human resource, finance, real property, and offerings; and the business activities. Additional subject areas could also be defined, such as impacts of budget reduction, benefits of opening a new branch, trends in government services, and so on. The subject areas could be numerous, and often overlap.

A *subject area* is a portion of the organization's contemporary architecture that represents an area of interest to the organization. It may represent the five critical resources, business activities, or other areas of interest to the organization. Subject areas could be numerous and may overlap.

Chronology stamps on subject areas avoid going through all the data in that subject area to determine the effective date of the subject area. Any time data in a subject area are added, changed, or deleted, the chronology stamp on the subject area is updated.

If historical data are maintained with chronology stamps, which is part of the contemporary architecture creation and maintenance process, a past historical version of the contemporary architecture or business data can be developed at any point in time. Successive historical versions of the contemporary architecture or business data provide a historical trend of the contemporary architecture or business data.

Version numbers could be used for major milestones of architecture development, such as Version 2.4 with a corresponding chronology stamp. Generally, lengthy version numbers, such as Version 2.3.1.6.4, are confusing and often difficult to maintain, because the lengthy version number has no inherent meaning to most people. Shorter version numbers with a corresponding chronology stamp are more meaningful.

Contemporary Architecture Benefits

The benefits of contemporary architectures are a resolution of basic problems with traditional architectures. Contemporary architecture definitions and the Contemporary Architecture Objective provide the new concept for contemporary architectures. An Architecture Trinity of descriptive, structural, and integrity components guide the design and development of contemporary architectures.

A distinction is made between the architecture data and architecture processes for defining and developing the contemporary architecture, and the business data and business processes contained in the contemporary architecture for understanding and operating the business.

Chronology stamps are used to formally manage contemporary architecture versions and the business data versions contained in the contemporary architecture. A history of architecture versions and business versions can be developed to show trends in evolution of the contemporary architecture and the business.

Contemporary architectures are a major step toward building an overarching construct for business understanding and agility so an organization to thoroughly understand and successfully operate its business.

141

CONTEMPORARY MODELS

Solving the basic problems with traditional models is a major step toward building an overarching construct for business understanding and agility. Solving the basic model problems and developing contemporary models includes definitions, model-driven architectures, architecture-driven models, the architecture-model relationship, contemporary model versions, data model patterns, and the benefits of contemporary data models.

Definitions

A *proper model* is a model that is complete, correct, organized, coordinated, and appropriate for developing or enhancing a proper architecture, or for portraying a portion of a proper architecture.

A *contemporary model* is a proper model of a contemporary architecture, either for building and enhancing that contemporary architecture, or for portraying that contemporary architecture.

The *Contemporary Model Objective* is to develop contemporary models that contribute to building and enhancing a contemporary architecture with model-driven architecture techniques, and to portray portions of a contemporary architecture to a recipient with architecture-driven model techniques.

Model-Driven Architectures

Contemporary models can be used to build and enhance contemporary architectures. A contemporary model cannot be independent of a contemporary architecture. Models that are independent of an architecture only lead to the rampant disparity seen in many public and private sector organizations today.

Model-driven architectures is a technique that develops contemporary models from an analysis of business needs and uses those models to build or enhance contemporary architectures.

The *Model-Driven Architecture Objective* is to develop and enhance contemporary architectures, for the entire scope of the organization's business, from multiple contributing contemporary models, that include all the detail necessary to thoroughly understand and successfully operate the organization's business.

Architecture-Driven Models

Contemporary models can also be used to portray contemporary architectures, such as the data resource architecture or processes resource architecture, at any level of detail, at any time, in any form, for any audience.

Architecture-driven models is a technique that prepares contemporary models by retrieving details from a contemporary architecture, for any scope of the business, and presenting those details to the intended audience using appropriate model presentation techniques.

The ***Architecture-Driven Model Objective*** is to prepare contemporary models from contemporary architectures, for any scope of the business, at any level of detail, at any time, in any form, for any audience, so they can thoroughly understand the business and successfully operate the business.

The Architecture – Model Relationship

The relationship between contemporary architectures and contemporary models is shown in Figure 10.3. An organization has a contemporary architecture for thoroughly understanding and operating its business, shown at the top center of the diagram. An organization's business needs are shown at the top left of the diagram. The business needs go through an analysis and a contemporary model is built for those business needs. That contemporary model is within a business scope and uses a specific model technique for the intended audience. The contemporary model is then used to build or enhance the organization's contemporary architecture to meet the business needs, shown by the up arrows.

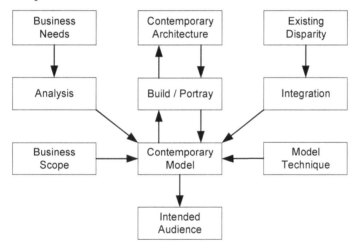

Figure 10.3. Contemporary architecture – model relationship.

An organization's existing disparity is shown at the top right of the diagram. That disparity goes through an integration process and a contemporary model is built to understand and manage the integration process. That contemporary model is within a business scope and uses a specific model technique for the intended audience. The contemporary model is then used to build or enhance the organization's contemporary architecture to support the integration process, also shown by the up arrows.

Both the business needs process and the existing disparity process are examples of the model-driven architecture technique, because contemporary models are used to build or enhance the contemporary architecture.

The contemporary architecture can be portrayed to an intended audience, through contemporary models, for a business scope, using specific model techniques, for an intended audience, shown by the down arrows. Portrayal of a contemporary architecture is an example of the architecture-driven model technique, because the contemporary architecture is portrayed to the intended audience through contemporary models.

The diagram in Figure 10.3 does not represent the storage and retrieval of business data or business processes in the contemporary architecture for understanding and operating an organization's business. It only represents defining and developing the contemporary architecture construct for the storage and retrieval of business data and processes.

A similar diagram could be developed for the storage and retrieval of business data and processes in the contemporary architecture to understand and operate the business. That diagram would include the final stages of the Data Resource Cycle and Processes Resource Cycle, the contents of the Business Understanding Framework, and so on.

Contemporary Model Versions

A basic problem with traditional models is managing model check-in / check-out and model versions. Many traditional models don't represent an architecture – they have become the architecture! That's the reason for the check-in / check-out process, so that multiple conflicting versions of the architecture are not created. Traditional model check-in / check-out is an old-school mindset that needs to be changed.

The first change is a concept that contemporary models are snapshots, are transient, and are never updated. Contemporary models represent the detail for building and enhancing contemporary architectures, and for portraying contemporary architectures at a point in time. Contemporary architectures are persistent and evolve over time. Contemporary models are not permanent, and do not change over time.

The second change is the addition of a chronology stamp to contemporary models. Each contemporary model has a chronology stamp indicating the point in time the model was prepared. The chronology stamp becomes the contemporary model version that represents the components from the contemporary architecture at that point in time, or the components to build or enhance a contemporary architecture at that point in time.

The *contemporary model version* is a chronology stamp that indicates the point in time when the contemporary model was prepared to enhance a contemporary architecture, or prepared to portray a contemporary architecture.

Each contemporary model must have a comprehensive description about what it represents. A chronology stamp without a corresponding comprehensive description does not completely solve the problems with traditional models. The chronology stamp resolves the point in time the contemporary model was prepared, but does not provide a detailed understanding about what the contemporary model represents. Both a chronology stamp and a comprehensive description are needed to resolve tradition model problems.

The chronology stamp on the data can be shown on a contemporary model portraying a contemporary architecture to show the point in time the data represent. However, inclusion of the data chronology stamps does not eliminate the need for a chronology stamp on the contemporary model.

Contemporary models can represent historical versions of the contemporary architecture at any point in time, similar to creating historical versions of data at a point in time. A point in time is selected and the contemporary architecture is searched for component chronology stamps on or before that selected point in time. A series of contemporary models at different points in time shows the evolution of the contemporary architecture.

Data Model Patterns

Many people talk about data model patterns. However, *data model pattern* has two different meanings.

First, *data model pattern* could mean the configuration format and notations for displaying data models to the intended audience. The appropriate term would be *data model format* that consists of data model format and notations. Model format and notations are explained in more detail in the Assisted Intelligence Chapter.

Second, *data model pattern* could mean the pattern of business data contained in a data model. The business data contained in data models have patterns, such as hierarchies, networks, parts explosions, menu preparation, mutually exclusive parents, recursions, and so on. Those business data patterns can be displayed on data models. The appropriate term would be *data pattern*.

The quality of a data model depends on how well the data model format meets the intended audience needs, and how well data patterns are displayed on that model. A high-quality data model emphasizes both data model format and data patterns. A low-quality data model has a confusing format, and masks or hides data patterns.

Contemporary Model Benefits

The benefits of contemporary models are a resolution of the basic problems with traditional models. Formal contemporary model definitions and the Contemporary Model Objective provide the concept for contemporary models. The techniques of model-driven architectures and architecture-driven models support the distinction between permanent contemporary architectures and transient contemporary models that portray a contemporary architecture. The architecture – model relationship resolves the confusion between traditional architectures and traditional models.

Model versions using chronology stamps eliminates the tedious and difficult check-in / check-out process for traditional models. The management of a large volume of persistent models is eliminated. Traditional model disparity is resolved, and formal models are prepared to meet intended audience needs. The distinction between model format and notation, and the patterns of model contents resolves confusion about the use of models.

Contemporary models are a major step toward building and maintaining contemporary architectures, and portraying contemporary architectures.

SYMMETRY AND PERSPECTIVE

The understanding of symmetry and perspective are crucial to understanding, building, maintaining, and using contemporary architectures and models. Symmetry and perspective are often misunderstood, and the terms are frequently confused and used inappropriately. Understanding symmetry and perspective includes formal definitions, the architecture – model relationship, the three architecture symmetries an organization faces, broken architecture symmetry, loss of architecture symmetry, broken model perspective, entropy and energy related to symmetry, and the benefits of architecture symmetry and model perspective.

Definitions

Symmetry is the shape, form, and makeup of an object, such as a cube, sphere, or blob.

Symmetry should not be confused with *symmetrical*. Every object has symmetry, but is not necessarily symmetrical.

Perspective is a specific perception of an object. When an object is perceived from different directions, it may appear different. The perspective of the object is different, but the symmetry of the object is the same. All perspectives are correct, even though each perspective may be different.

For example, when a cube or blob is viewed from different directions, that object looks different. The perspective of the object is different, but the symmetry of the object remains the same.

Contemporary architectures have a symmetry. Contemporary models portray a perspective of a contemporary architecture symmetry that currently exists, using architecture-driven model techniques. Contemporary models can also portray changes to build or enhance an existing contemporary architecture, using model-driven architecture techniques. Contemporary models represent a perspective of the contemporary architecture symmetry.

Architecture symmetry is the symmetry of an architecture. A *model perspective* is a perspective of an architecture symmetry.

Contemporary model perspective is a perception of a contemporary architecture symmetry represented by a contemporary model, either for enhancing a contemporary architecture or for portraying a contemporary architecture. Each contemporary model perspective is different, depending on the purpose of the model and the intended audience.

An *enhance model perspective* is a contemporary model perspective that enhances the contemporary architecture symmetry using model-driven architecture techniques.

A *portray model perspective* is a contemporary model perspective that portrays the contemporary architecture symmetry using architecture-driven model techniques.

A contemporary architecture represents the entire understanding and operation of the organization's business without format or notation, as explained earlier. Contemporary models provide perspectives to build and enhance or to portray that contemporary architecture, using a format and notation acceptable to the audience.

Architecture – Model Relationship

Several terms help clarify the relationship between contemporary architectures and contemporary models.

Invariance means an object appears different when the perspective changes. The features of the object are common to all perspectives and are valid from all perspectives.

For contemporary architectures and models, invariance means the contemporary architecture appears different with different contemporary models. The features of the architecture are common to all models and are valid for all models.

Complementarity means many different perspectives of an object are equally valid, and a person must choose one perspective that is valid and meaningful for that person at that point in time. Multiple perspectives define the whole object.

For contemporary architectures and models, complementarity means that contemporary models provide many different perspectives of a contemporary architecture that are valid, and a person must choose the contemporary model that is valid and meaningful for that person at a point in space-time.

Relativity means the same object can be represented in many different ways without loss of meaning.

For contemporary architectures and models, a contemporary architecture can be represented in many different contemporary models without loss of meaning about the contemporary architecture.

Due to constant change in the business niche and ongoing business niche observation over space-time, the contemporary architecture symmetry constantly changes. Any contemporary model that builds or enhances the contemporary architecture through model-driven architecture techniques changes the contemporary architecture symmetry. Subsequent contemporary model perspectives portray that different contemporary architecture symmetry.

That's the reason contemporary models that portray perspectives of the contemporary architecture symmetry are considered transient. As soon as a contemporary model that portrays a contemporary architecture is developed, the contemporary architecture symmetry could change from another contemporary model that enhances the contemporary architecture symmetry.

Three Symmetries

An organization faces three different architecture symmetries: the business environment architecture symmetry, the business niche architecture symmetry, and the organization's contemporary architecture symmetry. The progression from business environment architecture symmetry, to business niche architecture symmetry, to contemporary architecture symmetry narrows the scope and increases the organization's understanding of its business.

Business environment architecture symmetry is the architecture symmetry of the business environment with its complex set of interacting components, at a point in space-time. It has a wide scope and an organization has a limited understanding of the symmetry.

Business niche architecture symmetry is the architecture symmetry of the organization's business niche with its complex set of interacting components, at a point in space-time. It's a subset of the business environment architecture symmetry that *may be of interest* to the organization and the organization has a greater understanding of the symmetry.

The *contemporary architecture symmetry* is the symmetry of the organization's contemporary architecture at a point in space-time. It's a subset of the business niche architecture symmetry that *is relevant* to understanding and operating the organization's business.

Broken Architecture Symmetry

Competing, conflicting, and incomplete architectures are disparate and do not adequately represent an organization's understanding and operation of its business. The disparity can occur in any component of the architecture trinity – descriptive, structural, and integrity – and usually occurs in all three. Disparity can occur in either the data resource or the processes resource, and usually occurs in both.

The architecture disparity is referred to as broken architecture symmetry, because the formality of a comparate architecture is broken. The result is reduced understanding, and increased uncertainty, about the organization's business. Any architecture disparity is broken architecture symmetry!

Broken architecture symmetry is the existence of multiple, disparate, competing, conflicting, incomplete, or unclear contemporary architecture components that result in decreased understanding and increased uncertainty about the organization's business and its operation.

The resolution of broken architecture symmetry is to formally create and maintain proper architecture symmetry consisting of organization-wide data and processes architectures that resist anomalies and divergencies that lead to broken architecture symmetry. Avoidance of broken architecture symmetry is the justification for the formal development of proper architectures.

Proper architecture symmetry is the existence of a contemporary architecture, consisting of comparate, single, organization-wide data and processes architectures that result in increased understanding and decreased uncertainty about the organization's business.

Loss of Architecture Symmetry

An organization can develop a proper architecture symmetry, then lose that proper architecture symmetry and revert to a broken architecture symmetry by failing to rigorously maintain the proper architecture symmetry.

Loss of architecture symmetry is a loss of proper architecture symmetry that has been achieved by failing to rigorously maintain that proper architecture symmetry.

Loss of architecture symmetry is often difficult to detect, because the change from proper architecture symmetry to broken architecture symmetry is often very slow. Organizations don't notice the slow change until it's too late and they face the impacts of broken architecture symmetry. Recovery to a proper architecture symmetry is long and difficult.

Broken Model Perspective

Loss of proper architecture symmetry is not an architecture problem – it's a broken model perspective problem!

Models fail to maintain a proper architecture symmetry when building or enhancing a contemporary architecture, which leads to the broken architecture symmetry. What should be contemporary models to build and enhance contemporary architectures become traditional models that compromise contemporary architectures. Organizations revert to traditional models, often in an attempt to brute-force develop a comparate architecture.

The problem is referred to as a broken model perspective, because the model doesn't adequately or accurately build and enhance a proper architecture.

Broken model perspective is the use of traditional models, rather than contemporary models, to build and enhance a comparate architecture, resulting in a broken architecture symmetry.

Broken model perspective is often difficult to detect, because there is no independent test of reality. Traditional models and brute-force approaches slowly erode a proper architecture symmetry, leading to broken architecture symmetry. The resolution is to ensure that proper model perspectives are always used to build and enhance an organization's proper architecture symmetry.

Broken model perspective can also occur when a model doesn't adequately or accurately portray the proper architecture symmetry. Typically, traditional models are developed to portray the proper architecture symmetry. These traditional models become disparate and portray competing and conflicting perspectives of the proper architecture symmetry.

Eventually, the traditional models become persistent and begin to represent the architecture through a collection of models. The benefits of a contemporary architecture are lost. The organization has reverted to the problems with traditional models described earlier.

Proper model perspective is the consistent use of contemporary models to build and enhance the organization's proper architecture symmetry, and to portray perspectives of a proper architecture symmetry. It avoids the use of traditional models and brute-force approaches to build and maintain a contemporary architecture, and to portray a contemporary architecture.

Entropy and Energy

Building and maintaining an organization's contemporary architecture, and using contemporary models to build and portray the contemporary architecture are directly related to entropy and energy.

Entropy is the state or degree of disorderliness. It's a loss of order, which is increasing disorderliness. Entropy steadily increases over time, meaning that things become more disorderly over time.

In a closed system, such as an engine, entropy reaches a steady state. But in an open system, entropy steadily increases and does not reach a steady state. The business environment, business niche, and organization are open systems where entropy steadily increases without reaching a steady state.

Disparity is high entropy, meaning greater disorderliness. Comparity is low entropy, meaning lower disorderliness and greater orderliness.

A cooperative exchange exists between entropy and evolution. The three symmetries – business environment, business niche, and organization – continually evolve over time. That evolution is natural and results in increasing entropy. In addition to the natural entropy, organizations often create their own entropy by not using contemporary models and developing a contemporary architecture, leading to the problems described earlier.

Natural entropy is the entropy the occurs naturally as the business environment, business niche, and organization continually evolve over time.

Created entropy is the entropy an organization creates by not using contemporary models or formally developing a contemporary architecture.

Both natural and created entropy must be reduced to an acceptable level for an organization to thoroughly understand its business and successfully operate that business. Entropy can never be completely eliminated, because natural entropy is continuous. However, an organization can eliminate most, if not all, of the created entropy, and manage the ongoing natural entropy.

Maintaining an acceptable level of entropy requires energy. *Energy* is generally defined as the capacity for doing work; effort.

Energy is required to move from higher entropy to lower entropy, from disparity to comparity, and from uncertainty to understanding. A lower disparity requires less energy to achieve comparity, and a greater disparity requires more energy to achieve comparity. When comparity is built in from the beginning with contemporary models and a contemporary architecture, less energy is required to maintain that comparity. When comparity is routinely maintained as the business environment, business niche, and organization evolve, less energy is required to maintain comparity.

But when proper model perspective is lost and broken model perspective becomes routine, then contemporary architecture symmetry is lost and broken architecture symmetry evolves. Disparity runs rampant and comparity is lost. The result is loss of understanding and increased uncertainty about the business, and increased energy to regain proper model perspective and proper architecture symmetry.

The basic issue becomes how much energy an organization wants to expend to achieve and maintain an acceptable level of comparity for successful business operation. Traditional models build traditional architectures, and traditional models portray traditional architectures. A contemporary architecture cannot be built from traditional models, and contemporary models cannot be built from a traditional architecture.

An organization must start with contemporary models, build a contemporary architecture, and use contemporary models to portray that contemporary architecture. Maintaining proper architecture symmetry with proper model perspective from the beginning requires much less energy than achieving proper architecture symmetry later. Business understanding is maximized with minimum effort.

Symmetry and Perspective Benefits

Understanding architecture symmetry and model perspective is crucial to thoroughly understanding, being agile, and successfully operating the organization's business. Eliminating created entropy and routinely resolving natural entropy keeps disparity at a minimum and ensures ongoing comparity of the organization's contemporary architecture. Proper model perspective and proper architecture symmetry ensures comparity and minimizes impacts to business success.

ARCHITECTURE REGISTRIES

An architecture registry is a central location, usually maintained by a prominent organization, to store architectures from many different organizations. The architectures stored may be data architectures, processes architectures, or other architectures organizations may develop. Those architectures are made available to other organizations with the objective to seek commonality across organizations and to help organizations rapidly build their own architectures.

However, there can be hidden objectives and devious tactics behind some architecture registries, which will not be described. The problems with architecture registries, and a contemporary approach to managing an organization's architectures are described below.

Architecture Registry Problems

Architecture registries are an attempt to implement generic architectures across multiple organizations for a variety of reasons, such as sharing business understanding, ease of application development, and so on. However, generic architectures have three basic problems.

First, each organization does business differently, even within the same business discipline, and has the right to do business their own way. A regulatory organization may tell an organization *what* to do, but an organization has the right to determine *how* to do it. Organizations cannot be warped into the same mold.

Second, collecting a huge volume of architectures, from many different organizations, in many different business disciplines, is a massive effort. Most architectures are really a collection of model perspectives, and most model perspectives are implementation oriented and vary over time. Such a massive effort to build a generic architecture becomes nearly impossible, and likely would never get to end-of-job, even within a specific business discipline. But if it were accomplished, the result would likely have questionable results, and would not be meaningful or useful to specific organizations.

Third, acquiring a generic architecture avoids the learning process. An organization learns about their business by observing its business niche, determines how it wants to operate in that business niche, and develops its own unique contemporary architecture. Little benefit is gained from acquiring a generic architecture, because architecture acquisition severely compromises thorough business understanding.

Fourth, generic architectures are nearly impossible to build, because no independent test of reality exists. The only reality for an organization, is the reality it gains from business niche observation, the perceptions gained from observation, and the architecture developed from those perceptions.

In addition to these four basic problems with generic architectures, architecture registries have five additional problems that render those registries and their architectures ineffective.

First, a contemporary architecture symmetry does not have any format or notation. Model perspectives have a format and notation relevant to an intended audience at a point in time. When model perspectives are stored in an architecture registry, the specific format and notation may not be relevant to a wide variety of audiences. Attempting to store model perspectives in a variety of formats and notations relevant to many different organizations leads to massive redundancy.

Architecture registries, if they really contain *architectures*, should store the architecture symmetry without any format and notation. Organizations could then display that architecture using a format and notation that is relevant to that organization, using architecture-driven model techniques.

Second, many organizations are very concerned about the proprietary nature of their architectures, and are protective of their architectures. The organization's contemporary architecture represents the understanding and operation of its business. Organizations don't want to release that proprietary understanding to other organizations, particularly competing organizations.

Third, organizations with contemporary architectures have put considerable effort into developing those proper architectures. Many organizations are hesitant to give their contemporary architecture to other organizations. Organizations that contribute architectures that do not have proper architecture symmetry only contribute to the disparity.

Fourth, many architectures are incomplete, because they don't contain all components of the Architecture Trinity – description, structure, and integrity.

They usually contain the structure with component names, although those names are seldom formal and consistent across the organization. The definitions are not comprehensive and denotative. Many definitions are tautologies, such as, "Customer name is name of the customer." Seldom do architectures contain precise integrity rules to ensure quality, or have actions when a component fails integrity rules.

Fifth, most organizations have few formal names or comprehensive definitions, and usually have inconsistent name abbreviations. No universal thesaurus, or set of thesauri, exist to relate between names in a multitude of perspectives. Developing a universal thesaurus or set of thesauri is nearly impossible, because of the variety of names, synonyms and antonyms, homonyms, and abbreviations, in multiple human languages.

Contemporary Approach

The conclusion from these problems is that architecture registries and the *architectures* they contain are essentially useless for helping an organization thoroughly understand and successfully operate in its business niche. A far better approach would be for an organization to build contemporary architectures for its business, and learn about their business in the process. A unique contemporary architecture would be built with model-driven architecture techniques, and portrayed with architecture-driven model techniques.

An organization might consider collecting a set of architectures that *may be relevant* to their business, then formally integrating those architectures into their own unique architecture that *is relevant* to their business. However, the organization needs to develop the common context for architecture integration, as explained in the Simplexity Series of books. Also, that integrated unique architecture should be verified with business niche observation to ensure it represents the organization's reality.

An organization might consider collaborating with similar organizations to develop a contemporary architecture, particularly if they want to share data or processes. However, seeking commonality across a large discipline or many disciplines is usually quite difficult, and may not be worth the effort.

Organizations can accomplish far more, with far less effort, by routinely observing their business niche, thoroughly understanding their business, and developing their own contemporary architecture for understanding and operating the business.

The question often asked is, "How would vendors and consultants respond to organizations developing their own contemporary architectures?" Vendors and consultants would respond in one of two ways. They would reject the concept, because they have their own agenda, an investment in their existing products and services, and no desire to change. They would use whatever strategy and tactics necessary to quash the concept.

Or, they would embrace the concept, see a future return on investment, and develop software products and services to support the concept. They would develop products and services accordingly. Their products and services would support progressive organizations, and progressive organizations would purchase their products and services.

Maybe, hopefully, when the profession matures, emphasis will shift to developing technology-assisted comparity, containing assisted intelligence, to help organizations develop their own unique contemporary architecture. That topic is described in more detail in the Assisted Intelligence Chapter.

SUMMARY

Traditional architectures and models are fraught with problems that severely impact an organization's understanding of its business and the successful operation of that business. Resolution of the problems begins with understanding the distinction between architectures and models. Architectures store all the understanding detail without presentation format or notation, are persistent, and evolve over time. Models contain a subset of the detail with presentation format and notation suitable to the recipient, are transient, and do not evolve over time.

Generic architectures are problematic, because they compromise an organization's ability to thoroughly understand its business niche and how it chooses to operate in that business niche. A better approach is for an organization to develop its own contemporary architecture that represents its business understanding an operation in the business niche.

A contemporary architecture is a proper architecture that contains the thorough understanding of an organization's unique business. It is supported by the Architecture Trinity, consisting of a descriptive component containing names and definitions, a structural component containing components and the relations between them, and an integrity component containing integrity rules.

Contemporary architecture versioning is managed with chronology stamps. A chronology stamp is placed on architecture data or business data whenever those data are added, changed, or deleted. A chronology stamp can be placed on subject areas whenever any data in those subject areas are added, changed, or deleted. Chronology stamps can be used to track the history of architecture changes or business changes.

A contemporary model is a proper model of a contemporary architecture containing a subset of the detail for building and enhancing that architecture with model-driven architecture techniques, or for portraying that architecture with architecture-driven model techniques. Contemporary models are

155

transient and represent a snapshot at a point in time with a format and notation that are relevant to the recipient. Contemporary model versioning is managed with a chronology stamp indicating when the detail for the model was extracted from the contemporary architecture. Contemporary models avoid any check-in / check-out process.

Symmetry is the shape, form, and makeup of an object. Contemporary architectures have a symmetry that is built by, and portrayed by, contemporary models. Perspective is a specific perception of an object. Contemporary models provide a perspective of a contemporary architecture symmetry, either to build or to portray that architecture.

An organization faces three different architecture symmetries: the business environment architecture symmetry, the business niche architecture symmetry, and its contemporary architecture symmetry. The scope decreases and the understanding increases as an organization progresses through the three architecture symmetries.

The contemporary architecture symmetry can be broken when multiple, disparate, competing, incomplete, or unclear components are allowed. Maintaining comparate, single, organization-wide architectures that increase understanding and decrease uncertainty ensure proper architecture symmetry.

Contemporary model perspectives can be broken by using traditional modeling techniques that lead to brute-force development of architectures, which eventually leads to broken architecture symmetry. Consistent use of contemporary models ensures proper model perspectives, which ensures proper architecture symmetry.

Business understanding is increased, and uncertainty is decreased with contemporary architectures and models. An organization is better able to manage the constant change in its business niche and its business activities.

Entropy is the state or degree of disorderliness. Natural entropy steadily increases over time as the business environment, business niche, and organization evolve. Created entropy is caused by an organization not following contemporary architecture and model techniques. Energy is needed to reduce natural entropy and maintain comparity. Energy is also needed to resolve created entropy to achieve comparity. However, if comparity is built in from the beginning with contemporary architecture and contemporary model techniques, energy does not need to be wasted resolving created entropy.

Architecture registries have many of the same problems as generic architectures, plus additional problems. These problems make architecture registries useless for helping an organization thoroughly understand and successfully operate its business. Organizations have a far better chance understanding and operating their business if they routinely observe their business niche and develop their own contemporary architecture. Hopefully, as the profession matures, vendors and consultants will develop products and services that support organizations in the development of their unique contemporary architectures.

QUESTIONS

The following questions are provided as a review of the Architectures and Models Chapter, and to stimulate thought about architectures and models.

1. What are the basic problems with traditional architectures and traditional models?
2. How are those basic problems impacting an organization?
3. What is the difference between an architecture and a model?
4. What is a contemporary architecture?
5. What is the Architecture Trinity?
6. What are the components of the Architecture Trinity?
7. How does the Architecture Trinity support an organization's contemporary architecture?
8. How are contemporary architecture versions managed?
9. What are model-driven architectures?
10. What are architecture-driven models?
11. What are contemporary models?
12. Why are contemporary architectures persistent and contemporary models transient?
13. How are contemporary model versions managed?
14. What is the difference between symmetry and perspective?
15. How do symmetry and perspective pertain to contemporary architectures and contemporary models?
16. What are the three architecture symmetries an organization faces?
17. What are broken symmetry and broken perspective?
18. What are the problems with architecture registries?
19. How are entropy and energy related to contemporary architectures?
20. Are architecture registries beneficial or harmful for organizations?

Chapter 11
OVERARCHING BUSINESS CONSTRUCT

The overarching construct for business understanding and agility.

The Architectures and Models Chapter described the problems with traditional architectures and models, how contemporary architectures and models resolve those problems, architecture symmetry and model perspectives, and architecture registries. The Overarching Business Construct Chapter describes the overarching construct for business understanding and agility, each of the three tiers comprising that construct, and the underlying foundation supporting that construct. The chapter theme is to form the overarching construct for an organization to thoroughly understand and successfully operate its business.

OVERARCHING CONSTRUCT

You probably noticed the themes for business understanding and agility, with an overarching construct for that theme through the previous chapters. The overarching construct for business understanding and agility is a contemporary business construct, containing three tiers for thoroughly understanding and successfully operating the business, that is supported by an underlying foundation of theories, concepts, principles, and techniques.

Contemporary Business Construct

Overarching means to form an arch over or above; to be formal, extensive, comprehensive, all encompassing, and cohesive; and to prevail for the long term.

An overarching construct for an organization is a contemporary construct, because it is based on contemporary architectures, and contemporary models for building and for portraying those contemporary architectures. An overarching construct is a business construct, because it represents the thorough understanding and agile operation of an organization's business.

The *contemporary business construct* is an overarching construct, composed of contemporary architectures, for an organization to thoroughly understand and successfully operate its business. The construct consists of three tiers for business understanding, business support, and business operation, and is supported by an underlying foundation of theories, concepts, principles, and techniques.

A clarification needs to be made about terms. *A* contemporary business construct is the concept of an overarching construct that applies to all organizations. *The* contemporary business construct is unique to an organization and is built by the organization for its specific business. An organization builds only one contemporary business construct for understanding and operating its unique business.

Three Tier Construct

The contemporary business construct contains three tiers to thoroughly understand and successfully operate the organization's business. The three tiers are the Business Resource Tier, Business Support Tier, and Business Operation Tier. The contemporary business construct initial structure is shown in Figure 11.1. The Business Resource Tier and Business Support Tier contain segments, and each segment contains components for understanding and operating the business. The Business Operation Tier contains business activities. The three tiers and their segments are described in the next section.

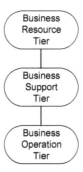

Figure 11.1. Contemporary business construct initial structure.

Underlying Foundation

The contemporary business construct is supported by an underlying foundation of theories, concepts, principles, and techniques. Concepts support the theories, principles support the concepts, and techniques implement the principles. The theories, concepts, and principles are common for all public and private sector organizations.

Typical theories are semiotic theory, set theory, dependency theory, normalization theory, and so on. These theories apply to both the data resource and the processes resource.

Typical data resource concepts are formal data names, comprehensive data definitions, data keys and data relations, data normalization, data integrity rules, and so on. Typical data resource principles are adequate data accessibility, appropriate data use, data integrity rule name, organization agility, realistic planning horizons, and so on. Refer to the Data Resource Simplexity series of books for all the concepts, principles, and techniques for data resource management. The data resource concepts and principles could be used as a pattern to develop processes resource concepts and principles.

The techniques are unique to each organization, depending on their operating environment and policies. Each organization develops its own techniques to implement the data resource and processes resource principles.

BUSINESS RESOURCE TIER

The top tier of the contemporary business construct is the Business Resource Tier. It consists of two segments for the data resource and the processes resource. Together, these two segments contain the thorough understanding about the organization's business and its successful business operation.

The Business Resource Tier could contain only one segment for the data resource, since processes are instructions that are stored as data. However, that narrow focus loses the major distinction between the facts about the business – the data, and the actions and decisions for business operation – the processes. Therefore, the Business Resource Tier consists of two equally important segments for the data resource and the processes resource.

The *Business Resource Tier* is the top tier of the contemporary business construct consisting of two segments for the data resource and the processes resource.

Each segment of the Business Resource Tier contains a set of data describing that segment. The data resource is self-documenting with data resource data. The data resource also documents the processes resource with processes resource data. The data resource and the processes resource are formally managed with processes documented in the processes resource. The close interaction between the data resource and processes resource is why the two resources are considered a combined critical resource of the organization.

Organization-wide architectures, the Data Resource Segment, the Processes Resource Segment, and the human resource are described below.

Organization-Wide Architectures

A *single organization-wide architecture* was defined earlier as a formally developed proper architecture, spanning the entire organization, which includes all related components, either data components or processes components, available to the organization, from within or without, in any form, that the organization needs to conduct business.

The two, single organization-wide architectures are the data resource architecture and the processes resource architecture. Each of these architectures is a single, proper architecture, that is integrated and normalized across the entire organization. The result is a high degree of comparity for both the data resource and the processes resource.

An organization has very few, if any, excuses or reasons for creating more than one architecture for their data resource, or more than one architecture for their processes resource. Doing so sets the stage for creating and perpetuating disparity. That created disparity makes the routine reduction of natural disparity more difficult. Therefore, single organization-wide architectures for the data resource and the processes resource are crucial to an organization's success.

Data Resource Segment

An organization's data resource typically began as a traditional data resource that was managed and documented in a variety of different ways. The traditional data resource was often disparate, and traditional data management perpetuated ongoing data disparity. A comparate data resource, within a single organization-wide data architecture, documented with data resource data, resolves that disparity and perpetuates comparity.

A *Data Resource Segment* is a segment of the Business Resource Tier that contains the facts about an organization's business.

The traditional data resource and contemporary data resource are described below.

Traditional Data Resource

A typical traditional data resource strategic structure is shown in Figure 11.2. Each component of the traditional structure is briefly described below. The Data Resource Simplexity series of books contains a detailed explanation of a traditional data resource structure.

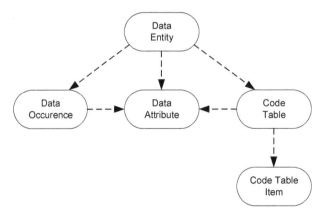

Figure 11.2. Traditional data resource strategic structure.

A *data entity* is a person, place, thing, event, or concept that is relevant to the organization. Examples of a data entity are Student and Vehicle.

A data entity contains one or more data attributes. A *data attribute* represents a specific feature – a fact – that describes or characterizes a data entity. Examples of data attributes are Student. Name, Student. Birth Date, Vehicle. Color, and Vehicle. Weight.

Notice the formal notation of data entity name, followed by a period, followed by the data attribute name. However, many traditional data resources did not have any formal naming conventions.

A data entity usually has multiple data occurrences. A *data occurrence* is a logical data record that represents the existence of an object or event.

Data occurrences contain the data values for data attributes in a data entity. Examples of data values in a data occurrence are Student. Name of *John Jones* and Vehicle. Color of *Blue*.

A *code table* is a data entity that contains a set of coded data values. A code table typically has data attributes for the coded data value, the name of the coded data value, and possibly other data related to the code table, such as a description, begin date, and so on.

A *code table item* is a specific coded data value, or logical record, in a code table. Examples of code table items are *M* for *Male*, *F* for *Female*, and *U* for *Unknown*.

Many organizations haven't progressed this far, and still use a physical file structure for their data resource that consists of data file, data record in a data file, data field in a data record, and data value in a data field.

Contemporary Data Resource

A contemporary data resource, developed with formal data resource management, and documented with data resources data promotes comparity. The Data Resource Segment strategic structure is shown in Figure 11.3. Each component of the structure is briefly described below. The Data Resource Simplexity series of books can be reviewed for a more thorough explanation of the data resource data, detailed definitions, and diagrams.

The strategic structure for the Data Resource Segment consists of data subject, data characteristic, data occurrence, data reference set, and data reference item. The change was made from *data entity* to *data subject* to align with the trend toward a subject-oriented data resource. If a data resource is subject oriented, the primary components of that data resource must be data subjects.

To avoid any confusion for formal data resource integration, *data attribute* was changed to *data characteristic*. *Code table* was changed to *data reference set*, because many code tables do not contain coded data values.

Code table item was changed to *data reference item* to align with *data reference set.*

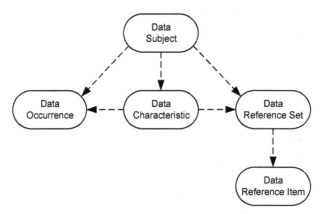

Figure 11.3. Data Resource Segment strategic structure.

A ***data subject*** is a person, place, thing, event, or concept that is relevant to the organization. Examples of a data subject are Student and Vehicle.

A ***data characteristic*** is an individual fact that describes or characterizes a data subject. It represents a business feature and contains a single fact, or closely related facts, about a data subject.

A ***data reference set*** is a set of data items for a general topic, such as gender or education level.

A ***data reference item*** is a single set of data values, data names, and data definitions representing a single data property in a data reference set.

A ***data property*** is a single feature, trait, or quality within a grouping or classification of features, traits, or qualities belonging to a data characteristic.

The Data Resource Segment strategic structure was enhanced to prepare for formal data resource integration. The enhanced strategic structure is shown in Figure 11.4.

Data subject, data characteristic, data occurrence, and data reference item are the same as described above. *Data characteristic variation* was added to represent variations in format or content of data characteristics. *Data reference set* was changed to *data reference set variation* to represent variations in domain, format, or content of data reference items.

A ***data characteristic variation*** is a variation in the content or format of a data characteristic. It represents a variant of a data characteristic, such as different measurement units, different monetary units, different sequences of a person's name, and so on.

A ***data reference set variation*** is a variation of a data reference set that has a different domain of data reference items, their coded data values, their names, or substantial difference in the data definitions.

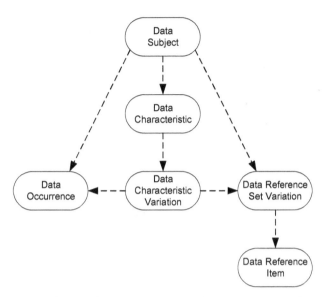

Figure 11.4. Enhanced Data Resource Segment strategic structure.

Processes Resource Segment

An organization's processes resource is typically a traditional processes resource that was designed, developed, and documented in a variety of different ways over many years. That traditional processes resource is usually disparate, and traditional processes management further perpetuates that disparity. A comparate processes resource, developed with formal processes resource management, and documented with processes resource data, resolves that disparity and perpetuates comparity.

The *Processes Resource Segment* is a segment of the Business Resource Tier that contains the sets of actions and decisions for operating the organization's business.

The strategic structure for the Processes Resource Segment, including elemental processes, business process components, business process connections, and business process logic, is described below.

Elemental Processes

A traditional processes resource is difficult to document, because of the disparity. A contemporary processes resource is much easier to document. Both traditional and contemporary processes resources can be documented and understood with processes resource data, as described below.

Process was defined earlier as a specific grouping of one or more sets of actions and decisions defining the logic that responds to an event. Conversely, a specific grouping of one or more sets of actions and decisions uniquely defines a process. Two or more processes cannot have the same specific grouping of sets of actions and decisions.

To thoroughly understand processes, an elemental process needs to be defined that is equivalent to a datum for the data resource. Information system is too general, and alphabetic characters, special characters, and numerals are too detailed. An elemental process is somewhere between these two extremes.

An *elemental process* is a set of logic consisting of one or more closely related sets of actions and decisions that can't be further divided and retain any meaning to business professionals. It's the lowest level of detail that business professionals perceive for managing their business.

The level of detail for an elemental process is organization specific, but should be consistent across the organization. Each organization defines their level of detail for understanding and managing processes, which may be different from other organizations.

Elemental processes are important for processes normalization and development of the single organization-wide processes architecture, and for processes denormalization for implementation. Processes development and implementation follows a sequence similar to the sequence for the development and implementation of data. The details of that sequence are beyond the scope of the current book.

Elemental processes are also important for processes resource integration, which is similar to data resource integration. The variability in traditional processes is determined, a common context is defined for processes integration, traditional processes are inventoried, and are cross-referenced to the common context. The details of processes resource integration are beyond the scope of the current book.

The important point is that elemental business processes must be identified so that business processes can be thoroughly understood, documented, and managed. Three approaches to understanding and documenting business processes are described below. No one approach is the best, and all three approaches are often used to thoroughly understand an organization's business processes.

Business Process Components

The first approach to understanding and documenting processes is understanding the components that make up each process. Elemental processes are combined to form larger process components, which are combined to form even larger process components.

A *combined process* is the combination of two or more elemental processes, or combined processes, to form a larger process. The combination of processes is dependent on the organization's business needs.

The recursive business processes is shown in Figure 11.5. The term *business process* is used, since the current emphasis is the business realm.

166

However, the diagram also applies to the non-business realm.

Figure 11.5. Recursive business processes structure.

Business process combination is viewed as a typical parts explosion or parts component structure, shown by the many-to-many recursive relation. A larger business process consists of many smaller business processes, and each smaller business process can be used to form many larger business processes. When a process changes, all manifestations of that process include the change. A recursive structure can go to any level of detail desired, and different processes can have different levels of detail.

The many-to-many relation is resolved with the addition of business process component, shown in Figure 11.6. The two relations between business process and business process component represent the parent business process and the subordinate business process. Business process type is added to identify the level of detail in the business process.

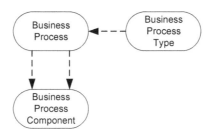

Figure 11.6. Business process component strategic structure.

Business process component identifies the elemental business process or combined business process that is combined with an existing elemental business process or combined business process to form a larger business process.

Business process type identifies the level of the resulting business process in the sequence from elemental business process to the highest-level abstraction of business process.

Business process type is organization specific. Each organization defines their own sequence of business processes from elemental processes to the highest level the organization desires, and uses that designation across the entire organization.

All business processes are formally named and comprehensively defined, from elemental business process to the largest combined business process. All business processes have a chronology stamp version.

Generally, an organization starts defining their business process components at a higher level, progressing to a more detailed level. However, an organization could start at a detailed level and progress to a higher level, or could start at any level and progress to higher levels of abstraction and lower levels of detail.

The main reasons for formally documenting business process components are to thoroughly understand business processes, to ensure the comparity of business processes, and to track all manifestations of a business process when a change is made. Tracking all manifestations of a business process could be eliminated by storing elemental business process components and combining them when needed to form a larger business process. However, that option is seldom feasible operationally, so tracking the combination of elemental business processes is the best option.

Business Process Connections

The second approach to understanding and documenting business processes is to understand the connections between business processes. The main reason for documenting business process connections is to understand how business processes are operationally connected.

The recursive business process structure was shown above in Figure 11.5. Business process connections form a typical network structure that resolves the many-to-many recursive relation, shown in Figure 11.7. A business process can connect with many other business processes, and each of those business processes can connect with many other business processes. Business process connections are not intended to show the logic of a business process or the flow through that logic.

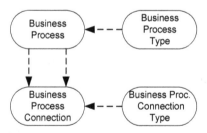

Figure 11.7. Business process connection strategic structure.

Business process connection represents the connection between two business processes.

Business process connection type identifies the type of connection between business processes, such as In-line, Called, and so on.

Generally, an organization starts defining their business process connections at a higher level, progressing to a more detailed level. However, an organization could start at a detailed level and progress to a higher level, or could start at any level and progress to higher levels of abstraction and lower levels of detail.

Business Process Logic

The third approach to understanding and documenting business processes is to understand the actions and decisions in process logic. The structure of business process actions and decisions is shown in Figure 11.8. Each business process contains many action sets and many decisions. A process action set can result from many process decisions, and a process decision can follow many process action sets, forming a many-to-many relation.

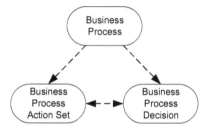

Figure 11.8. Business process logic actions and decisions.

An *action* is an act of will, a thing accomplished, a set of steps or tasks.

A *process action set* is a grouping of closely related actions representing the flow of process logic without a decision. It may end with a decision, which could be termination of a process.

A *decision* is a conclusion, determination, or resolution reached after consideration; the process of deciding something; the resolution of a question.

A *process decision* is a decision that results in a branch in the logic. Each decision follows the form of *When (condition) Then (action set)*.

Process logic is the combination of process action sets and process decisions, including comments, with the possible routes through those action sets and decisions.

Resolution of the many-to-many relation between process action sets and process decisions is resolved with business process logic connection, shown in Figure 11.9.

Business process logic connection is a connection between a business process action set and a business process decision.

Business process logic connections are not the same as state transitions described later. They represent the logic contained within a business process, not the state of business entities moving through a series of business processes.

An organization can go to any level of detail desired to document business process logic. Generally, documentation starts at a higher level and progresses to a more detailed level. However, an organization could start at any level and progress to higher levels of abstraction and lower levels of detail. Usually, a level of detail higher than specific business process logic is documented, with specific process logic documented in a process logic model. Details of process logic modeling are beyond the scope of the current book.

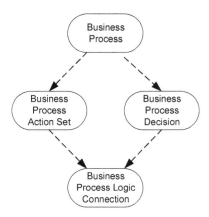

Figure 11.9. Business process logic strategic structure.

Human Resource

The data resource and the processes resource include the sum total of manual, automated, and human resource components, as described earlier. The data and processes in the human resource can't be structured or documented the same as the manual and automated data and processes. However, an organization can understand the data and processes contained in the human resource, often referred to as intellectual capital, and document that understanding in some form.

The manual and automated data and processes are persistent, but the data and processes in the human resource are transient. People join the organization bringing new data and processes – a gain in understanding. People also leave the organization – a loss of understanding. An organization needs to recognize that gain and loss of understanding, and plan accordingly.

BUSINESS SUPPORT TIER

The second tier of the contemporary business construct is the Business Support Tier. It consists of segments for tools and techniques that support business understanding and business activities. The segments are a bridge between business understanding and specific business activities. They are not specific business activities.

The *Business Support Tier* is the second tier of the contemporary business construct containing segments for tools and techniques that support business understanding and business operation.

The common business support segments are data flows, business rules, the Business Understanding Framework, state transitions, business workflows, and event-state. Each of these segments is described below. Other segments for tools and techniques that support business activities could be developed as needed for the business realm and the non-business realm.

The business support segments use the data and processes stored in the Business Resource Tier. Since data and processes are normalized within their respective organization-wide architectures, and the business support segments use those data and processes, the business support segments are also normalized across the organization.

The business support segments are not specific business operations or processes, such as project management, order fulfillment, inventory control, problem tracking, personnel management, and so on. Those are business activities for conducting the business. One common mistake organization's make is creating too many business support segments. An organization should not get carried away defining business support segments for specific business activities.

Data Flow Segment

Data are useless without processes that move and use those data. The movement of data into, within, and out of processes is referred to as a data flow, specifically input data, internal data, and output data. The *Data Flow Segment* is a segment of the Business Support Tier that contains the detail about data flows into, within, and out of business processes.

A *data flow* is a data set moving into a business process, an internal data set within a business process, or a data set moving out of a business process. A *data set* is a grouping of one or more data characteristic variations.

Data flows connect the data resource and the processes resource. Data can flow from one business process to another business process, from a business process to a data keep, and from a data keep to a business process. Data cannot flow from a data keep to another data keep without a process.

The data used within business processes that do not flow into or out of that business process are referred to as internal data or working data, because they are not visible outside the business process. These internal data should be documented as data flows, because they are seldom documented elsewhere.

The reasons for documenting data flows are to understand the data, and to identify where data are used by business processes so changes can be made. An excellent example of not documenting internal data flows is the Y2K date problem in the late 1990s. All locations of dates were not readily known, resulting in hours of searching source code to find data relating to dates. Horror stories abound about the use of undocumented internal data.

171

The initial strategic structure for data flows is shown in Figure 11.10. The dashed lines represent data relations between data entities, not a flow of data. A flow of data is represented by a solid line.

Figure 11.10. Data flow initial strategic structure.

Data Flow Type identifies whether the data flow is an input to a business process, internal data within a business process, or an output from a business process.

A data flow can contain many data characteristic variations, and a data characteristic variation can appear in many data flows. That many-to-many relation is resolved with Data Flow Characteristic Variation, as shown in Figure 11.11.

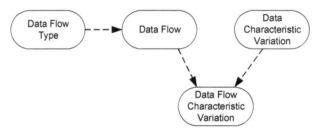

Figure 11.11. Data flow strategic structure.

Data Flow Characteristic Variation identifies a single data characteristic variation contained in a single data flow.

The data characteristic variations contained in a data flow can be documented two ways. First, the name of an external reference listing the data characteristic variations can be documented in Data Flow. The external reference could list the data characteristic variations, or could show the structure of the data characteristic variations in a data flow. Second, the individual data characteristic variations can be listed for a data flow. That listing typically does not show the structure of the data characteristic variations in a data flow. Either approach is acceptable, as long as an organization can determine the data being used by processes.

Business Rules Segment

Business rules ensure the quality and integrity of both data and processes used by the business. The ***Business Rules Segment*** is a segment of the Business Support Tier that contains the detail about business rules for data and for processes.

A *rule* was defined earlier as an authoritative, prescribed direction for conduct, or a usual, or customary, or generalized course of action or behavior; a statement that describes what is true in most or all cases; a standard method or procedure for solving problems.

A *business rule* is a set of one or more conditions, criteria, requirements, restrictions, or constraints placed on an organization's business to ensure the quality and integrity of the business.

Business rules are prescriptive, because they have a condition and an action for that condition. The typical format is a *When (Condition) Then (Action)* statement. For example, *When the sun sets Then turn on the lights.*

Some business rules don't have an explicit *When (Condition)*. For example, a business rule says, *A customer will always be treated with respect.* The implicit *When (condition)* might be *When an employee encounters a customer.*

Business rules can have multiple conditions in the form *When Condition A & Condition B & Condition C Then Action.* Business rules can also have multiple actions in the form *When Condition A Then Action 1 & Action 2.* Further discussion of business rules part of the underlying foundation of theories, concepts, principles, and techniques, and is beyond the scope of the current book.

Business rules apply to either data or processes. A *data rule* is a business rule pertaining to the quality and integrity of data in the data resource. A *processes rule* is a business rule pertaining to the quality and integrity of processes in the processes resource.

Data rules are stored as part of the data resource data so they are easy to access, understand, and manage by business professionals and developers. Any processes that add, change, or delete data must adhere to those data rules. Processes that do not adhere to the data rules contribute to the creation of disparate data.

Documenting data rules with the data, with processes manipulating the data, or any location other than the data resource data results in data rule redundancy, leading to difficulty accessing, understanding, and managing data rules. The result is data rules are not enforced and disparity increases.

Processes rules are stored as part of the processes resource data so they are easy to access, understand, and manage by business professionals and developers. Documenting processes rules in any location other than the processes resource data results in processes rule redundancy, leading to difficulty accessing, understanding, and managing processes rules.

Since the data resource and processes resource are normalized in their single organization-wide architectures, the data rules and processes rules are also normalized across the organization. You can see the reason for maintaining current, accurate, data resource data and processes resource data to ensure creation and maintenance of comparate data and processes.

The business rule initial strategic structure is shown in Figure 11.12. A business rule can apply to many data resource components or to many processes resource components. A data resource component can have many business rules, and a processes resource component can have many business rules. A business rule can originate from many business regulations, and a business regulation can support many business rules.

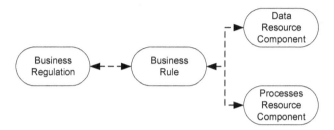

Figure 11.12. Business rule initial strategic structure.

A *data resource component* is any component of the organization's data resource. It can be a single datum or a set of datum.

A *processes resource component* is any component of the organization's processes resource. It can be anywhere in the structure of business processes.

A *business regulation* is any law, regulation, decree, order, mandate, dictate, directive, policy, guideline, and so on, that controls, regulates, or guides an organization's business and supports a business rule. It could be internal or external to the organization, and could describe a provenance of decisions and actions leading to the business rule.

The many-to-many relation between business rule and a data resource component or processes resource component is resolved with data rule and processes rule. The many-to-many relation between business regulation and business rule is resolved with business rule source. The business rule enhanced strategic structure is shown in Figure 11.13.

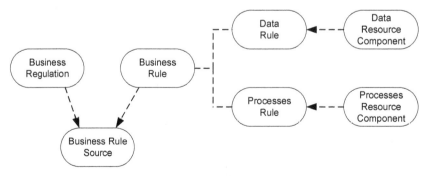

Figure 11.13. Business rule enhanced strategic structure.

A business rule can be either a data rule for a data resource component, or a processes rule for a processes resource component. A data resource component can have many data rules, and a processes resource component can have many processes rules, each of which is a business rule.

Business rule source identifies a single business regulation supporting a single business rule.

Data rules and processes rules can be developed for the non-business realm, such as physics, chemistry, biology, and so on. Usually, those rules are discovered and then documented, rather than documented and then applied as with the organization's business. The non-business regulation becomes a physical law, biological law, and so on. The strategic structure is similar to the strategic structure for the business realm.

Business Understanding Framework Segment

The Business Understanding Framework was described in Chapter 9. The *Business Understanding Framework Segment* is a segment of the Business Support Tier that contains the detail about the Business Understanding Framework.

The Business Understanding Framework consists of a framework dimension with six interrogatives, a specification level dimension, and a business activity dimension representing a seventh interrogative, as described in Chapter 9. The Business Understanding Framework strategic structure was shown in Figure 9.4.

A business activity can use many business processes, and a business process can be used by many business activities. The many-to-many relation between business activity and business process is resolved with business activity process, as shown in Figure 11.14. *Business activity process* identifies the business processes used by a business activity, and the business activities that use a business process.

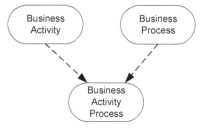

Figure 11.14. Strategic business activity process structure.

State Transition Segment

State transitions show the progression of a business entity through various states in its life cycle from an initial state to a terminating state. The *State*

175

Transition Segment is a segment of the Business Support Tier that contains the detail about the state transitions for business entities.

A *business entity* is any person, place, thing, concept, or event that goes through a life cycle of entity states from an initiating state to a terminating state.

A business activity is composed of one or more business processes. A business process consists of sets of actions and decisions, and manages business entities with those actions and decisions. A business entity transitions through various entity states during its life cycle, based on business process actions and decisions. Business process decisions determine whether a business entity stays in the same state or transitions to another state.

The transition of business entities through entity states can be displayed in a two-dimensional state transition matrix. The current business entity state is shown vertically on the left. The process decisions that determine whether a business entity stays in the same state or moves to another state are shown horizontally across the top. The cells in the matrix show the entity state resulting from the decisions, which may be the same entity state or a different entity state.

In state transition terms, the process decision is the input, and the resulting business entity state is the output. Typically, the process decision inputs and outputs are shown only for a normal or expected progression of a business entity through its life cycle. However, to be thorough and ensure business quality, all possible inputs should be shown for all possible current business entity states. In other words, the matrix should be exhaustive. Many unknown and unsuspected process decisions may be identified with an exhaustive matrix.

The state transition matrix can also be shown in data structure with nodes representing the entity states and arcs representing the transitions between the entity states.

The strategic state transition structure is shown in Figure 11.15. The structure represents the matrix described above. The life cycle for a business entity is represented by the state transition set. A state transition set belongs to a business activity, which contains the business processes that make the decisions determining a business entity's next state.

A state transition set is a set of related state transitions for a business entity during that business entity's life cycle.

Each state transition set has many entity states, as shown by the relation on the left between state transition and entity state. Entity state type qualifies entity state, such as the initiating state, an interim state, the terminating state, or reference to a more detailed state transition set.

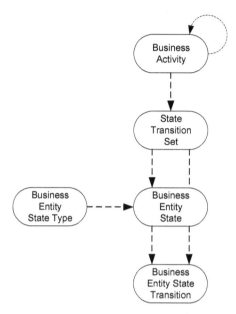

Figure 11.15. Strategic state transition structure.

Business entity state identifies a specific state in the life cycle of a business entity that progresses from the initial state, through one or more interim states, to a terminal state, or references a more detailed state transition set.

Business entity state type identifies the entity state as an initiating state, an interim state, a terminating state, or a reference to a more detailed state transition set.

Business entity state transition shows the current state of a business entity, and the state of a business entity resulting from a process decision. The relation on the left identifies the current state and the relation on the right identifies the state resulting from a process decision.

Business entity state transition is the movement of a business entity from one entity state to another, or back to the same entity state, based on a business process decision.

Some business entity states can be more detailed than others and are difficult to show in one state transition set. An entity state that is very detailed can reference another state transition set that shows that detail. The one-to-one relation between entity state and state transition set represents the reference from an entity state to a more detailed state transition set for that entity state. Multiple levels of reference between entity state and state transition set can be used to document business entity state transition detail.

Business Workflow Segment

Business workflows track the flow of work through a series of related business processes performed by organization units. The ***Business Workflow Segment*** is a segment of the Business Support Tier that contains detail about the flow of business, through business processes, that are performed by organization units.

Background

Business workflow is typically shown on a swim lane business workflow diagram. Organization units are shown vertically on the left side of the diagram. The sequence through time is represented horizontally on the diagram. Processes are shown as rectangles, and the flow between processes is shown by a solid line with an arrow pointing the direction of the workflow. Horizontal lanes show the organization unit responsible for performing the business process.

Each business workflow diagram represents a parent business process. The rectangles within the diagram represent subordinate business processes within that parent business process. A very detailed subordinate business process can reference its own parent workflow diagram that shows additional detail about its subordinate business processes. The result is a hierarchy of business workflow diagrams that match the functional decomposition of business processes. That functional decomposition was described earlier with the recursive many-to-many relation with business processes, which is resolved with business process components.

A business workflow diagram does not show business entities or business entity state transitions. The connection between business entity state transitions and business processes is the business processes used in business entity state transition diagram.

A business workflow diagram only shows *What* the flow is between business processes. It shows what process triggers another process, which triggers the next process in the business workflow. It does not show any *How*. The *How* is contained within the business processes.

The business flow on a business workflow diagram is always to the right. However, that rule often takes considerable space, and leaves large areas of white space on the diagram. To eliminate the white space, the flow often goes back to the left to the next sequential process. However, that's a model format and presentation technique. The structure of the business flow is the same, regardless of the presentation format and notation.

Another problem with traditional business workflow diagrams is the flow between processes branches to multiple processes. That branch in the flow shows a decision, which can only be made in a process. Decisions cannot be made independent of processes. The flow between processes must be

178

unbranched. Notations can be made on the flow between processes to indicate the result of decisions made in a process.

An organization unit is an actor that performs a process. The term *Actor* is not used, because *actor* is not defined anywhere within the architecture. Any organization unit or actor must be defined elsewhere in the architecture so business understanding segments can be connected.

Business Workflow Structure

Business workflow can be shown as a structure, the same as other segments. The basic business workflow structure is shown in Figure 11.16. A business workflow becomes a Business Workflow Set. A Business Workflow Set contains many business processes, and a business process can be contained in many different business workflow sets, forming a many-to-many relation.

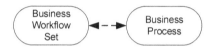

Figure 11.16. Basic business workflow.

A ***business workflow*** is a flow of work through a set of subordinate business processes for a parent business process which are initiated or performed by an organization unit. A preceding business process triggers a subsequent business process in the workflow.

A ***business workflow set*** represents a parent business process and shows the business workflow through the subordinate business processes in that parent business process.

The many-to-many relation between Business Workflow Set and Business Process is resolved with the addition of Business Workflow Process, as shown in Figure 11.17.

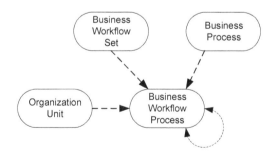

Figure 11.17. Addition of business workflow process.

Organization Unit identifies the organization unit responsible for performing the Business Workflow Process, which may be different for

179

different business workflows. An organization unit can be within the organization or in an external organization, but must be defined as an organization unit.

Business workflow process is the use of a business process in the workflow of a business workflow set.

A business workflow process can connect with many other business workflow processes, and each of those business workflow process can connect with many other business workflow processes, forming a many-to-many relation. That many-to-many relation is resolved with Business Workflow Process Connection, as shown in Figure 11.18.

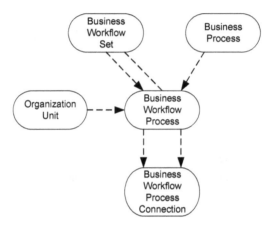

Figure 11.18. Business workflow strategic structure.

Business workflow process connection is the connection between two business processes in a business workflow set.

The first relation between Business Workflow Process and Business Workflow Process Connection identifies the preceding Business Workflow Process, and the second relation identifies the subsequent Business Workflow Process.

As described earlier, a Business Workflow Process can have a more detailed Business Workflow set that shows the flow of work through its subordinate processes. The one-to-one relation between Business Workflow Process and Business Workflow Set identifies the that Business Workflow Set.

Feedback loops can be shown as a workflow from a subsequent process back to a previous process, or to a resolution process. When an issue or problem arises, the workflow goes back for resolution, then moves forward again when the issue or problem is resolved. The decision for a feedback loop is made in a process, not on a flow, as described earlier. Only the feedback flow is shown in the workflow.

A business workflow can include events and the business processes they trigger. The distinction between business processes and events is the name. Business process names are formed with a verb-noun phrase, such as Calculate Penalty, Confirm Order, and so on. Business event names are a formed with noun-verb phrase, such as Vehicle Collision, Hazardous Spill, and so on. That simple addition makes the business workflow very powerful.

Business workflows can be developed for three different scenarios. Business workflows can be developed before the fact for a what should happen when an event occurs. Business workflows can be developed after the fact for what did happen during an event. Business workflows can be developed in real time while an event is evolving.

Event-State Segment

Cause and effect diagrams, also known as Ishikawa diagrams, fishbone diagrams, herringbone diagrams, and a variety of other names, were originally intended to diagram production problems and their contributing causes. The diagrams have a variety of different forms and notations, but are essentially a hierarchy of causes leading to a final effect, which is the production problem.

The technique can be used to understand a sequence of events and the states resulting from those events. Change *cause* to *event* and *effect* to *state*, and consider that an event causes a state, and that state can become an event that causes another state. Any situation is a network of events and states.

The *Event-State Segment* is a segment of the Business Support Tier that identifies events and the states resulting from those events.

An *Event-state* can be both a cause – the event – resulting in one or more effects – the states. The resulting state could become an event with a resulting state.

A typical scenario could be a chain of causes (events) and effects (states), such as an icy road, that results in a vehicle collision, a vehicle hits a tree, the tree hits power lines, the power lines pull down a utility pole, the utility pole breaks a fire hydrant, water washes the roadbed downhill, the sediment fills a community pool, and so on. An event results in a state, and that state can become an event that results in another state. The scenario can have branches, such as law enforcement response, medic response, power company response, water utility response, and so on.

Events don't lead to events, and states don't lead to states. Events lead to states, and states can become events. A state could result from many events, and an event could lead to many states. An event can be a non-happening, such as a fire sensor fails to activate the sprinkler system. Events and states can be good as well as bad.

Event-states are not the same as business entity transitions through

181

business entity states, as described in the State Transition Segment. However, the two segments are related, since the business entities could be involved in event-states. The business entity involvement is tracked through state transitions.

The Event-State initial strategic structure is shown in Figure 11.19. The many-to-many recursive relation shows that an Event could result from many States, and a State could result from many events.

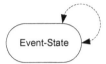

Figure 11.19. Event-state initial strategic structure.

The many-to-many relation is resolved with cause-effect designation, with two relations between event-state and cause-effect designation, as shown in Figure 11.20. The first relation identifies the event-state that is the cause, and the second relation identifies the event-state that is the resulting effect.

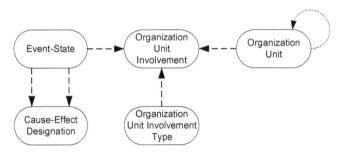

Figure 11.20. Event-state enhanced strategic structure.

Cause-effect designation identifies the event-state that is the cause, and the event-state that is the effect.

An organization unit can be responsible for an event-state, or have an interest in an event-state. An organization can be interested in many event-states, and an event-state can have many responsible or interested organizations. That many-to-many relation is resolved with Organization Unit Involvement, which is qualified with Organization Unit Involvement Type.

Organization unit involvement is the involvement of an organization in an Event-State. *Organization unit involvement type* is how or why an organization unit is involved in an event-state, such as Responsibility, Investigation, Interest, and so on.

Event-state works at any scale and time frame, from particles in the Large Hadron Collider, to continental drift on Earth, to evolution of the universe. It works on both good scenarios and bad scenarios, and in the business realm and the non-business realm. It can be used for causal modeling and for path diagrams. One caution, however, is not to confuse correlation with causation. A correlation does not always mean causation, but may indicate a causation. The causation must be proven.

Additional Segments

Additional segments could be added to the Business Support Tier for decision tables and decision trees; project management, such as IJ, PERT, and CPM; menu preparation, parts assembly, part disassembly; data provenance / data tracking; and any other tools and techniques an organization might use to support its business activities.

Non-Business Realm

The business understanding construct applies to the non-business realm, with some slight adjustments in terminology. *Business workflow* becomes *non-business workflow, business processes* become *biochemical processes, chemical processes*, and so on, for chemistry, physics, astronomy, and any other discipline. The concept of Business Understanding Tier segments applies to any discipline, with an appropriate change in terms and their definitions.

BUSINESS OPERATION TIER

The third tier of the contemporary business construct is the Business Operation Tier. It contains all the business activities needed for an organization to thoroughly understand its business and to successfully operate that business. The business activities in the Business Operation Tier use segments in the Business Support Tier, and use the Data Resource Segment and Processes Resource Segment in the Business Resource Tier.

The **Business Operation Tier** is the third tier of the contemporary business construct containing all the business activities an organization needs to successfully operate its business.

The contemporary business construct initial structure, shown in Figure 11.1, can be enhanced based on descriptions of the segments in the Business Resource Tier and the Business Support Tier. The contemporary business construct enhanced structure is shown in Figure 11.21.

The Business Resource Tier contains the Data Resource Segment and the Processes Resource Segment, shown at the top of the diagram. The Business Support Tier contains segments that use the data resource and the processes resource. The Business Operation Tier contains business activities that use the data resource and the processes resource, and use segments in the Business Support Tier to conduct the organization's business.

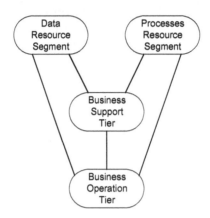

Figure 11.21. Contemporary business construct enhanced structure.

SUMMARY

The theme of business understanding and agility continues with the concept of a contemporary business construct. The construct is overarching, contemporary, and encompasses the organization's entire business. The construct consists of three tiers for the business resource, business support, and business operation. The construct is supported by an underlying foundation of theories, concepts, principles, and techniques.

The Business Resource Tier is the top tier and contains two segments for the Data Resource and the Processes Resource. These two segments contain the sum total of the organization's data and processes, including electronic and non-electronic data and processes, and the human resource. Each of those resources is normalized within a single organization-wide architecture to limit disparity and ensure comparity. The strategic structure for the data resource and the processes resource were described.

The Business Support Tier is the second tier and contains segments for data flows, business rules, the Business Understanding Framework, business entity state transitions, business workflows, and cause and effect of events known as event-states. Additional segments can be identified as needed for the organization's business. The segments also apply to the non-business realm, with slight changes in terms.

The Business Operation Tier is the third tier and contains all the business activities and organization needs to thoroughly understand and successfully operate its business. The business activities in the Business Operation Tier use the segments in the Business Support Tier, and the two segments in the Business Resource Tier.

Establishment and maintenance of an overarching contemporary business construct gives an organization the best chance of thoroughly understanding its business, being agile, and successfully operating that business.

QUESTIONS

The following questions are provided as a review of the Overarching Business Construct Chapter, and to stimulate thought about developing and maintaining an overarching business construct to thoroughly understand and successfully operate an organization's business.

1. Why are contemporary architectures important for thoroughly understanding and successfully operating an organization's business?
2. What is *a* contemporary business construct?
3. What is *the* contemporary business construct?
4. What are the three tiers in a contemporary business construct?
5. What is the underlying foundation for a contemporary business construct?
6. What is the Business Resource Tier?
7. What segments does the Business Resource Tier contain?
8. What is the purpose of each segment in the Business Resource Tier?
9. Why are organization-wide architectures for data and for processes necessary for the contemporary business construct?
10. What is the Business Support Tier?
11. What segments does the Business Support Tier contain?
12. What is the purpose of the segments in the Business Support Tier?
13. What additional segments might be added to the Business Support Tier?
14. What is the Business Operation Tier?
15. What segments does the Business Operation Tier contain?
16. What is the contemporary business construct enhanced structure?
17. How do the three tiers in the contemporary business construct interact to help an organization understand and operate its business?
18. How does the contemporary business construct apply to the non-business realm?
19. What are the results when a contemporary business construct is implemented in an organization?
20. What is likely to happen if a contemporary business construct is not implemented in an organization?

Chapter 12
BUSINESS UNDERSTANDING
INFRASTRUCTURE

A contemporary infrastructure for business understanding and agility.

The Overarching Business Construct Chapter described a contemporary overarching construct for business understanding and agility, consisting of three tiers, with an underlying foundation of theories, concepts, principles, and techniques. The Business Understanding Infrastructure Chapter describes traditional business architecture problems and business architecture trends, the architecture infrastructure concept, and the formality and benefits of that concept. The chapter theme is the contemporary concept of an architecture infrastructure for business understanding and agility.

TRADITIONAL BUSINESS ARCHITECTURES

Traditional business architectures are impacting an organization's understanding and operation of its business. The common problems with traditional business architectures, the basic problems and their impacts, the basic needs to resolve the basic problems, and business architecture trends are described below.

Common Problems

Most organizations are not sure what a business architecture represents, what it contains, how it is explained, or how it is used to understand and operate the organization's business. That lack of understanding about the development and use of a business architecture leads to fragmentated understanding, disparity, and created entropy.

The common problems with traditional business architectures that exist across many public and private sector organizations today are listed below. These common problems are in addition to the architecture and model problems described earlier.

Most organizations have multiple, conflicting, often disparate business architectures that are difficult to understand and manage.

Existing business architectures are seldom developed as organization-wide architectures that are normalized across the organization.

Relationships between separate business architectures seldom exist.

The drive toward rapid implementation of business needs often bypasses any formal business architecture.

Business reengineering, business transformation, business analysis, and the management of change are seldom done within a formal business architecture.

The full extent of the impacts of proposed or planned business changes are difficult to determine.

The concept, development, maintenance, and use of a formal, organization-wide, business architecture is not well understood.

Basic Problems and Impacts

The basic problems with traditional business architectures in most public and private sector organizations are listed below.

Not understanding what a formal business architecture contains, what it represents, what it provides, how it is developed and maintained, and how it supports an organization's business.

Not understanding the serious business impacts of disparate traditional business architectures, and the lack of any formal business architecture.

The impacts of the traditional business architectures problems are listed below:

Lack of consistent, integrated, thorough understanding of the organization's business and its operation.

Fragmentation of the business, increased business disparity, and decreased business agility.

Unknown and unexpected impacts of proposed or implemented business changes.

Basic Needs

The basic needs to resolve the basic problems with traditional business architecture are listed below.

A formal business architecture infrastructure for an organization to thoroughly understand and successfully operate its business.

A basic business architecture infrastructure that applies to all public and private sector organizations, but can be extended and expanded to meet each organization's specific needs.

A single, integrated, organization-wide, business architecture infrastructure for the entire organization, not just for selected business segments.

A business architecture infrastructure that supports business analysis, business transformation, business reengineering, and data and processes resource integration.

Business Architecture Trends

The term *BA* is often used by organizations, vendors, and consultants. However, the meaning of *BA* is not clear. It could mean *business activity*, *business analysis*, or *business architecture*. Confusion about the meaning of *BA* has clouded the real meaning and importance of business architectures.

Business architecture slowly evolved as a collection of architectures related to an organization's business. Numerous explanations and diagrams of those architectures evolved, with a variety of formats and notations. The result was a proliferation of architectures representing an organization's business.

Most of the architecture explanations were vendor product or consultant service oriented. The explanations used a variety of overly-complicated diagrams, and many terms that were not formally defined. The result perpetuated confusion about a formal business architecture.

Business frameworks evolved as an attempt to resolve the confusion about architectures. However, as explained in the Interrogatives and Frameworks Chapter, business frameworks brought their own set of problems that further confused the issue about the meaning of *business architecture*. Most organizations still didn't know what a business architecture represented or contained.

Two trends began to emerge about the meaning, contents, and use of a business architecture.

The first trend was *Arrival of the business architecture* (singular), which attempted to define the meaning of *business architecture*. Many presentations, articles, and books covered arrival of the business architecture. Most of the material was a rehash of existing material about business architectures packaged under a variety of different names, containing many overly-complicated diagrams, with a mixture of old and new terms that were not formally defined.

The second trend was *The emergence of business architectures* (plural). The trend had the same basic problems as the first trend. No formal definition of a business architecture was presented. Many presentations, articles, and books covered the emergence of business architectures, but no consistent explanation of the meaning, contents, or use of a business architecture was presented.

Amazing how everything changes, yet nothing changes!

ARCHITECTURE INFRASTRUCTURE CONCEPT

Each segment or business activity in the three tiers of the contemporary business construct has an architecture. Those architectures can be connected to form an architecture infrastructure for each tier, and the tier architecture infrastructures can be connected to form an architecture infrastructure for the business. Those architecture infrastructures are described below.

Architecture Infrastructure Tiers

The contemporary business construct, consisting of the Business Resource Tier, the Business Support Tier, and the Business Operation Tier, was described in the last chapter. The Business Resource Tier contains two segments for the data resource and the processes resource. The Business Support Tier contains multiple segments for understanding and supporting the business. The Business Operation Tier contains business activities to operate the business.

Each segment in the Business Resource Tier and Business Support Tier, and each business activity in the Business Operation Tier has an architecture. The strategic structures of those architectures were described in the last chapter. Architectures can be combined based on common data subjects in each architecture. The combination of multiple architectures is referred to as an architecture infrastructure.

An i*nfrastructure* is the resources required for an activity; the underlying foundation or basic construct of something; the organizational structure needed for some activity.

An *architecture infrastructure* is the infrastructure for a set of related architectures that represent some aspect of an organization's business. It contains both intra-architecture relations and inter-architecture relations.

The data resource segment and the processes resource segment in the Business Resource Tier form a business resource architecture infrastructure. The *business resource architecture infrastructure* is a set of two architectures for the organization's data resource and processes resource.

The multiple segments in the Business Support Tier form a business support architecture infrastructure. The *business support architecture infrastructure* is a set of individual business support architectures, connected by common data entities, that form an interconnected architecture infrastructure.

The multiple business activities in the Business Operation Tier form a business operation architecture infrastructure. The *business operation architecture infrastructure* is a set of individual business activity

190

architectures unique to each organization's data and processes that operate their specific business.

Business Understanding Infrastructure

The architecture infrastructures of each tier in the contemporary business construct can be combined based on common data subjects to form an architecture infrastructure for the business. The formal name of that architecture infrastructure is the Business Understanding Infrastructure. It's the formal construct for an organization to thoroughly understand, be agile, and successfully operate its business.

The name could have been Business Understanding and Operation Architecture, which is too long. The name could have been Business Operation Architecture, but that name avoids the thorough understanding emphasis. The name could have been Business Awareness Architecture, which includes both understanding and operating the business. But that name results in a BAA acronym, which is too close to the BA acronym and could be confusing. The name could have been Business Management Architecture, but management is the responsibility for running and controlling, which is basically operation, and which does not include thorough business understanding. Therefore, Business Understanding Infrastructure is the most appropriate name to emphasize the need for thorough understanding.

The *Business Understanding Infrastructure* is the single, organization-wide, contemporary architecture infrastructure for an organization's business understanding, so the organization can thoroughly understand its business, be agile, and successfully operate its business.

The Business Understanding Infrastructure is supported by an objective. The *Business Understanding Infrastructure Objective* is to provide an overarching architectural construct that supports the two major business functions to understand the business and to operate the business. It leads to a common understanding context that anyone in any public or private sector organization can use to carry out their business activities.

The Business Understanding Infrastructure strategic structure is shown in Figure 12.1. The solid lines between the segments are connections only. They are not data flows because they have no arrows, and are not data relations because they are not dashed. They are connections between the individual architectures based on common data subjects.

Starting at the top of the diagram, Business Rules are connected to data in the Data Resource, or processes in the Processes Resource. Data in the Data Resource and processes in the Processes Resource are connected by Data Flows. Processes in the Processes Resource are connected to Business Activity, Organization Unit, the Business Understanding Framework, and

Business Activity. Data in the Data Resource are connected to the Business Understanding Framework. Business Activity is connected to the Business Understanding Framework, Organization Unit, and Business Entity. More detailed connections could be developed based on the strategic architecture diagrams shown earlier.

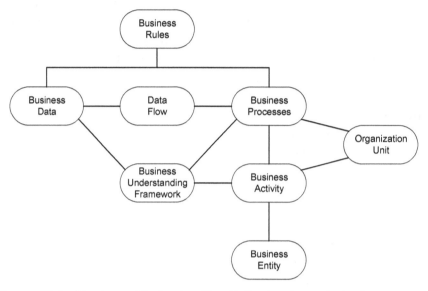

Figure 12.1. Business Understanding Infrastructure strategic structure.

A clarification was made in the last chapter that *A* contemporary business construct is applies to all organizations, and *The* contemporary business construct is unique to an organization based on its specific business. Similarly, *A* Business Understanding Infrastructure applies to all organizations, and *The* Business Understanding Infrastructure is unique to an organization based on its specific business.

The Business Understanding Infrastructure shown in Figure 12.1 can be expanded and extended to meet an organization's specific business needs. Expanded means adding more detail to a segment or business activity. Extended means adding more segments or business activities to a tier.

The data resource and processes resource in the Business Understanding Tier can be expanded to meet an organization's needs. Existing components should not be removed, because they could be useful as organizations gain understanding about its data and processes and begins to formally integrate its data and processes.

The Business Resource Tier cannot be extended, because there are no other segments to add. The data resource and processes resource are two interdependent segments. Neither segment can be removed, and no other segments can be added.

The Business Support Tier can be expanded by adding detail to the existing segments, and can be extended by adding additional segments to support the organization's business. The Business Operation Tier can be expanded by adding detail to the existing business activities, and can be extended by adding additional business activities.

An organization has only one Business Understanding Infrastructure that applies to the entire organization. Multiple Business Understanding Architectures become conflicting, overlapping, and incomplete, leading to fragmentation, disparity, loss of understanding, and less than successful business operation.

BUSINESS UNDERSTANDING FORMALITY

The Business Understanding Infrastructure has a formality based on architecture super-symmetry, model super-perspective, architecture separability, Business Understanding Infrastructure Laws, and Business Understanding Infrastructure Rules. That formality is described below, including impacts of violations of the laws and rules, and the benefits of building and maintaining a formal Business Understanding Infrastructure.

Architecture Super-Symmetry

Symmetry was defined earlier as the shape, form, and makeup of an object. *Architecture symmetry* was defined earlier as is the symmetry of an architecture.

Super-symmetry is the symmetry across multiple objects in a set of related objects, including relationships within and between the individual symmetries of those objects.

For example, an automobile has many component parts. Each component part has a symmetry. The automobile as a whole has a super-symmetry across those component parts.

Architecture super-symmetry is the super-symmetry across a set of related architecture symmetries.

The Business Understanding Infrastructure has an architecture super-symmetry across the architecture symmetries of the segments in Business Resource Tier and the Business Support Tier, and the architecture symmetries of the business activities in the Business Operation Tier. That architecture super-symmetry is similar to the super-symmetry for particles in a unified theory for quantum mechanics. It is the unified theory of architectures for an organization's business.

Model Super-Perspective

Perspective was defined earlier as a specific perception of an object. When an object is perceived from different directions, it may appear different.

The perspective of the object is different, but the symmetry of the object is the same. All perspectives are correct, even though each perspective is different.

A *super-perspective* is a perspective across multiple architecture symmetries in an architecture super-symmetry.

A model of a super-perspective, whether to portray the architecture or to enhance the architecture, is a model super-perspective. In other words, any model of a perspective across multiple architectures in an architecture super-symmetry becomes a model super-perspective. A **model super-perspective** is model of a super-perspective.

A model super-perspective can be across multiple architecture symmetries within a tier of the Business Understanding Infrastructure, or across multiple architecture symmetries in multiple tiers of the Business Understanding Infrastructure.

Every model, whether it represents a perspective or a super-perspective, must be formally named and comprehensively defined according to what it represents, as described earlier.

Architecture Separability

Architecture separability is a principle that parts of an object can be separated and considered on their own. The parts will not cease to exist or lose any of their features. The parts can be replaced to make the whole object without any loss of features.

Architecture separability is a principle that parts of an object can be removed, considered on their own, and replaced without any loss of features.

Architecture separability applies to objects that remain unchanged when a part is removed, and to a part that remains unchanged during the time it is removed from the object. A part can be removed from the object and replaced without change to the object, when neither the object or the part is changed while the part is removed.

For the Business Understanding Infrastructure, the object is the architecture symmetry or super-symmetry and the part is the model perspective or super-perspective. However, two problems occur when architecture separability is applied to the Business Understanding Infrastructure.

Fist, a model perspective or super-perspective is not a removal of part of the architecture. It is a copy or snapshot of part of the architecture at a point in space-time and the architecture remains intact. Multiple and often overlapping model perspectives can be taken of an architecture symmetry over a span of space-time without the architecture losing any of its features.

Second, the organization's business niche is very dynamic, and the business architecture is dynamic to stay current with that dynamic business niche. That change can't be stopped, or if it were stopped, would seriously impact the organization's business. After a model perspective is taken, the architecture symmetry continues to evolve to reflect an evolving business niche. The model perspective becomes out of synch with the architecture symmetry, no longer represents that architecture symmetry, and cannot be placed back into the architecture symmetry.

You see what happened with the models-as-architecture orientation and the model check-in / check-out process. It actively created and perpetuated disparity, and slowed down business understanding and operation. It prevented others from getting model perspectives of the architecture symmetry, and prevented widespread, current business understanding.

That's the reason for architecture-driven model techniques, and for model perspectives being transient. Model perspectives only represent a snapshot of the architecture symmetry at a point in space-time, and could become out-of-synch with the architecture symmetry.

Since model perspectives become out-of-synch with the architecture symmetry, they can only be placed back into the architecture symmetry with model-driven architecture techniques. Also, a model perspective can be used to formally enhance the architecture symmetry. That's the reason for model-driven architecture techniques.

Architecture separability fails for business architectures. That failure led to the creation of model check-in / check-out procedures, although most people did not recognize the reason behind that failure. Models were considered the architecture. When a model was checked-out, the architecture had to remain unchanged until the model was checked-in. When the model was checked-in, with or without modifying the architecture, then other models of that same architecture could be checked-out.

The problem with architecture separability is resolved with a principle of architecture non-separability. Parts of the architecture symmetry are not removed or replaced. Model perspectives portray snapshots of the architecture symmetry, using the architecture-driven model techniques. The architecture symmetry remains unchanged for other model perspectives to portray snapshots of the architecture symmetry, or for model perspectives to enhance the architecture symmetry.

Architecture non-separability is a contemporary principle that the architecture symmetry remains intact and evolves with the organization's business niche. Multiple, often overlapping, model perspectives can be taken of that architecture symmetry without impacting the architecture symmetry.

Architecture non-separability is a contemporary approach to maintaining architecture symmetry, allowing multiple model perceptions to portray that architecture symmetry, and formally managing model perspectives that

195

enhance the architecture symmetry, while allowing the organization's business to continue. It's a formality for maintaining comparity, reducing entropy, and reducing the energy to maintain comparity.

Business Understanding Infrastructure Laws

The Data Resource Laws and Processes Resource Laws described earlier support formal creation and maintenance of the two resource architectures for data and processes. The Business Understanding Infrastructure Laws support creation and maintenance of the Business Understanding Infrastructure.

Business Understanding Infrastructure Laws are laws that guide formal Business Understanding Infrastructure development, and ensure the integrity and quality of the organization's business understanding and operation.

First Business Understanding Infrastructure Law: The Business Understanding Infrastructure must adequately and accurately represent the entire business, and support the understanding and operation of an organization's business, from observation of the business niche to operation in that business niche.

Second Business Understanding Infrastructure Law: All architectures in the Business Understanding Infrastructure must be complete, including descriptions, structure, and integrity, according to the architecture trinity.

Third Business Understanding Infrastructure Law: The Business Understanding Infrastructure must adequately and accurately represent the architecture symmetries of the Business Resource Tier, the Business Support Tier, and the Business Operation Tier.

Fourth Business Understanding Infrastructure Law: All architectures in the Business Understanding Infrastructure must be understandable and readily available to anyone in the organization responsible for understanding and operating the organization's business.

Fifth Business Understanding Infrastructure Law: Any person involved in the understanding or operation of an organization's business must not disregard any of the Business Understanding Infrastructure Laws, nor through inaction allow any of the Business Understanding Infrastructure Laws to be disregarded.

Business Understanding Infrastructure Rules

Business Understanding Infrastructure Rules pertain to model perspectives for enhancing and portraying all architectures within the Business Understanding Infrastructure, using model-driven architecture techniques and architecture-driven model techniques. They support the

196

Business Understanding Infrastructure Laws.

Business Understanding Infrastructure Rules are rules that guide formal development and enhancement of the Business Understanding Infrastructure, and ensure the integrity and quality of the organization's business understanding and operation. They support the Business Understanding Infrastructure Laws.

The Business Understanding Rules are:

1. All architectures in the Business Understanding Infrastructure are persistent, and can be maintained and enhanced.
2. All models that enhance or portray the Business Understanding Infrastructure are transient and are not maintained or enhanced.
3. All models must support the Business Understanding Infrastructure Objective.
4. The Business Understanding Infrastructure must be developed and enhanced with models using model-driven architecture techniques.
5. The format and notation of model-driven architecture models must be oriented toward the contributor.
6. Multiple models from multiple contributors are necessary to create and maintain the Business Understanding Infrastructure.
7. All model-driven architecture models must be properly labeled with a chronology stamp, name, date, description, and any other information necessary for the contributor to thoroughly understand the model.
8. Minor corrections to the Business Understanding Infrastructure may be made without formal models.
9. The Business Understanding Infrastructure must be portrayed using architecture-driven model techniques.
10. The format and notation of architecture-driven models must be oriented toward the recipient.
11. All architecture-driven models must be properly labeled with a chronology stamp, name, date, description, and any other information necessary for the recipient to thoroughly understand the model.
12. Anyone involved in developing, enhancing, or using the Business Understanding Infrastructure is responsible for developing high-quality architectures and high-quality models.

Violations of Laws and Rules

Violation of the Business Understanding Infrastructure Laws and Rules result in impacts similar to violations of the Data Resource Laws and Rules, and the Processes Resource Laws and Rules. Understanding decreases, uncertainty increases, and disparity increases. Initial violations create a cascade of additional violations that impact an organization's chance of a successful business. Most violations are oriented toward brute-force development, as described earlier. Resources are wasted, entropy increases, and more energy is required to reduce entropy to be successful.

Individual violations of the Business Understanding Infrastructure Laws and Rules could be listed. However, that approach is past-oriented and focuses attention on failures. A better approach is to be future-oriented and focus attention on the formality that avoids any violations. When emphasizing formality, the right way to do things and pitfalls to avoid should be described.

Business Understanding Infrastructure Benefits

The Business Understanding Infrastructure is a single, integrated, organization-wide, overarching construct for an organization to thoroughly understand and successfully operate its business. It resolves the basic problems with traditional business architectures and meets the basic needs for a contemporary business architecture.

The theme through the book has been thorough business understanding, business agility, and successful business operation. The Business Understanding Infrastructure is the construct for that theme. It's the contemporary infrastructure of business architectures that resolves the problems with traditional business architectures, and provides the base for acquiring and storing the details about an organization's business.

The Business Understanding Infrastructure is the new paradigm that provides the formality for managing a dynamic business in a constantly changing business niche. It's the formality for an organization's architecture infrastructure that's supported by a foundation of theories, concepts, principles, and techniques. It's practical, because the business understanding and operation is contained in one place that is readily accessible.

The Business Understanding Infrastructure provides a base for data and processes resource integration, business analysis, business reengineering, and business transformation. It's the base for understanding complexity, planning business improvement, and making more informed business decisions to ensure business agility. It's a low-entropy, low-energy way to operate that leads to success.

The Business Understanding Infrastructure has been there all the time, to a greater or lesser degree. It has been confused or masked by presentations and publications with specific agendas, wrong orientations, informality, bad hype, and so on. People never saw the architecture infrastructure, because of technical orientations and an attitude of *Who needs architectures?*

The Business Understanding Infrastructure is a unified construct for business understanding and operation. It's a unified theory for an infrastructure of business architecture symmetries and model perspectives.

Albert Einstein's comment about J. Piaget's work applies to the Business Understanding Infrastructure: *It's so simple only a genius could have thought of it*.

SUMMARY

Traditional business architectures have two basic problems. First, organizations don't understand what a formal business architecture represents, how it's developed and maintained, and how it supports the organizations business. Second, organizations don't understand the serious business impacts of not having a formal business architecture. The basic needs are to develop a single, formal, organization-wide, business architecture infrastructure for understanding the organization's business, that supports business analysis, transformation, reengineering, and integration.

Two trends attempted to resolve these problems: *Arrival of the business architecture* and *The emergence of business architectures*. Both trends failed to provide any meaningful improvement in the concept and use of business architectures to help an organization understand and operate its business.

The contemporary business architecture concept is an architecture infrastructure encompassing the three tiers of the contemporary business construct. Each tier has an architecture infrastructure, and collectively those individual architecture infrastructures form an architecture infrastructure for the organization. The name of that combined architecture infrastructure is the Business Understanding Infrastructure. The objective is to support the two major business functions for thoroughly understanding and successfully operating the organization's business.

A basic Business Understanding Infrastructure was presented. That basic infrastructure can be expanded and extended to form the Business Understanding Infrastructure that meets an organization's specific business needs.

Each architecture in the Business Understanding Infrastructure has a symmetry. The combined symmetries across the entire Business Understanding Infrastructure forms an architecture super-symmetry. Models of an architecture are a model perspective. Models of an architecture super-symmetry represent are a model super-perspective.

Architecture separability states that a perspective can be taken from an architecture symmetry and replaced without altering that architecture symmetry, if the architecture symmetry is static. However, an organization's business niche is very dynamic, and the architecture symmetry is constantly changing to represent that constantly changing business niche. Model perspectives are only a snapshot that portrays the architecture symmetry using architecture-driven model techniques at a point in space-time, and is transient.

The architecture symmetry can only be enhanced with model perspectives using model-driven architecture techniques.

Business Understanding Infrastructure Laws and Rules guide development of the Business Understanding Infrastructure, and ensure the integrity and quality of the organizations business understanding and operation. Violations of those Laws and Rules lead to the basic problems that plague traditional business architectures, resulting in impacts on business understanding, agility, and success.

The Business Understanding Infrastructure is a new paradigm that provides the formality and practicality for an organization to manage its business and adapt to constant changes in its business niche. It's the unified theory for an infrastructure of business architecture symmetries and model perspectives that supports an organization's business. The Business Understanding Infrastructure has been there all the time, but has been masked by informality, bad hype, and personal agendas, and an attitude of *Who needs architectures*?

QUESTIONS

The following questions are provided as a review of the Business Understanding Infrastructure Chapter, and to stimulate thought about replacing traditional business architectures with a formal Business Understanding Infrastructure.

1. What are the basic problems with traditional business architectures?
2. What is needed to resolve those problems?
3. What have been the prominent trends with traditional business architectures?
4. Why have those trends with traditional business architectures not resolved the basic problems?
5. What is the business architecture infrastructure concept?
6. Why was the formal name of Business Understanding Infrastructure used?
7. What is the objective of Business Understanding Infrastructure?
8. What are the major components of the Business Understanding Infrastructure?
9. How can a basic Business Understanding Infrastructure be expanded and extended to meet an organization's specific needs?
10. How does architecture super-symmetry differ from architecture symmetry?
11. How does model super-perspective differ from model perspective?
12. How do architecture super-symmetry and model super-perspective apply to the Business Understanding Infrastructure?

13. What is the principle of architecture separability?
14. Why does architecture separability not apply to the Business Understanding Infrastructure?
15. What is the architecture non-separability principle that applies to the Business Understanding Architecture?
16. What are the Business Understanding Infrastructure Laws?
17. What are the Business Understanding Infrastructure Rules?
18. What are the impacts of violating those Laws and Rules?
19. What are the benefits of the Business Understanding Infrastructure?
20. Why should an organization develop a Business Understanding Infrastructure?

Chapter 13
BUSINESS UNDERSTANDING FORMATION

Create and maintain the Business Understanding Infrastructure.

The Business Understanding Infrastructure Chapter described traditional business architecture problems, business architecture trends, the architecture infrastructure concept, the formality of a Business Understanding Infrastructure, and the benefits of establishing a Business Understanding Infrastructure. The Business Understanding Formation Chapter describes the problems and with traditional information systems development, and the contemporary approach to creating and maintaining the Business Understanding Infrastructure. The chapter theme is to describe the formation of the Business Understanding Infrastructure for an organization to thoroughly understand its business, be agile, and successfully operate its business.

TRADITIONAL SYSTEM DEVELOPMENT

The problems with an organization's data resource and processes resource, and how those problems are resolved with organization-wide architectures, data resource management, and processes resource management have been described in previous chapters. However, those problems have not been resolved in most public and private sector organizations today. The problems are not with the creation of a combined data and processes resource, or with formal data resource management and processes resource management. The problems are with the traditional information system development processes, from business needs, through specification and design, system development, testing, implementation, and operation.

The common problems with traditional information systems development, the basic problems and their impacts, and the basic needs to resolve those basic problems are described below.

Common Problems

Many information system development methods have been promoted over the years by a variety of different organizations. Some methods have been more successful than others, but none have included the formal creation and maintenance of organization-wide data and processes architectures for an organization's thorough understanding of its business niche and successful operation in that business niche.

The common problems with traditional development methods described below are in addition to the problems with data and processes management described earlier. You may not agree with these common problems, and may violently object to the existent of these common problems. However, they are the problems observed, in one form or another, in a wide variety of public and private sector organizations, over many years, that are directly or indirectly impacting their business in one way or another.

Both business professionals and technology professionals can be in a brute-force development mode. *Brute-force development* was defined earlier as any action that bypasses or circumvents one or more phases in the Data Resource Cycle or Processes Resource Cycle. It's any action that jumps to a different state, or ignores the Data Resource Laws and Rules or the Processes Resource Laws and Rules.

Business professionals and technology professionals can be in a paralysis-by-analysis mode, which is the opposite of brute-force development. The over analysis is usually due to a genuine interest in developing complete formal designs of business needs, but may be due to an intentional delay. ***Paralysis-by-analysis*** is an on-going, ad nauseum, over-analysis of business data and processes, that unnecessarily delays development and implementation of the data and/or processes needed to support the business.

Extract-Transform-Load (ETL) is used to move data between databases or to create new databases from data in existing databases. ETL can be very useful for tasks like formal data resource integration. However, ETL can create huge quantities of redundant and disparate data, without formal design or documentation, if used improperly. Unfortunately, the latter is often the case in many organizations. The redundant data created by ETL often need to be maintained by a variety of bridges between databases to support business processes. A temporary or interim process using ETL frequently becomes a permanent process.

Business professionals often believe that if an application – processes and databases – is built for, and runs on, their desktop computer, that technology professionals are not involved or impacted, and they don't have to follow any formal data or processes resource management. However, sooner or later, technology professionals become involved and are impacted, because many desktop computers seldom work in total isolation. Eventually, they connect in some manner, require data, send data, store data, share processes, and so on, all of which usually involves technology professionals.

The flip side is technology professionals often prevent business professionals from independently building any applications, in an effort to avoid disparity they may need to manage. Many justifiable business needs cannot be met, because technology professionals don't have the time to build and operate an application, yet won't allow business professionals to build those applications.

Manual, non-electronic, and mechanical processes are seldom formally managed. However, those processes are just as important to an organization's successful operation as information systems. They must be managed with the same formality as information systems.

Business professionals don't always formally define their data and processes, or normalize their data and processes within organization-wide architectures. When they do, technology professionals often physicalize the data and processes design developed by business professionals. Such physicalizing violates the normalization of data and processes within their organization-wide architectures.

Business professionals often create designs lacking formal business decisions and integrity rules. Technology professionals often create business decisions and data integrity rules without consulting business professionals.

Business professionals often claim that technology professionals don't comprehend what's involved in understanding the dynamic business niche and conducting business in that business niche. The flip side is that technology professionals often claim that business professionals don't comprehend what's involved in constructing, implementing, and operating information systems.

The process for all types of information systems design, development, and operation is unclear, not well understood, and frequently misused. Business decisions are often changed or implemented by technology professionals without input from, or approval by, business professionals. The terminology for information systems design, development, and operation is vague, unclear, and confusing.

Organizations frequently define an organization structure, often with flashy, catchy, or popular names for organization units, without understanding the meaning behind those names, or how others interpret those names. Then they try to fit business activities into that organization structure, which only sets the stage for many of the problems described above.

The common problems with traditional systems development methods are summarized below.

Both business professionals and technology professionals are often in a brute-force development mode.

Business professionals and technology professionals are often in a paralysis-by-analysis mode.

Extract-Transform-Load (ETL) is often used inappropriately and outside any formal data resource design process.

Business professionals often develop applications – processes and databases – independent of any involvement of technology professionals.

Technology professionals often prevent business professionals from building applications without their involvement.

Manual, non-electronic, and mechanical processes are seldom formally managed or documented.

Business professionals often don't provide complete designs for data and processes, within organization-wide architectures, including formal business decisions and integrity rules.

Technology professionals often physicalize the data and processes, violating normalization rules and organization-wide architectures.

Technology professionals often create business rules and integrity rules without consulting business professionals.

Business professionals claim technology professionals don't comprehend what's involved in understanding and operating in a dynamic business niche.

Technology professionals claim business professionals don't comprehend what's involved in constructing, implementing, and operating information systems.

The process for system design and development is unclear and misused.

Business decisions are often changed or implemented by technology professionals without approval from business professionals.

The terminology for system development is unclear, confusing, inappropriate, frequently misunderstood, and misused.

The organization structure is often defined with catchy names before considering the detailed responsibilities of each organization unit.

Many times, I've heard each side – business professionals and technology professionals – exclaim, *They just don't get it!* when referring to the other side. These problems are not an issue of who's right and who's wrong, or who gets is and who doesn't get it. These problems are evidence of a disconnect between business professionals and technology professionals.

Basic Problems and Impacts

The basic problems with traditional systems development methods are listed below.

No formal, organization-wide, system development cycle from identification of business needs to implementation and operation.

The terminology for systems development, implementation, and operation is confusing, frequently misunderstood, and misused.

Business professionals and technology professionals often don't cooperatively work together toward a common business goal.

Business needs can't be readily implemented in an appropriate time frame.

Data and processes are not formally managed within a single organization-wide data architecture and single organization-wide processes architecture.

Business reengineering, transformation, and change management, and their impacts, are not well understood or easy to perform.

The impacts of the basic problems are the same impacts listed earlier: increased natural and created disparity, decreased understanding, increased uncertainty, excessive use of resources, business needs not being met, limited business agility, and ultimately a less than fully successful business.

Basic Needs

The basic problems with traditional systems development methods must be resolved for an organization to understand its business, be agile, and successfully operate its business. The basic needs to resolve the basic problems are listed below.

Define a formal development sequence for the Business Understanding Infrastructure from business needs to operation, that includes formal data resource management and processes resource management for all data and processes at the organization's disposal.

Define formal terms with comprehensive definitions to be used with the formal development sequence for the Business Understanding Infrastructure.

Determine the organization units responsible for different stages of the formal development sequence, and how business professionals and technology professionals work together to identify, define, and meet business needs.

CONTEMPORARY INFRASTRUCTURE FORMATION

Resolving the basic problems with traditional systems development methods and meeting the basic needs is accomplished by describing formation of the Business Understanding Infrastructure for an organization. The concepts and components of the Business Understanding Infrastructure were described in previous chapters. Those concepts and components are brought together into a formal method to create and maintain the unique Business Understanding Infrastructure for an organization.

Traditional terms and scenarios, contemporary terms, the contemporary approach, a contemporary workflow, and the benefits of creating and maintaining a Business Understanding Infrastructure are described below.

Traditional Terms and Scenarios

The basic problems with traditional systems development are deeply rooted in semantics, and the practices based on those semantics. The confusion about technology, about development, and about the difference between data and information, leading to traditional scenarios that result in a major disconnect within an organization are described below.

Confusion about Technology

Technology is widely defined as the application of scientific knowledge for practical purposes; machinery and equipment developed from the application of scientific knowledge; the knowledge of techniques and processes embedded in machines; the branch of knowledge dealing with the creation and use of technical means; the study and transformation of techniques, tools, and machines created by humans; the branch of knowledge dealing with engineering or applied sciences; the sum of techniques, skills, methods, and processes for the production of goods and services, or in accomplishing objectives.

Information technology is generally defined as the study or use of systems, especially computers and telecommunications, for storing, retrieving, and sending information; the use of any computers, storage, networking, or other physical devises, infrastructure, and processes to create, process, store, secure, and exchange all forms of electronic data, typically for enterprise operations.

The information technology definition refers to the study or use of computers, telecommunication systems, and physical devices; to both information and data, even though *information* is in the title; to storing, retrieving, and sending information, but not data; and to processes. It does not refer to the determination of business needs, or to the design or construction of data or processes. It does not refer to any non-electronic data or processes, or to the size of systems. A large part of an organization's business is done with non-electronic, non-automated, manual processes.

Confusion about Development

Develop is generally defined as to grow or cause to grow; to become mature, advanced, or elaborate; to come into existence or operation; to bring into being or activity; to grow to a more mature or advanced state.

It's a broad term that has a wide variety of meanings, including create, build, construct, make, generate, design, establish, and so on. The term can be used for everything from establishing business needs to building a database or information system. The term has many connotative meanings and many different agendas are hidden in those meanings.

Business professionals and technology professionals often hide behind the word *develop* as meaning anything related to developing processes and data. Both often believe *develop* includes the development of needs, specifications, and design, as well as development of the product from that design. Both may confound or confuse the term to suit specific agendas. Both often develop systems independent of any organization-wide data and processes architectures.

Business professionals often develop systems without technology professionals being involved. Technology professionals often change or compromise designs by business professionals. DevOps stands for Development and Operations, which is the development, implementation, and operation of systems, specifically processes and databases. DevOps evolved into IT, meaning Information Technology, but the concept of development and operations still remains.

Confusion about Data and Information

Data and information are still confused, and often used interchangeable. *Data* was defined earlier as individual facts, combined facts, or calculated facts that are out of context, have no meaning, and are difficult to understand. *Data in context* are data that have meaning and can be readily understood. *Information* was defined earlier as a set of data in context, with relevance to one or more people at a point in time or for a period of time. Information is more than data in context – it must have relevance and a time frame.

Something was lost moving from *Data Processing* to *Information Technology*. *Data Processing* was correct, because data and processes – the two basic resources that contain an organization's business understanding – are contained in that name and are used to develop data and processes to understand and to operate the organization's business. Technology got in the way of managing data and processes.

Traditional Scenarios

The development scenarios are different in different organizations. Sometimes, technology professionals want the formality of organization-wide data and processes architectures to make their job easier, but business professionals resist, or strongly resist. The business has become fragmented into different domains, with each domain having its own data and processes. The business professionals are comfortable with the business domain disparity across the data and processes, and don't want organization-wide data or processes architectures.

Business professionals are often concerned about the disparity of data and processes, and the lack of thorough business understanding. They want organization-wide data and processes architectures to resolve the business domain disparity. They often begin developing formal data and processes names and definitions within organization-wide architectures, only to be blocked by technology professionals. The technology professionals have become comfortable with the data and processes disparity.

Resistance to normalizing data and processes within organization-wide architectures, by either business professionals or technology professionals, encourages increasing data and processes disparity, and loss of thorough business understanding.

A Major Disconnect

You see what's happened. A major disconnect has occurred between business professionals and technology professionals. Each side is hiding behind a lack of semantic clarity. The scenarios differ from one organization to the next, but the disconnect is very real. That disconnect needs to be resolved.

As a professional friend once told during dinner, referring to a recent struggle in his organization: "The entire system design-construct-implement-operate scenario is like trying to use cats to herd turtles."

Contemporary Terms

Resolving the disconnect begins with resolving the semantic problems by defining contemporary terms. The second basic need listed above is to define formal terms with comprehensive definitions to support a contemporary approach for creating and maintaining a Business Understanding Infrastructure. Emphasizing *data* and *information*, abandoning the word *develop*, and revising the scope of *technology* are described below.

Emphasize Data and Information

The definitions for *data* and *information* must remain as defined earlier, and must be used appropriately by everyone in the organization. An organization will not make any progress toward formally managing data and processes without comprehensive definitions for *data* and *information*.

Abandon Develop

The term *develop* needs to be abandoned. The problems with *develop* cannot be resolved with a comprehensive definition. The wide use of *develop* for many tasks, the connotative meanings, and the hidden agendas are too ingrained to be resolved. The only alternative is to abandon the term. By extension, the terms *development* and *DevOps* also need to be abandoned.

More appropriate terms to use are *prepare*, *construct*, *deploy*, *operate*, and so on. *Prepare* could be any task related to understanding the business, stating specifications, and designing a product. *Construct* could be any task related to building a product according to the design. *Deploy* could any task related to installing or implementing that product. *Operate* could any task related to running the product to support the business. Other appropriate words would be *design*, *evaluate*, *form*, *build*, or any appropriate verb other than *develop*.

Revise Technology Scope

Technology has the same problem as *methodology* described earlier – it's literally the study of techniques. The problem is that *technology* applies equally to business professionals and to technology professionals. That problem cannot be resolved with a comprehensive redefinition of *technology* or *information technology*. The current perception is so fixed that it is nearly impossible to change.

The real issue with *technology* is that it applies to both sides – business professionals and technology professionals. Business professionals have a technology to observe the business, understand the business, and define business activities. Technology professionals have a technology to construct, implement, and operate systems. Technology applies to the entire sequence from observation of the business niche to implementation of data and processes to operate the business.

Technology is a huge and growing industry. The issue is not with the use of technology, but with losing track of the quality of data and processes, and the loss of business understanding. The issue is the technology of business needs and design versus the technology of system development and implementation. The issue has become *my technology versus your technology*. The real issue is technology outrunning thorough business understanding and successful business operation!

Contemporary Approach

The contemporary approach is to create and maintain a Business

Understanding Infrastructure for the organization. ***Create*** is generally defined as to cause something to happen; to invent something; to bring something into existence; to invest with a new form; to produce or bring about by a course of action or behavior. ***Maintain*** is generally defined as to cause or enable to continue; to keep in existence; to keep in good condition and working order; to preserve from failure or decline; to sustain against opposition or danger.

The contemporary approach to creating and maintaining the Business Understanding Infrastructure is based on the Business Niche Cycle, with its Understand Phase and Operate Phase, as described in Chapter 3. The Understand Phase and the Operate Phase represent the two basic business functions to thoroughly understand the business and to successfully operate the business. The Business Niche Cycle, combined with the Data Resource Cycle and Processes Resource Cycle, form the complete Business Cycle.

The Data Resource Cycle and the Processes Resource Cycle each have a Formalize Phase and a Customize Phase. The Formalize Phases formally normalize the data to proper data, and the processes to proper processes, within their respective organization-wide architectures. The Customize Phases formally denormalize proper data to implement data, and proper processes to implement processes as necessary for operational efficiency, without compromising the proper data or proper processes!

The relationship between the Understand Phase and the Operate Phase is shown in Figure 13.1. Briefly, the Understand Phase includes the Formalize Phases to formally normalize data and processes, and the Operate Phase includes the Customize Phases to formally denormalize data and processes.

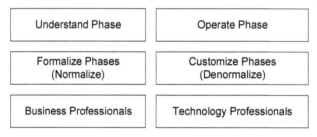

Figure 13.1. Understand Phase and Operate Phase Relationship.

The Formalize Phases are typically done by business professionals to support business needs. The Customize Phases are typically done by technology professionals for efficient operation of the business.

You probably thought the terms *Business Professionals* and *Technology Professionals* meant *business analysts* and *Information Technology*. You are correct – under the traditional concept. The problem is that the traditional concept is not working, and is seriously impacting business understanding and operation. It does not emphasize the creation and maintenance of the formal

Business Understanding Infrastructure for an organization.

The traditional concept is based on organization units, not on the skills and capabilities of individuals. The contemporary concept is based on the skills and capabilities of individuals, independent of organization unit. Those individuals must follow the formal processes for creating and maintaining the Business Understanding Infrastructure.

Business professionals are oriented toward business analysis, determination of business needs, and meeting those business needs. *Business analysis* is typically defined as enabling an organization to articulate needs and the rationale for change, and to design and describe solutions that deliver value. It includes taking the requirement aspects from beginning to end, using formal business analysis processes.

The operative word in that definition is *analysis*. *Analysis* is separation of the whole into its parts, an examination of a complex, its elements, and their relations; the separation of the ingredients of a substance; a statement of the constituents of a mixture. *Business analysts* are the business professionals that perform business analysis to identify and define business needs.

Implementation professionals are oriented toward the synthesis of solutions to meet business needs. *Synthesis* is to put together; the combination of parts or elements to form a whole; the production of a substance by the union of elements, or groups to form a whole. *Business synthesists* are the professionals that build and implement business solutions to meet business needs.

The word *technology* does not appear for either Business Professionals or Implementation Professionals. Technology applies to both responsibilities, as described above.

The contemporary concept is shown in Figure 13.2. The left is NeedSpec and the right is ConOps. Many people say, "I've never heard of those." That's good news, because there are no preconceived notions or connotative meanings about what those terms represent and people can better understand the contemporary approach. *NeedSpec* is an acronym for identifying business needs and designing the specifications to meet those business needs. It includes activities to observe the business niche, identify business needs, and design specifications to support those business needs.

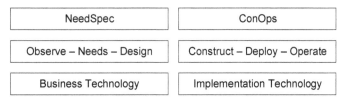

Figure 13.2. Contemporary concept for analysis and synthesis.

ConOps is an acronym for the construction and operation of systems to support business operation. ConOps includes activities to construct a solution according to the design specifications, deploy the solution ready for operation, and operate that solution to support the business.

The activities of NeedSpec and ConOps are summarized below.

NeedSpec activities:
> *Observe* the business niche
> Identify the business *needs*
> *Design* specifications to support business needs

ConOps activities:
> *Construct* solution according to the design
> *Deploy* solution ready to be operational
> *Operate* the solution to support the business

The people responsible for NeedSpec are skilled in business technology, and the people responsible for ConOps are skilled in implementation technology. These terms emphasize the fact that technology is involved in both NeedSpec and ConOps.

NeedSpec and ConOps do not represent organization units. They are business activities independent of organization structure. NeedSpec and ConOps refer to the skills and responsibilities of people, regardless of their location in the organization. Those people must follow the formal procedures for creating and maintaining the Business Understanding Infrastructure. Both must work together for a successful business.

Contemporary Workflow

The contemporary approach is supported by a contemporary workflow that extends from business niche observation to business operation in that business niche. The contemporary workflow is a seamless workflow, with feedback loops and responsibilities, to create and maintain the Business Understanding Infrastructure. The business workflow, responsibilities, feedback loops, testing, and ongoing cycles are described below.

Business Workflow

The contemporary business workflow to create and maintain the Business Understanding Infrastructure follows the Business Workflow Segment described in the Overarching Business Construct Chapter. Creating and maintaining the Business Understanding Infrastructure is a set of business processes and data that are no different than any other set of business processes and data. The workflow is a formal sequence that includes NeedSpec analysis and ConOps synthesis. All processes and data, automated and manual, large and small, must be developed within that formal business workflow.

The formal business workflow is unique for each organization depending on the type of business, the organizational structure, and the specific processes and data needed to understand and operate the business. Developing a formal business workflow that fits every organization would be nearly impossible.

The Business Cycle, Data Resource Cycle, and Processes Resource Cycle that are generic across all organizations were described in previous chapters. Adapting those generic cycles to a unique business workflow for a specific organization should be easy. Organizations have developed, and followed, much more intricate business workflows for other, often very detailed business activities. Why is defining a workflow to create and maintain the Business Understanding Infrastructure so difficult?

The *Business Understanding Workflow* is a seamless business workflow to create and maintain the Business Understanding Infrastructure. It includes all NeedSpec and ConOps activities from observing the business niche, the entire sequence of activities for observing the organization's business niche, identifying business needs, design specifications to meet those business needs, constructing a solution according to the design specifications, deploying that solution, and operating that solution to support the organization's business operation.

A single Business Understanding Workflow does not work for every organization. Each organization does business differently, and has the right to do business differently. Each organization prepares its own specific Business Understanding Workflow, based on how it wants to thoroughly understand and successfully operate its business. The Business Understanding Workflow formality must be followed, but can be adjusted based on the way an organization does business.

A *Specific Business Understanding Workflow* is a Business Understanding Workflow, developed by an organization, based on how that organization desires to thoroughly understand and successfully operate its business. It's follows the Business Understanding Workflow formality, but is specific to a particular organization.

Each project to design, acquire or create, and maintain a business activity within an organization has different needs for understanding the business and successfully operating the business. The organization's Specific Business Understanding Workflow is adjusted to meet those different project needs. The Specific Business Understanding Workflow formality must be followed, but can be adjusted based on the project details.

A *Project Business Understanding Workflow* is a Specific Business Understanding Workflow for building or maintaining a business activity, that has been adapted to a specific project. It follows the Specific Business Understanding Workflow formality, but is unique to a project.

A Project Business Understanding Workflow can be supported by formal project management, using whatever project management technique is appropriate for the project. Note that project management can be a segment of the Business Support Tier, as described in the Overarching Business Construct Chapter.

Each production operation of a business activity has different needs for operating the organization's business. The organization's Specific Business Understanding Workflow is adjusted to meet those production needs. The Specific Business Understanding Workflow formality must be followed, but can be adjusted based on production details.

A *Production Business Understanding Workflow* is a Specific Business Understanding Workflow that has been adapted for production operation of a business activity. It follows the Specific Business Understanding Workflow, but is unique to production operation.

Responsibilities

Organization units traditionally had specific responsibilities for identifying business needs, forming designs to meet those business needs, constructing systems to meet the designs, and operating those systems. The responsible people have been referred to as *business professionals* – business analysis, and *technology professionals* – IT. However, as described earlier, *technology* applies to all responsibilities. Also, technology has become readily available to nearly everyone in an organization. That trend leads to the terms *business technology* for NeedSpec, and *implementation technology* for ConOps. These terms resulted in a conflict between organization structures and responsibilities.

An organization can structure its human resource any way it deems appropriate, and has the right to structure its human resource as it considers appropriate. The issue becomes how the organization structure is involved in creating and maintaining the Business Understanding Infrastructure and operating the organization's business. The issue is best resolved with a contemporary perspective of organization structure, complete with organization unit definitions and responsibilities.

The primary emphasis of the contemporary perspective is creating and maintaining the Business Understanding Infrastructure, so an organization can remain agile and be successful. That emphasis requires following formal processes, for all business activities, regardless of the size or scope of the business activity. No business activity is exempt from following formal processes for data and processes resource management.

One example is implementing a major production system for the organization, either acquired or designed and built in-house. Many different organization units are responsible for various phases of the project, from defining business needs to production operation.

A second example is the evolution of simulation systems. A small group of business professionals design and build a simulation system, which involves many different trials and adjustments until a suitable simulation is achieved. That simulation system can then be put into production.

A third example is individual, automated or non-automated processes performed by employees, for both routine and non-routine business activities. Most organizations have a plethora of small business processes, performed by individuals, that keep the organization operational.

Numerous other examples exist in the spectrum from large, automated, production applications to small, manual processes performed by individual employees. The creation and maintenance of all business activities must follow formal processes for data and processes management.

Specific responsibilities for both Project Business Understanding Workflows and Production Business Understanding Workflows cross organization units. Different organization units have different responsibilities for different phases of project activities and production operation. Organization units and specific project tasks are orthogonal to each other. Organization units roll-in and roll-out of a project as necessary to complete the project. That roll-in and roll-out is shown on the business workflow, and is supported by project management.

Each organization unit has a responsibility to create and maintain the organization's Business Understanding Infrastructure. If any organization unit shirks their responsibility, or compromises another organization unit's responsibility, the Business Understanding Infrastructure is not complete and correct. The thorough business understanding is lost, agility is compromised, and the organization drifts toward a less than successful business operation.

Feedback Loops

The Business Understanding Workflow includes feedback loops. The concept of feedbacks has been around a long time. The first feedback loop was defined in 2000 BCE by the Greek mathematician Ktesibios of Alexandria, who built a self-controlling water clock. Nature has many feedback loops. Your body has feedback loops, such as when you are hot, you sweat to cool. A furnace thermostat is a feedback loop.

Many people discover feedback loops, write about feedback loops, talk about feedback loops, and so on. But those are personal discoveries, because the concept has been known for years.

Feedback loops can be negative or positive. A *negative feedback loop* gains control. A *positive feedback loop* loses control.

A good example of a negative feedback loop is the steam engine governor developed by Watt. When the engine runs too fast, the governor closes the steam valve, and the engine runs slower. When the engine runs too slow, the governor opens the steam valve, and the engine runs faster. The negative feedback loop maintains a constant engine speed.

A good example of a positive feedback look is when the steam engine runs too fast, the governor opens the steam valve and the engine runs faster. That situation is referred to as a run-away system, and usually ends in disaster. When the steam engine runs too slow, the governor closes the steam valve and the engine runs slower. Eventually the engine stops.

Two examples of positive feedback loops organizations encounter are brute-force development and paralysis-by-analysis.

Brute-force development builds and implements processes and databases quicker with less delay, which is rewarded, which perpetuates brute-force development, and so on. However, the run-away development leads to rampant disparity, increased created entropy, increased uncertainty, and business failure from the lack of formality and single organization-wide architectures. The organization tries to keep up with operational systems to support the business without thoroughly understanding the business.

A major driver of brute-force development is automated software design and development tools. Another major driver is the rush to production operation to support the business. Both drivers are oriented toward implementation, not toward thorough business understanding.

Paralysis-by-analysis is a continuous cycle of specification and design that delays data and processes development and implementation. Observation leads to discovery, which leads to design, which leads to questions, which leads to discovery, and so on, while the organization tries to keep pace with understanding constant change. The reward is discovery and development of organization-wide architectures, which may lead to better business understanding and business practices, but perpetuates a runaway analysis cycle without any data or processes development or implementation.

A major driver of paralysis-by-analysis is the desire to gain a thorough business understanding and prepare complete design specifications to support that business understanding. Another major driver is the complete development of single organization-wide architectures to reduced disparity.

The Business Understanding Workflow eliminates positive feedback loops. It's a balance between brute-force development and paralysis-by-analysis with negative feedback loops. Too much development without thorough business understanding triggers a negative feedback to gain business understanding. Too much analysis without any development triggers a negative feedback to continue with development.

In spite of the connotative meaning of *negative feedback* as bad, and *positive feedback* as good, the opposite is true. *Negative feedback* is good and *positive feedback* is bad. Too much analysis pushes the cycle toward synthesis, and too much too much synthesis pushes the cycle toward analysis. The result is a balance between paralysis-by-analysis and brute-force development.

Testing

Testing is broadly defined as the action or process of checking someone or something; inquiring into something thoroughly and systematically; the means by which the presence, quality, or genuineness of something is determined; the procedure leading to proof or disproof, or to acceptance or rejection; the actual testing of a product to meet quality control standards; stress testing a product to see if the actual results match the expected results; a process to evaluate the functionality of a product with an intent to find whether the product met the specified requirements or not, and to identify the defects to ensure that the product is defect-free; quality assurance.

The common perception is to test a product after it has been constructed, before it is implemented and put into operation. However, that test is rather late in the business workflow, allowing errors and problems accumulate. A far better approach is to continually test through the entire Business Understanding Workflow, to catch and resolve errors and problems as early as possible.

Testing begins with NeedSpec activities, which include business niche observation, the identification of business needs, and preparation of design specifications. The business niche observations and consensus are reviewed to make sure they were done properly. The business needs are reviewed to make sure they are valid. The design specs are reviewed to make sure they adequately cover the business needs.

Testing continues through the ConOps activities, which include construction according to the design, deployment in preparation for production operation, and production operation. Data and processes integrity rules are checked. Process testing and stress testing are done to make sure the product will support production operation. Production operation is checked for accuracy and efficiency.

Through both NeedSpec activities and ConOps activities, the data resource and processes resource must be constantly checked to ensure that all data and processes are normalized within their organization-wide architectures, and are properly documented with data resource data and processes resource data.

When a failure, problem, or issue arises, the business workflow cycles back to the previous process, or to a resolution process, to be resolved. When the failure, problem, or issue is resolved, the business workflow moves forward again. Those cycle-backs are tracked through project management.

As described earlier, identification of a failure that causes a cycle-back occurs within a process on a business workflow. The cycle-back flows from that process to a previous process, or other process that will resolve the failure. The decision is made in the process, not on a workflow between processes.

The regular, consistent testing from business niche observation to production operation ensures that an organization thoroughly understands their business and successfully operates that business.

Ongoing Cycles

The design process is never complete, due to the dynamic business niche. An organization faces ongoing change, because the business niche never becomes static. At some point the design must stop and construction must begin. Additional business changes go into the next design cycle. If not, an organization moves into a paralysis-by-analysis mode.

Cycles of design and construction are created to match the rate of business change. That's the Business Niche Cycle that each organization must go through to ensure the business is current with the business niche changes. Each organization determines the frequency of the cycles, depending on how current the organization wants to be with the business niche. Each cycle moves through the Business Understanding Workflow from business need to implementation and operation.

Changing the organization's business changes the business niche where the organization operates, because the organization is part of its business niche. That changed business niche often creates additional business needs that contribute to the next cycle of needs, design, construction, testing, implementation, and operation. That cycle is ongoing.

The business needs must be real, or perceived to be real. Business professionals sometimes claim they have a need, but that need has no justification – which is the *Why* interrogative. If the *Why* interrogative is not answered, a cycle of paralysis-by-analysis is created, because the business need is not thoroughly understood.

Benefits

The benefits of creating and maintaining the Business Understanding Infrastructure are a reduction of disparity and uncertainty, an increase in thorough business understanding, increased agility, and rapid support of changing business needs. Created entropy is eliminated and natural entropy is managed at an acceptable level.

Every organization faces a turnover of people, including retirement, resignations, promotions, new hires, and so on. New people often struggle to understand the data and processes due to lack of a thorough business understanding. That struggle to understand data and processes results in wasted resources that could be put into more productive activities. The creation and maintenance of a Business Understanding Infrastructure reduces or eliminates those wasted resource.

The cycle from identification of business needs during business niche observation to production operation with a data and processes resource is shortened and takes less effort. When an organization slows down and does things right, the desired results are achieved quicker with less effort. When all business projects and operation follow a formal business understanding workflow, with organization units performing specific roles, the Business Understanding Infrastructure is maintained.

A Business Understanding Infrastructure cannot be bought off-the-shelf, borrowed from another organization, or copied from a repository. It must be created and maintained by the organization, for the organization. An organization must go through the process of creating and maintaining its own Business Understanding Infrastructure to reap its full benefit.

The Business Understanding Infrastructure is the unified theory for thorough understanding, agility, and successful operation of the organization's business.

SUMMARY

Traditional systems development is fraught with problems that are common across many organizations. Those problems impact the organization by decreasing understating, increasing uncertainty, limiting business agility, and ultimately impacting the organizations business success. Resolving those problems requires the creation and maintenance of a Business Understanding Infrastructure.

The creation and maintenance of a Business Understanding Infrastructure begins with revised terminology to help resolve a major disconnect between business professionals and technology professionals. The difference between *data* and *information* is clarified. *Develop* is overused, has lost its meaning, and is often used to support individual agendas. It should be abandoned and replaced with more specific verbs, like *design, evaluate, form, build,* and so on. *Technology* applies to all aspects of an organization's business and is not limited to specific organization units.

The contemporary approach is to create and maintain an organization-wide Business Understanding Infrastructure. That approach includes NeedSpec and ConOps functions. NeedSpec is an acronym for identifying business needs and designing specifications to meet those business needs. ConOps is an acronym for construction and operation of systems.

Business Understanding Workflows are created for the sequence of events through NeedSpec and ConOps. Organization units have specific responsibilities for activities within those workflows. An organization unit cannot shirk their responsibility or compromise another organization unit's responsibility.

Feedback loops can be negative or positive. A positive feedback loop loses control, while a negative feedback loop gains control. All Business Understanding Workflows must emphasize negative feedback loops to avoid paralysis-by-analysis and brute-force development.

Testing is done routinely through the Business Understanding Workflow, including both NeedSpec and ConOps. When any failure arises, the business workflow cycles back to the previous process or a resolution process for resolution.

The design and implementation of systems is an ongoing process that is never complete. The business niche constantly changes and an organization's business must constantly adapt to those changes. Cycles of design, construction, and implementation must be established to avoid paralysis-by-analysis and brute-force development.

The benefits of creating and maintaining a Business Understanding Infrastructure are reduced disparity, reduced uncertainty, increased business understanding, management of entropy at an acceptable level, increased business agility, and rapid support of dynamic business needs. The Business Understanding Infrastructure is the unified theory for thorough business understanding, agility, and successful business operation.

QUESTIONS

The following questions are provided as a review of the Business Understanding Formation Chapter, and to stimulate thought about developing and creating and maintaining the Business Understanding Infrastructure for an organization's unique business.

1. What are the basic problems with traditional system development methods?
2. What is needed to resolve those basic problems?
3. What are the terminology problems that need to be resolved?
4. How are those terminology problems resolved?
5. What is the contemporary approach to resolve the basic problems?
6. What is purpose of NeedSpec?
7. Who is primarily involved in NeedSpec?
8. What is the purpose of ConOps?

9. Who is primarily involved in ConOps?
10. What is the Business Understanding Workflow?
11. What is the difference between Specific, Project, and Production Business Understanding Workflows?
12. What are the organization unit's responsibilities for the Business Understanding Workflow?
13. What are feedback loops?
14. What is the difference between a negative feedback loop and a positive feedback loop?
15. Which feedback loops do the Business Understanding Workflow eliminate and promote?
16. When should testing be done?
17. What happens when testing fails?
18. Why are ongoing cycles of development necessary?
19. Why should paralysis-by-analysis and brute-force development be avoided?
20. What are the benefits of creating and maintaining a Business Understanding Infrastructure?

Chapter 14
ASSISTED INTELLIGENCE

Using computer technology to support infrastructure development.

The Business Understanding Formation Chapter described the problems with traditional systems development and the contemporary approach to creating and maintaining the Business Understanding Infrastructure. The Assisted Intelligence Chapter describes the concept of assisted intelligence and the possibilities of using assisted intelligence for creating and maintaining the Business Understanding Infrastructure. The chapter theme is to use computer technology to assist individuals that are using their intelligence to create and maintain the Business Understanding Infrastructure.

ASSISTED INTELLIGENCE

Assisted intelligence is a concept I've used for many years during my professional venture to assist in completing a variety of design and development tasks. It has become a powerful concept to design and build a wide variety of systems. It's also a key component of creating and maintaining the Business Understanding Infrastructure. The overarching construct and underlying foundation, the concept of assisted intelligence, and a theme of building on the shoulders of giants are described below.

Construct and Foundation

The Business Understanding Vision was defined earlier is an overarching construct for business understanding and agility, supported by an underlying foundation of theories, concepts, principles, and techniques to create and maintain that construct. The overarching construct is the Business Understanding Infrastructure described in detail in the preceding chapters. The underlying foundation of theories, concepts, principles, and techniques supports the creation and maintenance the overarching construct.

The construct for the underlying foundation is shown in Figure 14.1. Theories, such as set theory, semiotic theory, graph theory, relational theory, and so on, form the base of the underlying foundation. Concepts, such as formal names, comprehensive definitions, proper structure, precise integrity rules, and so on, are based on the theories. Principles for names, definitions, structure, and integrity rules, are based on the concepts. Techniques are based on the principles and are unique to each organization.

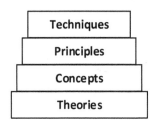

Figure 14.1. Construct of the underlying foundation.

The theories, concepts, principles, and techniques for the data resource are described in the Simplexity series of books. They have been used extensively to create and maintain the data resources for a variety of different public and private sector organizations. An equivalent set of theories, concepts, principles, and techniques could be developed for the processes resource, using the theories, concepts, principles, and techniques for the data resource as a pattern.

Assisted intelligence directly supports human intelligence to use the underlying foundation for the creation and maintenance of the organization's Business Understanding Infrastructure. Assisted intelligence could also support operation of the business, but that's another topic beyond the scope of the current book.

The Concept

Technology-driven disparity is a basic problem with both data and processes. *Technology-driven disparity* was defined earlier as the use of technology to drive the development of disparate data or disparate processes without any regard for formal theories, concepts, principles, or techniques, or any formal data resource or processes resource development. It usually considers current needs without any consideration for future needs.

Stopping the problems associated with technology-driven disparity involves a major emphasis on technology-assisted comparity. *Technology-assisted comparity* was defined earlier as the use of technology to assist the formal development of comparate data and processes resources, rather than drive the development of disparate data and disparate processes resources. It's a major feature of substance-driven style that directly supports the cognitive processes of data and processes resource management.

Technology-assisted comparity is supported by assisted intelligence, which is the subtitle of this book and was briefly described in the Preface. Understanding technology-assisted comparity and assisted intelligence begins with the definition of intelligence.

Intelligence is broadly defined as the ability to acquire and apply knowledge and skills; the ability to accomplish complex goals; the ability to learn or understand, or to deal with new or trying situations; the skilled use of reason; the ability to apply knowledge to manipulate one's environment, or to think abstractly as measured by objective criteria; the capability for learning, reasoning, understanding, and similar forms of mental activity; the aptitude for grasping truths, relationships, facts, meanings, and so on.

Intelligence is difficult to define, because it's a human trait representing the intellectual power of humans. In my college years, I learned that inanimate objects cannot possess intelligence. Then artificial intelligence evolved, with many articles and discussions about the meaning of artificial intelligence that ranged from the statement *Artificial intelligence is neither artificial nor intelligent*, to terms like *near artificial intelligence* and *far artificial intelligence*.

Artificial intelligence is evolving, but cannot observe the business niche, determine how the organization needs to conduct or change its business to be agile and successful, and create and maintain the Business Understanding Infrastructure. It cannot resolve the huge and burgeoning data and processes disparity. Those tasks require human intelligence, which can be supported by assisted intelligence for the routine tasks.

Assisted Intelligence is the appropriate use of technology to assist human intelligence in the performance of tasks, specifically the creation and maintenance of the Business Understanding Infrastructure. It supports the shift from technology-driven disparity to technology-assisted comparity.

One reason assisted intelligence hasn't been used to a greater extent is the lack of formality in most development methods today. Assisting informality in any way is an extremely difficult task, and seldom achieves any reliable benefits. Assisting informality supports technology-driven disparity, rather than technology-assisted comparity.

The formality of the Business Understanding Infrastructure supports technology-assisted comparity and benefits from assisted intelligence. The formality allows assisted intelligence to perform the routine tasks that people should be doing, which frees people to perform the intelligent tasks. It allows people to work smarter, not harder, to understand the business.

The technology for assisted intelligence exists today. Organizations don't need to wait for some panacea that will support creation and maintenance the Business Understanding Infrastructure. Organizations only need to evolve from traditional methods to contemporary concepts, begin using assisted intelligence, and reap the benefits.

On the Shoulders of Giants

A common phrase today is *On the shoulders of others*. The essence of that phrase is to build on the ideas and work of those that came before you; to build on what others have learned and accomplished.

The best-known use of this phrase is *Standing on the shoulders of giants,* written by Isaac Newton in a letter to his rival Robert Hooke, in 1676. *"What Descartes did was a good step. You have added much several ways, and especially in taking the colours of thin plates into philosophical consideration. If I have seen a little further it is by standing on the shoulders of Giants."*

However, Isaac Newton didn't originate the phrase. The 12th century theologian and author John of Salisbury used a version of the phrase in a treatise on logic called *Metalogicon*, written in Latin in 1159. Translations of this difficult book are quite variable, but the essence of what John of Salisbury said is: *We are like dwarfs sitting on the shoulders of giants. We see more, and things that are more distant, than they did, not because our sight is superior or because we are taller than they, but because they raise us up, and by their great stature add to ours.* The phrase may even pre-date John of Salisbury, who was known to have adapted and refined the work of others before him.

Another prominent phrase is from Sir Winston Churchill: *Those who fail to learn from history are doomed to repeat it.* The phrase is an adaptation from George Santayana: *Those who cannot remember the past are condemned to repeat it.* Santayana's statement is a modification of Edmund Burke's phrase: *Those who don't know history are destined to repeat it.*

Not building on the shoulders of others, and not learning from history, results in organizations repeating mistakes, creating disparity, and wasting energy. Creating and maintaining the Business Understanding Infrastructure with assisted intelligence is the least energy approach that maintains entropy at a low and manageable level that allows an organization to remain agile. It's a collective effort by everyone in the organization.

ASSISTED INTELLIGENCE POSSIBILITIES

Assisted intelligence can provide support for many aspects of creating and maintaining the Business Understanding Infrastructure. A few of the more important tasks are model reengineering, model management, architecture management, normalizing and denormalizing data and processes, data and processes documentation, data and processes resource integration, business support segments, process testing, and a variety of other possibilities. Each of these is described below.

Model Reengineering

One current trend today is people arguing about model format and notation. I've seen it many times at conferences and professional meetings, where a person presents a problem with data or processes in their organization and another person draws a model to understand the problem. A third person draws the model with a different format and notations, followed by yet another person using their format and notations. Time is spent drawing competing models and arguing about model formats and notations. That time could be better spent on understanding the person's business and developing models to represent that business.

People often have their own favorite format and notations for models. Many of those formats and notations are from prominent modeling methods, and many are personal choices. The only way to reasonably manage different sets of model formats and notations is through model reengineering. *Model reengineering* is the process of taking a model prepared using one format and set of notations and converting it to a model with another format and set of notations.

Model reengineering begins with the identification of seven basic model configuration parameters that apply to all models.

Model notation: The symbols and notations used on a model.

Model format: How the symbols and notations are laid out in the model, such as upper left with detail to the lower right, detail down and out, core in the center with surrounding detail, random, and so on.

Model style: How the model is packaged, such as segmented, butcher paper, drill-down, and so on.

Model phase: The schema the model represents, such as business schema, data view schema, proper schema, deploy schema, or implement schema.

Model scope: The portion of the business that the model represents, such as a business area, business segment, business activity, and so on.

Model tier: The level of specification detail for the model, such as strategic, tactical, or detail.

Model content: The details contained in the model, such as names, definitions, structure, keys, attribute roles, diagram, integrity rules, and so on.

The process is to identify each person's preferred model configuration parameters. Each person develops a model in private, such as on a personal computer, using the preferred model configuration parameters they know and understand. Technology converts those personal models to data resource data representing the data resource architecture, or processes resource data representing the processes resource architecture. Those data resource data or processes resource data are then displayed as personal models to other people using their preferred configuration parameters.

The model reengineering could be done locally in the same room, or remotely at different locations. It could be done in real time, over a span of time, or across time zones where people make their contributions to an evolving model.

Assisted intelligence supports model reengineering by storing details in the architecture symmetry, then displaying personalized model perspectives of that architecture symmetry to individuals. The process avoids arguments about model format and notations, and emphasizes business understanding. People don't need to meet in one location at the same time. Maximum business understanding can be achieved in minimum time with minimum effort. One benefit observed in some organizations is a voluntary migration to a common set of model configuration parameters.

An additional feature would be to have consultants and vendors agree to the concept of different model configuration parameters and present their models using model configuration parameters acceptable to the audience. Consultants and vendors that agree to use model configuration parameters would have a better opportunity to sell their services and products than those that don't agree to acceptable model configuration parameters.

Model Management

Assisted intelligence can produce models representing perspectives of the architecture super-symmetry can be produced for any perspective of the architecture super-symmetry, using architecture-driven model techniques. Multiple perspectives are be produced without altering the architecture super-symmetry. The complete architecture super-symmetry is available for other perspectives.

Models can be produced on demand, for perspectives of the current or historical architecture super-symmetry, for any scope of the business, with any level of detail, at any time, to any location, using model configuration parameters preferred by the recipient.

These just-in-time, any-oriented models support on-demand business understanding and operation, because on-demand is in demand with today's fast-paced business. The model recipient has no uncertainty about the model validity, because the model is a perspective of the architecture super-symmetry. Two chronology stamps show the date of the material in the model and the date the model was produced. That formality beats traditional approaches to developing and maintaining individual models, with check-in / check-out and versioning.

The arrangement of components and relations between those components on a model has evolved over the years. Years ago, models were hand-drawn using a plastic template. Minor changes were made by erasing and redrawing components and relations. Major changes required redrawing the entire model.

Currently, models can be drawn on a computer screen where the components and relations between the components are rubber-banded. Dragging components around the screen automatically moves the relations between components. Occasionally, relations need to be moved so they don't go through components. A person can adjust the model to be meaningful to the recipient.

The next step is to designate the components and their relations for a model, such as a subject area or project, identify the model configuration parameters, and let assisted intelligence draw the model. The resulting model is meaningful to the recipient. No hand-drawn models and no rubber-banding to adjust the models.

I have visions of Star Trek: Computer, show me a strategic data model of personnel recruitment, using my model configuration parameters. Computer, move Employee to the center. Computer, remove affirmative action data. Computer, ... That's assisted intelligence!

Architecture Management

The Business Understanding Infrastructure is an architecture super-symmetry, unique to the organization's business, that is created and maintained with models using model-driven architecture techniques. That unique architecture super-symmetry may be large, but it is finite and has no configuration parameters. The model perspectives used to create and maintain that architecture super-symmetry are unlimited, depending on the business needs, and those models have model configuration parameters.

Assisted intelligence can support creating and maintaining a proper architecture super-symmetry using model perspectives. It can ensure that model perspectives for enhancing the architecture symmetry are appropriate, check the thesaurus for proper names, check the existing architecture symmetry for similarities or discrepancies, identify the impact of changes or enhancements to the architecture super-symmetry, identify any ripple effects of changes and enhancements, check for the complete architecture trinity, including structure, descriptions, and integrity, and anything else to ensure a proper architecture super-symmetry. When all changes and enhancements are acceptable and confirmed by human intelligence, assisted intelligence can adjust the architecture super-symmetry accordingly.

The organization's unique architecture super-symmetry is created and maintained from business niche observation, from the organization's existing data and processes architectures through formal integration, from generic architectures appropriate for the organization's business, or from any combination of those three. The Data Resource Cycle and Processes Resource Cycle are used based on business niche observation. Formal data resource integration and processes resource integration are used for the organization's existing data resource and processes resource. Appropriate components from generic architectures are selected and enhanced according to the architecture trinity. Assisted intelligence can support all these tasks.

Normalizing and Denormalizing

Data are normalized to proper data within a single organization-wide data architecture in the architecture super-symmetry. Data can be denormalized in one or more ways to implement data for operational efficiency, without compromising the proper data. Processes are also normalized to proper processes within a single organization-wide processes architecture in the architecture super-symmetry. Processes can be denormalized to implement processes for operational efficiency, without compromising the proper processes.

Assisted intelligence can support normalizing and denormalizing data and processes. In many situations, both the data and processes need to be denormalized for operational efficiency. Human intelligence decides what to normalize and assisted intelligence does the normalizing. Human intelligence also decides what to denormalize and assisted intelligence does the denormalizing.

Typically, the structure is denormalized, and other components of the architecture trinity are denormalized accordingly. For example, the data structure may be denormalized. Data names will be formally abbreviated, data definitions may be changed, and data integrity rules may be changed accordingly. The same is true for processes.

Assisted intelligence can support formal name abbreviations according to an abbreviation algorithm and set of word abbreviations. It can support changes in integrity rules according to the structure changes, and ensure that denormalization is complete and appropriate, by identifying multiple random and competing denormalizations that could lead to the creation and maintenance of many bridges between databases.

Assisted intelligence can support the identification and documentation of multiple bridges between databases, the timing of data across the bridges, the sequence of bridges, and the processes involved in moving the data across bridges. It can identify similar denormalizations, and identify the degree of denormalization for data or processes, which are indications of disparate data or processes.

Data and Processes Documentation

All phases in the Data Resource Cycle connect to data resource data in a

Data Resource Guide, shown in Figure 4.2. All phases in the Processes Resource Cycle connect to processes resource data in a Processes Resource Guide, shown in Figure 5.2. Assisted intelligence can support building, maintaining, and accessing both the Data Resource Guide and Processes Resource Guide during all phases of the Data Resource Cycle and Processes Resource Cycle.

Assisted intelligence can ensure that all components of the Architecture Trinity are maintained for both the data resource and processes resource, including description, structure, and integrity components. It can scan data or processes according to the Architecture Trinity, identify any missing, weak, or conflicting components, and flag them for correction or enhancement. It can scan the thesaurus for any conflicts, for appropriate names and comprehensive definitions, for names that are alias names, and for precise data integrity rules and integrity rule lockouts.

Assisted intelligence can routinely scan the organization's data and processes to ensure both data and processes are fully documented in the Data Resource Guide or Processes Resource Guide. That process has been done by several organizations to identify data and processes that are not properly documented, document them, and flag them for review or enhanced documentation. Technical professionals know their operating environment and can easily develop processes to routinely scan data and processes.

Assisted intelligence could support creation of a combined Data and Processes Resource Guide to support combined data and processes resource management. Many components of the Data Resource Guide and Processes Resource Guide are the same. When an organization rises to that level of understanding, it has made a huge leap toward thorough business understanding and successful business operation

Resource Integration

Assisted intelligence can support the integration of disparate data and disparate processes into their respective organization-wide architecture. The approach to integrating disparate data into a comparate data resource is to:

Document the existing disparate data resource in the Data Resource Guide as data bases, data files, and data fields.

Determine the variability in that disparate data resource.

Build the initial common data architecture that will become the single organization-wide data architecture for the organization.

Cross-reference the existing disparate data resource to the common data architecture, and enhance the common data architecture as necessary.

Plan integration of the disparate data depending on the data and processes involved.

The Data Resource Simplexity series of books provides the process details and examples for data resource integration. A similar process with examples could be developed for processes resource integration, based on the data resource integration process.

The integration can be done by subject area, business activity, or any other grouping appropriate for the organization. The integration can be done for either the data resource, the processes resource, or both. However, when one resource is changed, the other resource is impacted. Assisted intelligence can identify the impact of integration on the data resource and the processes resource. Human intelligence can prepare a plan for integrating the data resource and/or the processes resource with minimum impact on the organization's business operation.

Business Support Segments

Business support segments are tools and techniques that support business understanding and business operation. Common business support segments are business workflows, data flows, business rules, the Business Understanding Framework, state transitions, cause and effect, project management, decision tables and decision trees, data provenance and data tracking, menu preparation, parts assembly and part disassembly, and other tools and techniques. Assisted intelligence can support any of the business support segments.

All of these business support segments are connected in the architecture super-symmetry. Any change to one component could have a ripple effect to other components. The addition of a new component or removal of a component could have an impact on other components. Assisted intelligence can support the management and use of business support segments within the context of the architecture super-symmetry.

Business support components can be connected, such as business workflows for a project and project management for that project. Project management could be monitored for alerts about paralysis-by-analysis or brute-force development. Workloads for organization units could be monitored against business activities through peak times and slack. State transitions and cause and effects can be used to track any business activity, whether planned or unplanned. The list of possible interactions goes on, and assisted intelligence can support any of the business support components.

Process Testing

Assisted intelligence can support the testing of processes before implementation. The concept is to test each process against the business specification before implementation and find any discrepancies from the specifications. Any discrepancies result in the process cycling back for resolution. The process was put into operation only when it passed the test.

A number of years ago, I met a person at an international conference who was responsible for testing all production applications before implementation. He had developed a test harness for every major application in the organization. Any change to an application was independently made to its test harness. An application was put into the test harness and had to pass before it could be implemented. If an application failed, it cycled back for adjustments until it passed. Any failure resulted in an independent review of the application and the test harness against the design specifications.

He was very secretive about the nature of the test harness. My interpretation was that it tested every function of the application, every possible valid input, and every possible invalid input. It only tested processes. It did not test any observations of the business niche, or normalization of data or processes within organization-wide architectures.

My concern was at what point the specifications split to go to process development and to the test harness development. He assured me the processes were totally independent and very thorough, and that no production application failures had occurred.

Other Possibilities

Assisted intelligence can support a variety of other tasks. The possibilities are limited only by one's imagination. If you know what needs to be done and it's a routine task, then assisted intelligence can perform that task. It's the human intelligence that determines what needs to be done.

Assisted intelligence can prompt a person about a task that needs to be performed. It can identify problems or deficiencies in a design and make suggestions for improvement. It can assist with routine tasks from business niche observation to operating the business.

Assisted intelligence can support business reengineering, business transformation, change management. It can identify the business impacts of proposed changes to the Business Understanding Infrastructure. It can support business analysis with as-is versus to-be designs.

Everything is connected in the Business Understanding Infrastructure through the architecture super-symmetry. Assisted intelligence can ensure consistency and continuity through the entire architecture super-symmetry. It can go through the architecture super-symmetry and identify possible problems, such as data not used, data used and not defined, processes not used, processes used and not defined, organization units and processes don't match business workflows, state transitions that don't match business workflows, and so on.

Any routine task to enhance and improve the architecture symmetry and model perspectives about the organization's business can be supported by assisted intelligence. Any routine task to portray the architecture symmetry to anyone in the organization, at any time, in any form, can be supported by assisted intelligence. If the task is known and routine, assisted intelligence can perform that task, leaving people are free for the intelligent tasks of thoroughly understanding and successfully operating the business.

An entire book could be written about the possibilities and details for how assisted intelligence can be used to support creation and maintenance of the Business Understanding Infrastructure. But that's another professional venture which is best left for those that follow what I started. Others can take the concept and ideas, and run with them to achieve the new norm of formal data and processes resource management.

BENEFITS

The benefits of assisted intelligence are the same as the benefits described in previous chapters, plus support for human intelligence to perform the routine tasks for creating and maintaining the architecture super-symmetry of the Business Understanding Infrastructure that is unique to an organization's business. That support provides real-time, on-demand architecture super-symmetry to support an organization's unique business.

The technology for assisted intelligence is available today. The process of assisting human intelligence is very detailed, but is easy, effective, and efficient. Why is it so difficult for a professional discipline to achieve assisted intelligence?

SUMMARY

The trend in many organizations today is technology-driven disparity that impacts the organization's business success. That trend needs to change to technology-assisted comparity that ensures the organization's business success. The change involves creating and maintaining a unique Business Understanding Infrastructure for an organization.

Creating and maintaining the architecture super-symmetry of the Business Understanding Infrastructure's is a very detailed and time-consuming process based on established theories, concepts, principles, and techniques. The process relies on human intelligence to understand the organization's business niche, determine the organization's business activities, and operate the business. However, many tasks in that process are routine and don't require human intelligence. Those routine tasks can be performed by assisted intelligence, leaving human intelligence available for the really hard-thinking tasks.

Models can be reengineered according to an individual's model configuration parameters, so time can be spent on understanding the business rather than arguing about model format and notation. Just-in-time, any-oriented models can be produced on demand with architecture-driven model techniques, so people can thoroughly understand and successfully operate the organization's business. The architecture super-symmetry can be created and maintained with model-driven architecture techniques.

Routine tasks in the Data Resource Cycle and Processes Resource Cycle can be performed, such as normalizing and denormalizing data and processes, and documenting data in the Data Resource Guide and processes in the Processes Resource Guide.

The complete architecture trinity can be maintained for data and processes, existing data and processes can be scanned, and the Data Resource Guide and Processes Resource Guide can be enhanced accordingly. A combined Data and Processes Resource Guide can be created and maintained.

Disparate data can be formally integrated into a comparate data resource, and disparate processes can be formally integrated into a comparate processes resource.

Business support segments, such as business workflows, data flows, business rules, the Business Understanding Framework, state transitions, cause and effect, project management, decision tables and decision trees, data provenance and data tracking, process testing, and so on, can be supported. Business analysis and the impacts of proposed changes, such as business reengineering, business transformation, change management can be supported.

Many other possibilities for the use of assisted intelligence are limited only by one's imagination. Routine tasks can be performed by assisted intelligence, so human intelligence can be used for real hard-thinking tasks about thoroughly understanding and successfully operating the organization's business.

The technology for assisted intelligence is available today. Organizations can make use of that technology without further delay. Progressive organizations will take that opportunity and be successful. Other organizations won't. The choice is up to the organization.

QUESTIONS

The following questions are provided as a review of the Assisted Intelligence Chapter, and to stimulate thought about using assisted intelligence to support the creation and maintenance of the organization's Business Understanding Infrastructure.

1. Why is it necessary to shift from technology-driven disparity to technology-assisted comparity?
2. What is the difference between human intelligence and assisted intelligence?
3. What is the meaning of *On the shoulders of others*?
4. What is the underlying foundation of the Business Understanding Infrastructure?
5. What is model reengineering?
6. Why is model reengineering important?
7. What are the model configuration parameters?
8. Why is model management important?
9. How can assisted intelligence support model management?
10. Why is architecture management important?
11. How can assisted intelligence support architecture management?
12. Why is on-demand, real-time modeling important?
13. How can assisted intelligence support the normalizing and denormalizing of data and processes?
14. How can assisted intelligence support data and processes documentation?
15. How can assisted intelligence support data resource integration and processes resource integration?
16. How can assisted intelligence support the business support segments?
17. How can assisted intelligence support process testing?
18. What other aspects of the Business Understanding Infrastructure can be supported by assisted intelligence?
19. What are the benefits of assisted intelligence?
20. Why is assisted intelligence not used by more organizations today?

Chapter 15
AGILE BUSINESS CULTURE

Business agility requires a sound paradigm and a proactive culture.

The Assisted Intelligence Chapter described the concept of assisted intelligence and the possibilities for using assisted intelligence to support creation and maintenance of the Business Understanding Infrastructure. The Agile Business Culture Chapter describes the culture of an agile business that is necessary for an organization to support creation and maintenance of the Business Understanding Infrastructure so it can remain agile and be successful in its business operations. The chapter theme is to understand the cultural components necessary to support an agile and successful organization.

BUSINESS AGILITY

Agility has been a common theme through the previous chapters, but agility has not been described in the context of a culture supporting data and processes resource management. The emphasis has been on thorough business understanding to support business agility and success. The emphasis now needs to be placed on the culture of business agility and success. An agile culture preamble, an agile business culture, and the relationship between culture and technology are described below.

Agile Culture Preamble

Two sentences from *Rime of the Ancient Mariner* highlight the need for agility: *Water, water everywhere, and how the boards did shrink. Water, water everywhere, nor any drop to drink.*

Those two sentences can be adapted to the fundamental data and processes problems. *Data, data everywhere, and how the bases did grow. Data, data everywhere, nor any understanding.* Well, maybe not *nor any understanding*, but certainly not a *thorough understanding* of the organization's business. Without a thorough business understanding an organization cannot be agile, and without agility an organization cannot be fully successful.

A comment my grandson makes when he encounters a particularly difficult situation is also appropriate for agility. *It's like having a tiger by the tail. As long as you hold tight and are quick enough to stay behind the tiger, you are okay. But if you lose your grip on the tail or don't stay behind the tiger, you are in deep trouble.*

The tiger is the organization's business in its dynamic business niche, the grip on the tiger's tail is a thorough understanding about the business, and staying behind the tiger is remaining agile. When an organization loses business understanding – the grip on the tiger's tail, or business agility – staying behind the tiger, it will fail to be fully successful. Many organizations today have lost their grip on the tiger's tail, can't stay behind the tiger, or both.

An Agile Business Culture

Data and processes resource management is supported by a data and processes resource culture. *Data and processes resource culture* was defined earlier as an organizational culture that supports formal data and processes resource management. It includes lexical richness, good hype, substance-driven style, and technology-assisted comparity, as well as other cultural aspects that promote thorough business understanding and successful business operation.

Culture has many very broad and lengthy definitions. Sociologists generally define culture as consisting of values, beliefs, languages, communications, and practices that people share and that define them as a group. Synonyms for culture include philosophy, values, principles, beliefs, attitudes, viewpoints, moralities, ethics, opinions, ideas, trust, and confidence.

Agility was defined earlier as the quality or state of being agile. *Agile* was defined earlier as able to move quickly and easily, able to think and understand quickly, energetic, flexible, adaptable, iterative, and evolving. *Business agility* was defined earlier as the state of an organization being agile in its business understanding and operation.

Agile business culture is an organization mindset to achieve business agility, based on thorough business understanding, that is created and maintained in the Business Understanding Infrastructure, and leads to business success.

Culture and Technology

A relationship exists between culture and technology. Traditionally, technology has been driving the culture in most organizations. The question becomes: Why is the technology driving the business culture?

One reason technology is driving the business culture is that many managers today are not trained in management concepts, principles, and techniques. Many managers became managers by rising through the technical ranks, and they tend to take a technology orientation rather than a cultural orientation. Managers need to have management training and experience, and apply that training and experience to thorough business understanding and agility.

Another reason technology is driving the culture is that technology is prominent today, and technology is definitely needed for today's fast-paced business environment. The problem is that people are enamored with technology and want to apply that technology to their work, which is appropriate. They tend to apply the technology outside any formal construct, which results in the rampant disparity seen in many organizations today.

Many organizations want to manage constant change effectively and efficiently to be agile and successful. Yet disparity reigns supreme in most organizations, which impacts agility. The question becomes: What dark energy is driving organizations to disparity?

That dark energy is technology for technology's sake. It's putting technology before culture, which is creating the disparity, and impacting business agility and success.

Organizations are not abusing technology. Organizations are using technology to abuse citizens and customers, under the guise of better serving those citizens and customers.

The orientation needs to change from technology driving the culture to culture driving the technology. A formal construct for understanding and operating an organization's business is supported by the technology – the assisted intelligence described earlier. That new orientation is a cultural issue.

THE CONTEMPORARY PARADIGM

Facing the cultural issue begins with understanding the new paradigm for business understanding, agility, and success. Many features of the paradigm were described in previous chapters, and don't need to be repeated. Other features of the paradigm are being in the right paradigm, hype versus goals, goals and understanding, business understanding principles, quality and maturity, formality and practicality, elegance and simplicity, and entropy and energy. Each of these is described below.

The Right Paradigm

A statement that adequately characterizes data and processes management in most organizations today is: *You're in the wrong paradigm!* You are in a traditional paradigm that results in the problems described earlier, and the business impacts described earlier.

Organizations need to move to *The right paradigm*, a contemporary paradigm consisting of data and processes resource management supported by a data and processes resource culture. That move is a paradigm shift for the organization.

The name of that contemporary paradigm is the same as the title of this book: The Business Understanding and Agility Paradigm. The ***Business***

Understanding and Agility Paradigm is data and processes resource management, supported by a data and processes resource culture, to create and maintain the Business Understanding Infrastructure for an organization, so the organization can be agile and successful in its business.

The Business Understanding and Agility Paradigm is self-consistent. It is based on a clear-cut scheme that is mathematically consistent, where only one answer can be obtained for the architecture super-symmetry. Business agility and success are based on a self-consistent scheme.

A self-inconsistent scheme can't be agile or successful. Traditional paradigms are self-inconsistent, where multiple answers can be deduced depending on a person's desires and agenda. Many people rely on the self-inconsistency of traditional paradigms to promote their personal viewpoints and agendas.

The Business Understanding and Agility Paradigm is plausible and relevant. *Plausible* means it's probable, reasonable, valuable, credible, believable, and worthy of approval and acceptance. *Relevant* means it's appropriate for the current situation, and has significant and demonstrable benefits.

The Business Understanding and Agility Paradigm is based on semiotic theory. Semiotic theory consists of syntax, semantics, and pragmatics. Syntax is the form, semantics is the meaning, and pragmatics is the practicality. Syntax and semantics become the formality of the paradigm, and pragmatics becomes the practicality of the paradigm.

The Business Understanding and Agility Paradigm is a unified paradigm. It's the unified theory for thorough business understanding, agile operation, and a successful business. It is not a hypothesis to be proven. It is a sound concept with an overarching construct and an underlying foundation of established theory, supported by concepts, principles, and techniques.

The success of the Business Understanding and Agility Paradigm depends on an organization culture that ensures the overarching construct and underlying foundation of the Business Understanding Infrastructure are accepted and followed.

Hype Versus Goals

Many organizations face a dilemma whether to follow the short-term hype to get things done fast, or to establish long-term goals to do things right. Considering the current data and processes disparity in most organizations resulting from short-term hype and lack of long-term goals, the answer should be obvious. However, many organizations still follow short-term hype leading to disparity, rather than seeking long-term goals leading to disparity.

Many organizations are still stuck in the meta-data fiasco and an infinite regress problem. Many organizations still manage data and processes separately. Many organizations still don't formally manage their data and processes in single organization-wide architectures, resulting in disparate or massively disparate data and processes. Many organizations are still oriented toward brute-force development, or are stuck in paralysis-by analysis. These organizations appear to be surviving, but are not as successful as they could be. Many organizations are sacrificing the future for the present, resulting in increased disparity, higher entropy, and decreased agility.

A relationship exists between Good, Quick, and Cheap. If you want something Good and Quick, it won't be Cheap. If you want something Quick and Cheap, it won't be Good. If you want something Cheap and Good, it won't be Quick. The Business Understanding and Agility Paradigm is a balance of all three, oriented toward business understanding, agility, and success.

People are still talking about data lakes, data vaults, data mining, data administration, data governance, and other fads, ad nauseum. Those are all traditional, refined traditional, and super-refined traditional hype, that results in increased disparity, which impacts on business understanding and agility. None of them are contemporary, leading to business understanding, agility, and success.

Data science is an evolving discipline, but disparate data and disparate processes hamper data science. Successful data science needs comparate data and comparate processes. Successful data science needs to avoid all the current hype, like big data, data mining, data vault, data lakes, data administration and governance, and so on. Successful data science depends on a sound paradigm for formally managing an organization's data and processes.

The existing problems in many organizations are often blamed on current situations, such as bad weather, fuel shortages, labor shortages, and on, and on. The current pandemic situation is a ready-made blame for the current situation in many organizations. The pandemic is causing impacts to be sure, but it's not responsible for all the poor business practices. Current situations are easy scapegoats for hiding problems with traditional business practices.

Organizations need to set long-term goals for comparity, and move incrementally toward those long-term goals, with interim mid-course corrections. That's a goal-oriented culture. The same applies to the professional organizations. They need to promote long-term goals for comparity, and encourage professionals to move away from current hype and toward those long-term goals.

Goals, Understanding, and Operation

Long-term business goals, a thorough business understanding, and business operation have a strong relationship. Establishing long-term business goals requires a thorough business understanding, and a thorough business understanding requires establishing business goals. Neither can be successful without the other.

A Business Understanding Infrastructure that supports the business must begin with an understanding of the business and the data and processes needed to support the business. That understanding requires that the business goals be known, so the understanding supports those business goals. Without knowing the business goals, the understanding may not fully support the organization's business

Knowing the business goals and having a thorough business understanding does not guarantee business agility and success. Business operation plays a key role in moving from business understanding to business success. The best business goals and a thorough business understanding are for naught if the business operation – decisions and actions – is flawed. That's why the Business Understanding Infrastructure includes both business understanding and business operation.

An organization must know the business goals, have a thorough business understanding, and have effective and efficient business operation to be agile and successful. The combination of those three allow an organization to work smarter, rather than harder.

Business Understanding Principle

David Hume identified three principles of understanding. The first principle is resemblance – identifying the similarity between objects and events. The second principle is contiguity – the spatial and temporal proximity of events. The third principle is cause and effect – events must be contiguous in space and time, and cause must be prior to effect.

These three principles are how causality is separated from coincidence. Causality must have a relationship between objects and events, a proximity or closeness in time or space, and a cause prior to an effect.

For example, a woman sneezes in San Francisco and a deadly automobile crash occurs on the New Jersey Turnpike is coincidence. The two situations have no relationship, are not close in time or space, and have no cause prior to effect. However, a person getting hit in the nose with a baseball, and their nose starts bleeding is causal. The two situations have a relationship, are close in space or time, and have a cause prior to an effect.

Law enforcement uses those rules when investigating a crime. Many investigators say, *I don't believe in coincidence.* That statement is made in the context of a possible relationship, a possible proximity in space and time, and a possible cause prior to effect. Those are not the criteria for causality, although further investigation may prove a causality.

The three principles of understanding are useful for many aspects of the Business Understanding and Agility Paradigm. They apply to everything from business niche observation, to thoroughly understanding the business, to creating and maintaining the Business Understanding Infrastructure, to being agile and successfully operating the organization's business.

Quality and Maturity

The Business Understanding and Agility Paradigm has high quality and maturity, and the resulting Business Understanding Infrastructure has high quality and maturity. Quality and maturity go hand-in-hand. High quality cannot exist without maturity, and maturity cannot exist without high quality.

Quality is the degree of excellence; fit for a purpose; meets a high standard. *Maturity* is the state of being mature; being fully developed; having reached the most advanced stage of development.

Quality is related to both form and function. *Form* is the Business Understanding Infrastructure. It's the architecture super-symmetry that contains the business understanding. *Function* is business operation according to that Business Understanding Infrastructure. It's implementation of the architecture super-symmetry to operate the business.

Quality of form is how well the Business Understanding Infrastructure represents the organization understanding of its business niche. *Quality of function* is how well the organization follows the Business Understanding Infrastructure to operate the business.

An organization must have high quality of form to have high quality of function. An organization cannot have high quality of function without high quality of form. But an organization can have high quality of form, but low quality of function. It can have a high-quality Business Understanding Infrastructure, but not be following that Business Understanding Infrastructure to operate the business.

High quality function must be both effective and efficient. *Effective* is doing the right thing. *Efficient* is doing the thing right. Effective is following the Business Architecture Infrastructure. Efficient is how well the Business Architecture Infrastructure is followed.

An interesting twist is that developing the form is a function. If the function to develop the form is not high quality, the form won't be high quality. If the form is not high quality, the function to operate the business according to that form won't be high quality. That's the crux of the problem, and is where most organizations fail.

The longer an organization waits to achieve quality and maturity, the greater the cost of that quality, and the greater the impact on the business. Achieving quality and maturity early requires far less energy, is far less expensive, and has far less impact on business success.

Formality and Practicality

The Business Understanding and Agility Paradigm is both formal and practical. Many people ask: *Why all the formality? Who needs formality? Why not do your own thing and get it done quick? That's being practical!*

Formality is the quality or state of being formal. *Formal* is relating to or involving the outward form, structure, and relationship of elements; according to established form. *Informal* is the lack of formality.

Formality begins at a high level and encompasses current and future concepts, principles, and techniques. It supports a wide variety of scenarios and must use proper terms with comprehensive definitions that are readily understood by everyone involved.

Practicality means in a practical manner. *Practical* is of, relating to, or manifested in practice or action; capable of being put to good use. *Impractical* is not practical; incapable of dealing sensibly or prudently with practical matters.

Any paradigm, concept, method, or technique must be a balance between total formality with little practicality, and total practicality with little formality. As formality increases, practicality is compromised, and as practicality increases, formality is compromised. Formality without practicality is impractical and leads to business stagnation and failure. Practicality without formality is informal and leads to disparity and failure.

Formality and practicality form a continuum. The *formality-practicality continuum* is a range from total formality without practicality, to total practicality without formality.

An organization needs to establish a balance between total formality and total practicality somewhere in the formality-practicality continuum that is optimal for their business. Business agility and success can be impacted by too much formality with too little practicality, and by too much practicality with too little formality. When that balance is established, assisted intelligence can support creation and maintenance of the Business Understanding Infrastructure.

Formality-practicality balance is a point in the formality-practicality continuum that is that is optimal for the organization's business.

Formality evolves over time. At a point in time, a lack of formality is recognized and formality is established. But moving forward in time and looking back often shows a lack of formality and a need for additional formality. That process can be frustrating, but is necessary.

Elegance and Simplicity

The Business Understanding and Agility Paradigm is characterized by elegance and simplicity. *Elegance* is the quality of neatness; pleasingly ingenious; dignified propriety; exhibiting refined form or style. *Simplicity* is easy to understand or do; uncomplicated.

The paradigm follows Albert Einstein's statement that everything should be as simple as possible, and no simpler. It is simple because it is self-consistent, and it is elegant because it is simple. It may be very detailed, but it is elegant and simple.

Elegance and simplicity are related to formality and practicality. Elegance is the formality, and simplicity is the practicality of the paradigm.

Entropy and Energy

The Business Understanding and Agility Paradigm reduces entropy and minimizes the energy necessary to maintain a lower entropy. *Natural entropy* was defined earlier as the entropy the occurs naturally as the business environment, business niche, and organization continually evolve over time. *Created entropy* was defined earlier as the entropy an organization creates by not using contemporary models or formally developing a contemporary architecture.

Natural entropy exists, whether the paradigm is self-consistent or self-inconsistent, and energy is needed to reduce that entropy. Created entropy should be largely eliminated because it's unnecessary, and unnecessary energy is required to resolve that entropy. When the existing disparity is resolved with formal integration, which requires large energy, the only entropy should be natural entropy.

A self-consistent paradigm results in lower created entropy, and requires less energy to maintain that low entropy. A self-consistent paradigm is a low-energy situation. Any self-inconsistent paradigm results in higher created entropy, which requires more energy to reduce that entropy. A self-inconsistent paradigm is a high-energy situation.

Any changes an organization makes to its business niche or its business requires energy. Those changes need to be evaluated to determine the energy required to make the change, which can be evaluated against a return on investment for making those changes. Usually, the energy expended on business change is the cost of staying agile.

ACCEPTANCE AND PERSISTENCE

The best paradigm possible is useless unless it can be instilled in an organization, is accepted and takes hold, resolves problems and provides benefits, and persists over time. Persistence and endurance, mutations, memes, and memeplexes, the Laws of Ecology, the filters against folly, feedback and acceptance, imagination, the web of business, six kinds of scientists, employees and rules, nudge theory, where to begin, an understanding notation, and final thoughts are described below.

Persistence and Endurance

How does an organization make the Business Understanding and Agility Paradigm take hold, become persistent, and endure over time? How does an organization ensure the paradigm endures ongoing trials and tribulations of an organization business, and the onslaught of current hype? Without some mechanism to make the paradigm persist and endure, all the efforts to create the paradigm will have been for naught.

Persistence is a firm course of action; the ability to stay the course; continuing to exist or endure over a prolonged period in spite of opposition, obstacles, or discouragement. *Endurance* is the ability to withstand hardship or adversity; to remain active over a long period of time; to resist adversity.

An organization must choose to accept the Business Understanding and Agility Paradigm and make a paradigm shift. Then the paradigm can be sold based on its features, benefits, and successes over time. When people see the benefits and want to achieve a new paradigm, that paradigm has a much greater chance of being persistent and enduring. Ordering implementation of any new paradigm likely results in failure.

The topics described below help an organization make the paradigm shift.

Mutations, Memes, and Memeplexes

The orientation of the Business Understanding and Agility Paradigm is based on ecology, with the business environment, business niche within that business environment, organizations within that business niche, and organisms within that organization. The business environment evolves as all components interact. The concept of mutations can be used to understand that evolution.

Mutations are random errors in gene copying that cause a small change. Macromutations are mutations with a large impact. Changes in an organization could be viewed as mutations or macromutations. Changes in organisms, such as departing and arriving; ideas from organisms, imagination, fresh ideas and visions, and changes in organism conduct, such as agendas, are mutations or macromutations that affect the organization's evolution.

Organization evolution is a cycle of stress, mutation, and selection. Agility is how well organisms survives in the organization, and how well the organization survives in the business niche. Agility and survival are related to an organization's constant observation of its business niche.

The concept of memes could also be used to understand an organization's evolution. Memes are self-replicating elements of culture that are passed on by imitation. Memes come in two types.

The first type of meme is when a person looks at a picture, sets it aside, and makes a copy. That person passes their copy to another person, who makes a copy. The process continues through numerous people. The successive copies continue to deteriorate in the sense that they don't match the original picture. The mutations accumulate.

The second type of meme is when formal instructions are prepared to build some object. The object may not be made exactly according to the instructions, but the next person is likely to correct the mistake based on the formal instructions. The mutations don't accumulate in the sense that the instructions are self-correcting.

A memeplex is a set of mutually compatible or related memes. Memes are supportive within a memeplex, but are hostile to rival memeplexes. Memes are selected against a population of memes in an organization's meme pool.

Memeplexes are constantly competing in an organization's meme pool. An organization needs to select the best memeplexes for promoting the business understanding and agility. Organizations need to establish an environment where the good memeplexes are prominent, and the hostile memeplexes are not. Organizations need to evaluate good and bad memeplexes, and constantly select the best memeplexes for supporting the Business Understanding and Agility Paradigm.

Laws of Ecology

Barry Commoner identified four basic and inescapable Laws of Ecology to describe the web of life on Earth.

The First Law of Ecology states that everything is connected to something else. Everything is a network of relationships with interconnections and interactions, and one thing can never be done in isolation. Relationships act on one another, have surprising consequences, influence behavior, and have cycles and feedback loops, with constant adjustments for stability and balance. Organisms have accumulated stress, which depends on complexity, and requires constant adjustment. Successful organisms resist greater stress.

The Second Law of Ecology states that everything must go somewhere. It follows the principles of conservation of energy, and that matter is indestructible. It pertains to the relationships between matter and energy, matter–energy conversion, and the states of matter. Nothing is wasted, and where matter and energy go may cause impacts.

The Third Law of Ecology states that nature knows best. Man-made changes are likely to be detrimental, because the extent of all relationships and interactions is not known. The full impact of any change is not known. Random changes are likely to lead to problems or disaster, because the full ramifications of change are not known.

The Fourth Law of Ecology states that there is no such thing as a free lunch. Every gain is won at a cost. No gain is made without a cost, which may be delayed, but is not avoided. What is gained and what is lost by every change must be evaluated.

The First Law of Ecology applies to understanding the organization's business, and creating and maintaining the architecture super-symmetry. The Second Law of Ecology applies to understanding the relationship between entropy and energy. The Third Law of Ecology applies to understanding how the organization operates in its business niche. The Fourth Law of Ecology applies to understanding how the organization changes its business niche or its business.

Filters Against Folly

Garrett Hardin's excellent book *Filters Against Folly* describes three filters to be used against folly relating to ecological problems. The three filters are literacy, numeracy, and ecolacy.

Literacy qualifies things with a description. It uses a written and/or spoken language to provide meaning that is readily understood. It requires a person skilled with words.

Numeracy quantifies things with numbers. It provides quantities, proportions, rates, trends, and so on, that support the literacy.

Ecolacy recognizes that everything is tied to everything else in some manner. It's about complex relationships, and both the short term and long-term impacts of not recognizing those relationships. It's about *then what* after some action is taken, or not taken. Notice that ecolacy is very similar to the First Law of Ecology.

The greatest folly is accepting expert statements uncritically, without question. Other opinions must be sought to find the true picture of reality. All perceptions of the complete world must be determined, which includes observing the organization's business niche, the observer state, and the perceptions gained by the observer.

Agendas often remove or ignore many relationships, which can be very complex. Agendas may appear to clarify and focus, but often leave out or remove something in favor of the agenda. The assumptions, biases, and prejudices in agendas should be thoroughly understood. The best approach is to apply the three filters against folly to any agenda.

Most controversies are resolved by taking a close look at agendas.

Organizations need to carefully look at agendas, because they often lead to folly, and folly leads to tragedy. Looking into agendas directs attention toward substantive issues, and away from personalities and agendas.

The three filters clarify agendas, but also leave something out. Know the filters, what they leave in, and what they leave out. Use the filters to identify the assumptions, biases, and prejudices. Use the seven interrogatives along with the three filters to evaluate all agendas. All three filters must be used to develop a fitness against folly for the Business Understanding and Agility Paradigm to be successful.

Feedback and Acceptance

Feedback about the Business Understanding and Agility Paradigm are very bimodal. Those wanting to make a difference readily accept the paradigm. Those feeling threatened in any way reject the paradigm. Very few responses are in the middle.

A few feedbacks are along the line of: That's a lot of new material to get my head around. The best answer is to explain that the material is new and different, but is a more formal approach to managing data and processes as critical resources. When the paradigm is understood, formal management is much easier and the resulting data and processes support the organization's business.

A few feedbacks criticize the new terms and denotative definitions, particularly in a discipline flooded with terms and definitions. Explain that the new terms with denotative definitions have no connotative meanings, which helps people fully understand and use the paradigm.

When people begin to connect the multitude of traditional terms with weak definitions to the contemporary terms with denotative definitions, they begin to understand the new paradigm. That understanding as a positive trend. A learning curve, to be sure, but a positive trend.

A few feedbacks claim the paradigm is not following or supporting current trends, meaning not following current hype and specific agendas. The simple answer is, "Yes, of course." That simple answer tends to make the person think about the current problems. A lengthy answer tends to make the person resistant to the paradigm.

Acceptance comes from professionals wanting to support clients and customers. Most professionals want more detailed techniques, and are interested in assisted intelligence to perform routine creation and maintenance tasks. Rejection comes from those with specific agendas that are contrary to the organization's agendas and feel threatened by the new paradigm that is contrary to their agendas.

Imagination is the Only Limit

An organization's possibilities and potential for success is only limited by the imagination of its people. The Business Understanding and Agility Paradigm provides the construct for acquiring and documenting business understanding, and using that understanding to be agile and successful. But the employees must provide the imagination to acquire the business understanding and use it to build an organization that is agile and successful.

Imagination requires genius to visualize things, think with their bodies, to transform ideas and patterns into visual ones, to move from illusion to reality, and to explain that reality in a way that others can understand. It requires a combination of internal imagination and external experience.

An excellent book that supports imagination is *Sparks of Genius: The 13 Thinking Tools of the World's Most Creative People*.[1] The 13 tools are summarized below.

Observing: All knowledge begins with observation. All knowledge is acquired through observing and paying attention to what was observed. That's the substantiation for emphasizing ongoing observation of an organization's business niche.

Imaging: Recalling and seeing in the mind, visual thinking and blue-sky thinking, and sensing properties never touched. It includes imagination and portraying images to others in a meaningful way.

Abstracting: Paring down complicated things to simple principles and acronyms, some of which are accepted and some are not accepted. The difficulty is finding an abstraction to fit audience. Many times, the audience is too results-oriented to accept any abstraction. Abstracting is a talent for seeing simplicity in very complex things, seeing the underlying simplicity to a theory. It's the ability to remove the excess to reveal the critical essence.

Recognizing Patterns: The discovery of existing patterns that exist in structures. Being able to recognize existing patterns is the first step to creating new patterns.

Many people don't know the origin of HAL, the computer in Arthur C. Clarke's movie *2001: A Space Odyssey*. Many people think HAL stands for Heuristically programmed ALgorithmic computer. Actually, each letter in HAL is one letter before IBM in the alphabet, but many people didn't see the pattern.

Here's a pattern you should easily recognize. What's the pattern with the letters above the line and below the line?[2]

---

[1] Robert and Michelle Root-Bernstein, New York, Houghton-Mifflin Company, 1999.
[2] The patterns are explained in the Summary at the end of the chapter.

$$\frac{A \quad\quad E \quad\quad I \quad\quad\quad O \quad\quad\quad U}{BCD \quad FGH \quad JKLMN \quad PQRST \quad VWX} \,Y\, Z$$

Here's a second pattern that may be a little more difficult to recognize. What's the pattern with the letters above and below the line?

$$\frac{A \quad\quad EF \quad HI \quad KLMN \quad\quad\quad\quad T \quad VWXYZ}{BCD \quad\quad G \quad J \quad\quad\quad OPQRS \quad U}$$

Here's a third pattern that may be more difficult to recognize. What's the pattern with the letters above and below the line?

$$\frac{A \quad\quad EF \quad HI \quad\quad LMNO \quad\quad RS \quad\quad\quad X}{BCD \quad\quad G \quad JK \quad\quad\quad PQ \quad\quad TUVW \quad YZ}$$

Forming Patterns: Combining simple elements in unexpected ways to form recognizable patterns that represents something meaningful to an audience. Forming patterns usually follows the ability to recognize patterns and show various options with patterns. Some basic examples of forming patterns are Bill Ding, Lincoln Logs®, Tinker Toys®, Erector Set®, Legos®, and so on.

Analogizing: Realizing two apparently different things share important properties or functions, which lies at the heart of most new theories and inventions. An analogy is a correspondence of inner relationship or of function between different phenomenon. It's a similarity of shared properties, a resemblance between things based on observed characteristics, or a relationship between observed properties. Analogies are imperfect, but allow a bridge between the unknown and known.

Body Thinking: Thinking that occurs through sensations and awareness. A person feels ideas emerging, thinks with their whole body, puts themselves there during an event.

Empathizing: Losing yourself in the study and becoming the thing you are creating. Get into another's mind and understand what are they thinking and reasoning, why they are acting, how they produce something. For inanimate objects, what would an electron want to do, what would DNA do to replicate.

Dimensional Thinking: Taking things from a flat plane to three dimensions, four dimensions, or more. Interpreting things in multiple dimensions. Scaling things from a subatomic level to the universe. FORTRAN allows seven dimensions, and theoretical physics allows nine or ten dimensions, but most people can't visualize beyond three or four dimensions.

Modeling: Displaying new patterns and concepts. Developing functional, theoretical, and imaginary models that represent some object or event. What was, is now, or will be, in a variety of forms and notations, suitable to a recipient. Modeling is crucial for creating perspectives to build or portray data and processes architectures.

Playing: Working through a new concept, challenging the limits of a novel idea, playing with an idea, running scenarios, and fooling around to understand and learn something new.

Transforming: Translating between one form of thinking and another, becoming aware of problems, and expressing the solution clearly. It involves transformational thinking, where the more unexpected the transformation, the more likely a surprising insight will result. It's transforming from traditional methods to contemporary methods to move from disparity to comparity,

Synthesizing: Experiencing sensations in multiple ways at the same time. An integration of knowledge to work not serially as in transformational thinking, but simultaneously to understand in a holistic somatic way. It's putting all the associated parts together by first analyzing problems with traditional approaches. It's the ultimate form of emergent understanding, since the route to understanding is often circuitous and indirect. It recognizes that understanding builds on understanding.

Web of Business

The web of life is a set of objects, relationships, and processes linking living things to the physical and chemical environment. It doesn't have the rigor of physics, but it does have generalizations that are evident and were formalized into the four Laws of Ecology. The web of life is the basis for an organization's web of business.

The organization's web of business is a set of components and interactions between those components representing the organization's business. It's a network of relationships with interconnections and interactions that influence behavior and have surprising consequences. It's a set of objects, events, relationships, and rules related to an organization's business, where the current state and an interacting set of probabilities result in a future state. It's a web of causes and effects that is often influenced by human volition.

When an organization understands that web of business, documents that understanding in the Business Architecture Infrastructure, and operates the business according to that understanding, it has established the base for an agile and successful business.

Six Kinds of Scientists

Dr. Bruce West identified four different kinds of scientists in *Where Medicine Went Wrong*. Leapers are like Einstein and Newton who create new paradigms that leap into the future. Creepers investigate findings predicted by existing models that are not yet established. They creep toward proof. Sleepers pass on what they and others have previously learned. Keepers refine and redo experiments of well-known phenomena and existing paradigms, and object to new theories. They keep the status quo.

Two additional kinds of scientists could be added to Dr. West's list. Beepers modify, rearrange, rename, add new terms, and so on, to something that already exists and present it as their own. They are beeping their own horn in an attempt to be a leaper. Peepers make a personal discovery of something that already exists, but is new to them. They think it's great, write about it, and present it as if they were an expert. They are wannabe creepers.

Traditional data management and traditional processes management certainly has a lot of beepers and peepers, with very few leapers and creepers.

The leapers and creepers should take the lead in promoting the Business Understanding and Agility Paradigm. The sleepers, keepers, beepers, and peepers should be leveraged as necessary to understand the Business Understanding and Agility Paradigm, and be encouraged to support the leapers and creepers.

Employees and Rules

An organization has three classes of employees. The first class is employees that operate the business without understanding the business. They are clueless about the business. The second class is employees that understand the business and operate the business accordingly. They are business aware. The third class is employees that understand the business understanding and operate the business accordingly. They are architecture aware.

The employees that take the lead in promoting the Business Understanding and Agility Paradigm should be both business aware and architecture aware.

Many data and processes were developed based on ignorance and denial. They were not engineered according to formal design methods, and are fragile in a dynamic business environment. That fragility limits an organization's agility to respond to changing needs, and may lead to a point-of-no-future.

The disparity with data and processes are the result of both acts of commission and acts of omission. The iatrogenic principle says that the healer should cause no harm, either by what they do or by what they do not do. The healer in this situation is the developer of data and processes. They harm the business by not following the formality for properly managing the organization's data and processes resource.

The employees responsible for creating and maintaining the Business Understanding Infrastructure should be those that follow formal design methods and cause no harm to the organization.

An organization has two broad sets of rules. One set of rules people follow without necessarily understanding the basis for the rules. The other set of rules people follow because they understand the basis for the rules. The basis for all rules in the Business Understanding and Agility Paradigm are made very clear so that employees can understand, accept, and follow those rules.

Nudge Theory

Nudge theory emphasizes slowly nudging people in a new direction. That new direction is toward the Business Understanding and Agility Paradigm. People can be nudged away from bad memeplexes and toward good memeplexes. Slowly nudging people in a new direction goes well with positive results, the aha syndrome, and success motivation. People accept the nudge when they see positive results that support their business activities.

However, nudge theory can be used for three different forms of hype promotion. Positive hype promotion flaunts the benefits of a paradigm for the recipient as well as the promoter. Questionable hype promotion flaunts the benefits of a paradigm for the promoter, which may or may not benefit to the recipient. Negative hype promotion flaunts the benefits of a paradigm for the promoter, but to the detriment of the recipient.

Positive hype promotion needs to be emphasized, while questionable and negative hype promotion need to be discredited or blocked. Questionable and negative hype promotion slowly nudge people toward other paradigms, many of which violate one or more of the Data Resource Laws and Rules, the Processes Resource Laws and Rules, and the Business Understanding Infrastructure Laws and Rules.

Questionable and negative hype promotions nudge people toward the promoter's objectives, according to the promoter's agendas, whether or not the promoter's objectives match the recipient's objectives. Competing hype promotions lead to a nudge battle. Unfortunately, nudge battles occur in many organizations, both from within and from outside the organization, more times and more subtly than most people will ever know.

I have been aware of many nudge battles, and have seen many very devious tactics involved in the, often not so gentle, nudges that include intimidation, coercion, manipulation, and threats. But that's in the realm of conflict management, which is beyond the scope of the current book.

Where to Begin

Okay! I get it! How do I start?

That's the expression I hear from organizations that understand the new paradigm, are impacted by traditional data and processes, and want to make a change.

When an organization buys into the Business Understanding and Agility Paradigm, what does it do first? Where does it begin understanding and gaining control of their business? Knowing where to begin implementing a new paradigm is critical if an organization wants to be successful with that new paradigm,

Steven Covey states, *Begin with the end in mind*. The end is successful business operation. Successful business operation requires business agility, which requires thorough business understanding, which requires creating and maintaining the Business Understanding Infrastructure. An organization starts with the Business Understanding Infrastructure.

The first step is to realize that a paradigm shift involves unweaving the old paradigm and reweaving the new paradigm. The traditional paradigm based on current hype leading to disparity is unwoven and rewoven into the contemporary paradigm that leads to comparity. The self-perpetuating disparity unwoven and rewoven into self-perpetuating comparity.

One risk building the Business Understanding Infrastructure is that people find what they believe to be basic architectures and put those traditional architectures in the Business Understanding Infrastructure. That approach leads to a broken architecture symmetry. Traditional architectures need to be unwoven and rewoven into the Business Understanding Infrastructure.

The second step is to realize the evolution from traditional data management and traditional processes management to combined data and processes resource management. That evolution is:

From traditional data management to data resource management.

From traditional processes management to processes resource management.

From separate data and processes management to combined data and processes resource management.

From style-driven substance to substance-driven style.

From lexical challenge to lexical richness.

From bad hype to good hype.

From technology-driven disparity to technology-assisted comparity.

257

From a disparate culture to a comparate culture.

The third step is to realize the current problems cannot be tackled from the downstream side. Trying to resolve existing disparity with formal integration won't succeed, because created disparity grows faster than formal integration can solve that disparity. The created disparity must be stopped before any formal integration can begin.

The general sequence to shift from a traditional paradigm to the Business Understanding and Agility Paradigm is:

Design the initial Business Understanding Infrastructure.

Start with data, since processes are generally more disparate than data.

Pick a small subject area or a problem subject area for data.

Design the initial Data Resource Guide.

Start understanding and documenting the existing data within single organization-wide data architecture.

Pick a small subject area or problem subject area for processes.

Design the initial Processes Resource Guide.

Start understanding and documenting the existing processes within a single organization-wide processes architecture.

Design a business workflow for the new paradigm.

Continue expanding the Business Understanding Infrastructure.

When an organization gets started, there is seldom any problem identifying additional subject areas. Typically, people see the benefits of the new paradigm and want their subject area to be next.

A few general guidelines help the paradigm shift.

Provide specific examples that are relevant to the organization's business to explain the paradigm. Using examples that are not relevant to the organization's business tend to turn people away from the new paradigm.

Move into the new paradigm incrementally, with mid-course adjustments. No objective is achieved in one try.

People typically know the solution to their own problems. When people thoroughly understand the problem, the solution is usually very clear. Sometimes, a person from outside the organization with low knowledge and high objectivity is needed to help identify to the solution.

The full potential of the Business Understanding and Agility Paradigm remains untapped in most organizations today.

An Understanding Notation

A shorthand understanding notation helps people understand the Business Understanding and Agility Paradigm and explain the paradigm to others. In many cases, the understanding notation works better than lengthy textual descriptions to provide a more visual understanding of the paradigm. A few understanding notations are shown below, with a textual description below the notation.

⌃ Architecture Trinity = {Descriptive = {Names, Definitions}, Structure = {Components, Relations}, Integrity = {Integrity Rules}}

The Architecture Trinity consists of the set containing Descriptive, Structure, and Integrity components. Descriptive consists of Names and Definitions, Structure consists of Components and Relations, and Integrity consists of Integrity Rules

⌃Audience (Contributor) => Model perspective => Architecture symmetry

An Audience contributor provides a model perspective to enhance the architecture symmetry

⌃ Architecture symmetry => Model perspective => Audience (Recipient)

The architecture symmetry provides model perspectives for an audience recipient.

⌃↑ Agility => ↓ Fragility => ↓ Entropy

Increased agility leads to decreased fragility, which leads to decreased entropy

Refer to Appendix D for the meaning of the symbols used in the understanding notations, and a set of understanding notations for the Business Understanding and Agility Paradigm. These understanding notations can be used as shown, or modified to meet a specific organization's need. Additional understanding notations can be created as necessary for people to understand the Business Understanding and Agility Paradigm.

Final Thoughts

Roger Penrose's excellent book *Fashion, Faith, and Fantasy in the New Physics of the Universe* describes the evolution and future of theoretical physics. His *fashion* is fashionable versus unfashionable, a popular trend, a manner of doing something. His *faith* is a belief founded on authority, authority has a strong influence on our thinking, complete confidence in someone or something. His *fantasy* is fantastical, beyond belief, activity of imagining things, especially things that are impossible or improbable/

The title of his book is a most appropriate phrase for the Business Understanding and Agility Paradigm: The faith, fashion, and fantasy of thorough business understanding, agility, and success.

Fashion is the current mode of understanding an organization's business and managing its data and processes that lead to disparity, high entropy, limited agility, and limited success.

Faith is the belief that the Business Understanding and Agility Paradigm will help an organization evolve to a future environment of comparity, low entropy, and business understanding, agility, and success.

Fantasy is the belief that something miraculous and fantastical can happen for an organization to understand its business, achieve agility, and become successful in its business endeavor.

Two guiding thoughts about fantasy. First, the only real failure is not to try. Second, a mistake is absolute proof that somebody tried to do something.

I'll end with a proverb that is as appropriate today as it was when it was written, although in a different context.

For Want of a Nail is a proverb reminding us that apparently unimportant acts or omissions can have grave and unexpected consequences. The full proverb is: *For want of a nail, the shoe was lost. For want of a shoe, the horse was lost. For want of a horse, the rider was lost. For want of a rider, the battle was lost. For want of a battle, the kingdom was lost. And all for the want of a horseshoe nail.*

Does that proverb apply to your organization's business understanding, agility, and success?

SUMMARY

The patterns on Pages 252 and 253 are 1) vowels are above the line and consonants are below the line, with Y being a consonant, but sometimes a vowel; 2) letters above the line are all formed with straight lines, and those below the line have some curved lines; and 3) the letters above the line are prefixed with *an*, and those below the line are prefixed with *a*, when pronouncing the letter.

A data and processes resource culture supports data and processes resource management. That culture must be agile to emphasize that agility is the link between thorough business understanding and business success. The emphasis of the Business Understanding and Agility Culture is to switch from technology-driven culture to culture-driven technology.

The Business Understanding and Agility Paradigm is the right paradigm. It is self-consistent, plausible and relevant, and based on semiotic theory. It is the unified theory for thoroughly business understanding, agile operation, and success.

The Business Understanding and Agility Paradigm is based on long-term goals, thorough business understanding, and effective and efficient business operation. It is based on three principles for business understanding, has quality of form and of function, and ensures that function is both effective and efficient.

The Business Understanding and Agility Paradigm is a balance between formality and practicality. It is elegant and simple, and produces elegant and simple results. It maintains low entropy with minimum energy, by eliminating created entropy and keeping natural entropy to a low level.

The Business Understanding and Agility Paradigm is persistent and endures the adversity of short-term hype in favor of long-term goals. It is based on mutations, memes, and memeplexes, where good memeplexes are selected for promoting the paradigm. It is supported by the Three Laws of Ecology and uses the Filters Against Folly to sort through agendas and select agendas appropriate for the organization's goals.

The Business Understanding and Agility Paradigm relies on imagination as the only limit to an organization's potential, and utilizes the 13 thinking tools to support imagination. It promotes a web of business that constantly changes as components in the business niche interact. The six kinds of scientists are utilized to promote the paradigm. Employees that are both business aware and architecture aware are encouraged to promote the paradigm. The paradigm uses nudge theory and follows the iatrogenic principle of doing no harm.

Making a paradigm shift begins with the end objective of business success. The evolution from traditional to contemporary is outlined, a general sequence of activities is presented, and basic guidelines are presented. A understanding notation for the paradigm is introduced, and final thoughts about fashion, faith, and fantasy for the Business Understanding and Agility Paradigm are presented.

QUESTIONS

The following questions are provided as a review of the Agile Business Culture Chapter, and to stimulate thought about developing and maintaining an agile business culture.

1. Why is an agile business culture necessary?
2. Why should culture drive technology?
3. What is the new paradigm?

4. What is the difference between a self-consistent paradigm and a self-inconsistent paradigm?
5. Why is a new paradigm shift needed?
6. How are hype, goals, and understanding related?
7. How are quality and maturity related?
8. Why do formality and practicality need to be balanced?
9. How are entropy and energy related?
10. What roles do mutations, memes, and memeplexes play in making the paradigm persistent?
11. What are the Laws of Ecology?
12. What are the filters of folly?
13. How is imagination the only limit to an organization's potential for s successful business?
14. What are the 13 tools of imagination?
15. What is the organization's web of business?
16. How are the six kinds of scientists used to promote the paradigm?
17. How are the three classes of employees used to promote the paradigm?
18. How is nudge theory used to promote the new paradigm?
19. How does an organization get started with a new paradigm?
20. How does an understanding notation help people understand the new paradigm?

POSTSCRIPT

As I near the end of his book, and my professional venture, I look back at the memories. Most of the memories are good, but a few are not so good. I focus on the good memories.

I've been praised and received awards, and have been referred as a *Visionary thought leader*. I've also been personally chastised and demeaned in private and in public for my thoughts, ideas, and approaches, mostly by individuals that feel very threatened by what I present. I've also seen many individuals that initially felt threatened, but saw the light and adopted new approaches, leading to business success.

Many people have promoted what I put forth. Many people have copied what I have put forth and modified it into their own agenda. Others have openly criticized what I have put forth in public and in private.

I was at an international conference and presented a new concept about data provenance to track the quality and integrity of data, similar to the provenance of artwork. I had never read or heard about such a term applied to data. The closest term was *data tracking* oriented to identifying the source of data and the flow of data. Several subsequent presentations in the same conference suddenly had the term *data provenance* in their presentations as a new approach to tracking and identifying the quality of data, but no details. Interestingly, *data provenance* was not in the handouts of their presentations. So much for professionalism in data management.

At another international conference, I presented a new diagram about the relationships between various aspects of formal data resource management. The details of the diagram aren't important. A vendor booth that evening had the same material on an easel, with the same terms, in a diagram with a slightly different structure. That diagram was not present in the vendor booth the evening before. A subsequent presentation in the same conference had yet another diagram with the same notation, but in yet another format, claiming it to be a new approach to managing data.

That may be progress, although I'm concerned about not giving credit where credit is due. Maybe that's my academic background. Data resource managements and processes resource management seem to be plagued with rampant plagiarism.

I've met many excellent professionals along the way. Most have welcomed what I have done and encouraged me to continue. A few have been skeptical of my ideas, but wished me the best of luck in what I was trying to accomplish.

I remember one prominent professional I met early in my venture who was working on data reengineering from one database management system to another. He listened very intently to my ideas about formal data resource integration within a common data architecture. When I finished, he said the concept sounded fascinating, but he had no idea how I would ever implement such a concept. I went on to successfully implement formal data resource integration, within an organization-wide data architecture, in several organizations. The process is documented in the Data Resource Simplexity series of books.

I recently saw an ad for a Director of Architecture Development that was relatively local, where I could drive without the hassle of air travel. The title sounded promising, but the description was oriented toward developing and integrating databases, and required many years of experience with several database products. I thought that odd for a director position.

I called them about the description, without letting them know who I was or my experience. The person explained the job in detail, which was basically managing massively disparate databases across multiple database management systems, with new databases coming on a regular basis. He asked if I was interested, because they really needed someone to pull things together with a database architecture. I commented that the job sounded like a Director of Brute-Force Development. After a few harsh words about me not understanding the nature and magnitude of their problem, the conversation ended. As I hung up the phone, I wondered if they understood the nature and magnitude of their problem.

I was contacted by a new government agency that was formed from the merger of several smaller government agencies. The new agency wanted to integrate their data to carry out their new mission and charges. The task sounded interesting and challenging, and I do enjoy challenges. But after further investigation, I found that each former agency had a huge disparity of data. The merger of agencies formed a constellation of data disparities.

I like challenges, but I'm not a masochist. I declined, because I didn't see that task going to end-of-job during my professional venture. I also didn't see the people involved in the integration effort interested in learning new concepts and carrying out the task with a formal data resource architecture integration. I saw they were only interested in merging multiple disparate databases.

These two contacts illustrate the fact that organizations are still operating without formal data resource or processes resource management. Many organizations are still technology-driven rather than business-driven; implementation-driven rather than formality-driven; and short-term oriented rather than long-term driven. Many organizations are still unconcerned about thorough business understanding and successful business operation.

As I write these last pages, we are going through a global pandemic, triggering both a health crisis and an economic crisis. I see a change in the way most organizations could do business, moving well into the information age, and into the near artificial intelligence age. I see the agricultural age school structure begin to move into an information age school structure, and hopefully into the near artificial intelligence structure. I believe students are more up to the change than teachers.

I remember Mark Twain's statement, "Don't let schooling interfere with your education." Change *schooling* to *schools* and you have the current situation: Don't let schools, or the lack thereof, get in the way of education.

I see educators trying to decide how children should learn. I often wonder what would happen if children were asked for input about how they would like to learn, and educators really listened to what they had to offer. The result might be most informative.

All aspects of society are changing as we work through the global pandemic. No segment of society is immune from the impacts of the pandemic. Recovery from the impacts will last for five years or more, until society stabilizes to a new norm. The old norm is gone, never to return. The current norm is one of constant change that will slowly evolve to a new norm.

My parents went through the Spanish Flu as children and lived through the Great Depression. I was born near the end of the Great Depression and grew up in the War Years. My children have been through a few economic slumps and are facing the impact of climate change. My grandchildren are growing up in a global pandemic and living with climate change. I wonder what is waiting for them in the years to come.

The situation gets directly to the topic of agility. Is society agile enough to adapt to rapid and severe changes, like climate change, a global pandemic, raging wildfires, and severe storms? Do organizations thoroughly understand their business well enough to rapidly adapt to change and survive? Can organizations understand dynamic situations and adjust their business to survive those changing situations? Some will, and many won't.

I see a trend toward doing things smarter. Smarter requires a better understanding, and better understanding is based on good data and processes – the facts and the decisions/actions.

I've been on a professional venture for over 60 years, beginning with writing simulation programs in college. I encountered many problems with unclear parameters and algorithms for simulations that were not well understood, and early simulations failed. When those parameters and algorithms were well understood, progress was made toward successful simulations. That scenario was the beginning of my professional venture.

Many people ask what I'll do now. I'll continue outdoor recreation, back-country hiking, biking, cross-country skiing, and kayaking. I'll have the freedom to read, and think, and continue writing children's books. I'll help my boys and grandkids with their projects. I'll enjoy a quiet retired life, but I'll always remember the exciting and challenging professional venture with data and processes resource management.

I'll miss the challenge of meeting with clients, understanding their problems, and helping them solve those problems. However, I definitely will not miss the travel, shuttles, airports, airplanes, rental cars, hotels, restaurants, and so on, that go with the travel. The mountains are far more appealing.

I wish you all the very best in your future endeavors. Keep pushing the frontiers of formal data and processes management ahead. Keep learning and promoting new ideas and concepts. Keep building on the shoulders of others, and giving credit to those that came before you. Keep striving to improve and create a formal profession.

I'll end with mindful optimism – the expectation that good things will happen, if you plan carefully and work hard for them. That's how I feel about the formal management of data and processes as a combined, critical resource to thoroughly understand and successfully operate a business.

I sincerely hope you feel the same way.

Appendix A
COMMON DATA PROBLEMS AND NEEDS

Common Data Problems
Masses of disparate data.

Lack of data understanding.

Lack of data awareness – unknown existence of data.

Low quality data.

Early implementation without formal design - synthesis without analysis.

Business is described in implementation terms.

Business decisions made by technicians at implementation.

Data management is personality oriented, inbred, and not building on the shoulders of others.

Lexical challenge with data management terms.

Lack of formal data names and comprehensive data descriptions in in-house applications and purchased applications.

Technical orientation rather than business orientation.

Focus on current needs while ignoring future needs.

Data modelers forcing their views on clients.

Application vendors forcing their designs on clients.

Data resource design products not robust.

Data management not a formal discipline.

Data management not properly located in organization.

Data names not consistent across all models.

Multiple denormalizations of data.

Common Data Needs
Stop further creation of disparate data.

Resolve existing disparate data.

Increase awareness of data as a critical resource.

Increase data understanding – reduce data uncertainty.

Improve data quality.

Establish proper data resource management terms.

Establish formal data names and comprehensive data definitions for all in-house and purchased applications.

Business drives development of data resource.

Decisions from business before implementation.
Consider both present data needs and future data needs.
Establish formal data resource management discipline.
Incorporate features from other disciplines as necessary.
Determine where data resource management fits in organization.
Improve vendor-client relations.
Can't dictate organization structure – organization's decision.
Can designate skills and sequence of events.
Can't dictate vendor-client relations – professional ethics.
Can set a foundation for formal data resource management.

Appendix B
COMMON PROCESSES PROBLEMS AND NEEDS

Common Processes Problems

Both manual processes and automated processes must be considered.

Both process logic and workflow through organization units must be considered.

Many detailed business decisions are made during process development often without the knowledge of, or any review and approval by, business professionals.

Processes are not thoroughly documented so they can be readily understood and easily revised.

Many processes are known only by a few people in the organization.

No single source exists for the documentation of all processes that anyone in the organization can readily access.

Processes are not formally named, and informal process names are not consistently used across processes and automated systems.

Processes don't use formal data names, and informal data names are not consistently used within or across processes and automated systems.

Working data within processes are not formally named or denotatively defined.

The names, formal or informal, of processes are not used consistently across all process models.

The business specifications and vendor product generation specifications for processes are lost, discarded, or not kept current with development.

Processes are not developed within a single processes architecture

Many processes are redundant, often competing, and often have slightly different logic.

Processes have flawed logic and/or flow.

Processes frequently don't have any design oriented toward the business.

Design specifications for processes are often in a form used for development and implementation.

Development of processes often begins with a conceptual design and jumps to development and implementation.

The change history for processes is not consistently tracked and documented.

Processes are tightly coupled with their own unique databases

Processes and data are not formally managed together.

Processes management terms are weak and poorly defined.

The management of processes is informal and is not built on the shoulders of others.

The development of processes is often based on hype and initial apparent successes, without knowledge of initial failures or long-term impacts.

Many business rules are documented with the data, rather than with the processes.

Purchased applications seldom fully meet client needs as specified.

Clients are often forced into predesigned purchased applications.

Common Processes Needs

Process decisions need to be made during business process design.

Process decisions need to include input from business professionals.

Process decisions need to be reviewed and approved by business professionals before process development.

Business rules need to be appropriately located with processes and data.

Business process design needs to be oriented toward the business.

Business process design specifications need to be readily understandable by business professionals.

Business process design specifications and system generations specifications need to be kept up to date.

Business process design specifications need to be retained for future reference.

Process design and development need to follow a formal design and development cycle from business understanding through implementation.

Processes need to be thoroughly documented.

Process documentation needs to be readily understood by anyone in the organization.

Process documentation needs to be maintained in one location and be readily available to anyone in the organization.

Processes need to be managed within the single organization-wide processes architecture.

The processes architecture and the data architecture need to remain independent of each other during design.

Processes need to have formal business and implementation names.

Formal business and implementation process names need to be used consistently across all processes and all process models.

Process names in purchased applications need to be cross-referenced to the organization's formal process names.

Processes need to be denotatively defined.

Processes need to have a formal set of process integrity rules.

The orthogonal structure of processes and data need to be maintained up to physical development.

Implementation development of processes and data needs to be coordinated.

Appendix C
FIVE-SCHEMA CONCEPT

Figure C.1 shows the relationship between the Five-Schema Concept described in the Data Resource Simplexity series, and the Data Resource Cycle. The top of the diagram shows a counter-clockwise cycle starting with the Business Niche at the top center. The Observe Phase leads to Preliminary Data, through the Realize Phase to Business Data, through the Formalize Phase to Proper Data, through the Customize Phase to Implement Data, and though the Utilize Phase to Operational Data that support the Operate Phase in the Business Niche.

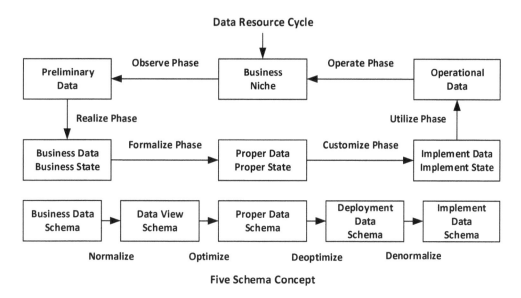

Figure C.1. Five-Schema Concept and Data Resource Cycle.

The bottom of the diagram shows the Five-Schema Concept beginning on the left with Business Data Schema, progressing to Data View Schema, to Proper Data Schema, to Deployment Data Schema, and to Implement Data Schema. The Data Resource Cycle and the Five-Schema Concept match with the Business Data, Proper Data, and Implement Data.

When the Five-Schema Concept was first defined, which was before the Data Resource Cycle was defined, the Business Data Schema are normalized to Data View Schema, which are optimized to Proper Data Schema in an organization-wide data architecture.

The tradition at that time was *logical data*, which was used for the organization-wide data architecture. That term has since been changed to Proper Data in the organization-wide data architecture.

The Proper Data Schema are deoptimized to Deployment Data Schema, which are denormalized to Implement Data Schema for different operating environments. Deoptimization is the process that can create multiple Implement Data Schema from the single Deployment Data Schema, depending on the intended operating environment.

The tradition at that time was *physical data*, which was used for the operational data. That term has since been changed to Implement Data for implementation and operation.

Appendix D
UNDERSTANDING NOTATION

A shorthand notation helps people understanding the Business Understanding and Agility Paradigm, and explain that paradigm to others. These understanding notations are a quick and convenient way to understand the paradigm without long textual statements. People can readily understand the paradigm in less time with a shorthand notation.

Examples of the understanding notations are shown below. However, this is not a compendium of all possible understanding notations. Organizations can create understanding notations and use them as they see fit to explain the Business Understanding and Agility Paradigm.

The symbols used in the understanding notation are shown below. The symbols are not formal math symbols, statistical symbols, or logic symbols. They are symbols used to help understand the paradigm. Words can also be used in the notations as necessary.

⋏	identifies an understanding notation
→	*yields, produces, leads to*
←	*requires, mandatory for*
↑	*increases, increased*
↓	*decreases, decreased*
↔	*the range from – to, between*
!	*caution, beware*
¬	*not, does not, no, none*
?	*to question, ask*
∴	*therefore,* or *conclusion*
=	*equal to, equals*
≠	*not equal, does not equal*
<	*less than*
>	*greater than*
+	*add, plus* (mathematical)
&	*and* (non-mathematical)
{ }	*a set containing*
=>	*progression, sequence, provides*
<=>	interact with
∨	*supported by, characterized by*

^   *supports, maintains, characterizes*

The understanding notations are shown below. They can be used as shown, or can be modified to be more meaningful to the audience. Additional notations can be prepared as necessary. However, don't go overboard creating a plethora of symbols and notations that confuse people and turn them away from the paradigm. The symbols and notations are intended to draw people into the paradigm by helping them understand the paradigm.

Problems and Needs:

⌃ TDM = Traditional Data Management

⌃ TDM Problems = {Lexical challenge, Style-driven substance, Bad hype, Technology-driven disparity}

⌃ DRM = Data resource Management

⌃ DRM Needs = {Lexical richness, Substance-driven style, Good hype, Technology-assisted comparity}

⌃ TPM = Traditional processes management

⌃ TPM Problems = {Inappropriate business decisions, Inadequate business rules, Unacceptable design and development, Informal data and processes names, Incomplete processes documentation}

⌃ PRM = Processes resource management

⌃ PRM Needs = {Appropriate business decisions, Adequate business rules, Acceptable design and development, Formal data and processes names, Complete processes documentation}

⌃ Fundamental problems = {Data & processes = {Separate resources, ¬ critical resources, management ¬ integrated, ¬ vision}}

⌃ Fundamental needs = {Data and processes {Unite resources, Critical resources, Resource Management, Resource Culture, Understanding vision}}

Business Understanding

⌃ Ecological perspective = {Business environment => Business niche => Organization}

⌃ Business Niche Cycle = Business niche => Understand Phase => Operate Phase => Business Niche

⌃ Business Understanding Sequence = Business environment => Business niche => Preliminary data and processes => Data and processes architecture => Data and processes

⌃ Business Cycle = {Business Niche Cycle, Data Resource Cycle, Processes Resource Cycle}

⤷ Business functions = {Understand Business Function, Operate Business Function}

Data Resource Management:

⤷ Data Resource Management = {Data Resource Method, Data Resource Method Objective, Data Resource Cycle, Data schema, Data Resource Data, Data Resource Laws, Data Resource Rules}

⤷ Data Resource Method Objective = {Right data, Right people, Right place, Right time, Right form, Right cost}

⤷ Data Resource Cycle = {Initial State = {Preliminary Data} => Realize Phase => Business State = {Business Data} => Formalize Phase => Proper State = {Proper Data} => Customize Phase => Implement State = {Implement Data} => Data Keep => Utilize Phase = {Operational Data}}

⤷ Data schema = {Business Schema, Data View Schema, Proper Data Schema, Deployment Data Schema, Construct Schema}

⤷ Data Resource Data <=> {Understand Phase, Realize Phase, Formalize Phase, Utilize Phase, Operate Phase}

⤷ Data Resource Laws = {First Law (Identification), Second Law (Normalization), Third Law (Denormalization)}

⤷ Data Resource Rules = {12 Rules}

Processes Resource Management:

⤷ Processes Resource Management = {Processes Resource Method, Processes Resource Method Objective, Processes Resource Cycle, Processes Resource Data, Processes Resource Laws, Processes Resource Rules}

⤷ Processes Resource Method Objective = {Right processes, Right people, Right place, Right time, Right decisions, Right actions}

⤷ Processes Resource Cycle = {Initial State = {Preliminary Processes} => Realize Phase => Business State = {Business Processes} => Formalize Phase => Proper State = {Proper Processes} => Customize Phase => Implement State = {Implement Processes} => Processes Keep => Utilize Phase = {Operational Processes}}

⤷ Processes Resource Data <=> {Understand Phase, Realize Phase, Formalize Phase, Utilize Phase, Operate Phase}

⤷ Processes Resource Laws = {First Law (Identification), Second Law (Normalization), Third Law (Denormalization)}

⤷ Processes Resource Rules = {12 Rules}

Business Niche:
> ⮭ Business niche components = {Objects, Events, Relationships, Rules, Features, Actors, Triggers, Responses}

Business Niche Observation:
> ⮭ Business Niche Observation Cycle = {Business Niche => Discover Phase => Possibility State => Comprehend Phase => Actuality State = {Mental vision} => Chronicle Phase => Mental Model State = {Mental model} => Consensus Phase => {Data Resource Initial State, Processes Resource Initial State}
> ⮭ Business Niche Scoping = {Observation scoping = {Business Niche Segment}, Data and processes scoping = {May be of interest, Are of interest, May be relevant, Are relevant}}
> ⮭ Observer problems = {Unsure of interest / relevance, Self-fulfilling prophecy, Erroneous perceptions = {Illusion, Omission, Hallucination}, Structure distinction}

Interrogatives:
> ⮭ Interrogative roles = {Ongoing queries for understanding, Identify data and processes, Identify business activity}
>
> ⮭ Traditional interrogatives = {What, How, When, Where, Who, Why}
> ⮭ Traditional primary interrogative = What
> ⮭ Traditional associate interrogatives = {How, When, Where, Who, Why}
>
> ⮭ Contemporary interrogatives = {Which, What, How, When, Where, Who, Why}
> ⮭ Principle contemporary interrogative = Which
> ⮭ Associate contemporary interrogatives = {What, How, When, Where, Who, Why}
>
> ⮭ Which = Business activity designation
> ⮭ What = Business activity description
> ⮭ How = Data and Processes
> ⮭ When = Time component of space-time
> ⮭ Where = Location component of space-time
> ⮭ Who = Participants / Actors
> ⮭ Why = Motivation / Justification
>
> ⮭! Traditional interrogative What ≠ Data
> ⮭ Contemporary interrogative What = Business activity description
>
> ⮭! Traditional interrogative How ≠ Processes
> ⮭ Contemporary interrogative How = Data & Processes

Frameworks:

⚑Traditional Framework dilemmas = {How Dilemma, What Dilemma, Topic Dilemma}

⚑ Business Understanding Framework = {Business activity = {Which}, Framework interrogatives = {What, How, Where, When, Who, Why}, Specification level}

Architectures and models:

⚑Contemporary Architecture = {Persistent & {Descriptive, Structure, Integrity} & ¬ {Format, Notation}}

⚑Contemporary Model = {Transient & Architecture subset & {Format, Notation}}

⚑Architecture Trinity = {Descriptive = {Names, Definitions}, Structure = {Components, Relations}, Integrity = {Integrity Rules}}

Model-driven architectures:

⚑Contributor Audience => Model perspective => Architecture symmetry

Architecture-driven models:

⚑Architecture symmetry => Model perspective => Recipient Audience

⚑Model configuration parameters = {Notation, Form, Style, Phase, Scope, Tier, Content}

Architecture symmetries:

⚑Architecture symmetries = {Business environment symmetry, business niche symmetry, contemporary symmetry.

Overarching Construct & Underlying Foundation:

⚑Contemporary business tiers = {Business Resource Tier, Business Support Tier, Business Operation Tier}

⚑Business Resource Tier = {Data Resource Segment, Processes Resource Segment, Human Resource Segment}

⚑Business Support Tier = {Data Flow Segment, Business Rules Segment, Business Understanding Framework Segment, State Transition Segment, Business Workflow Segment, Event-State Segment, other segments}

⚑Business Operation Tier = {Business activities}

⚑Underlying Foundation = {Theory, Concepts, Principles, Techniques}

Business Understanding Infrastructure:

⚑Business Understanding Infrastructure = {Architecture super-symmetry, Model super-perspective, Business Understanding

⮽ Infrastructure Laws = {5 Laws}, Business Understanding
Infrastructure Rules = {12 Rules}}
⮽ Create & Maintain = {NeedSpec = {Observe => Understand =>
Design}} => {ConOps = {Construct => Deploy => Operate}} =>
Business Success

Paradigm and Culture:

⮽ Business Understanding and Agility Paradigm = {Data and Processes
Resource Management, Data and Processes Resource Culture}

⮽ Critical Resources = {Data and Processes, People, Finances, Real
property, Offerings}

⮽ Filters Against Folly = {Literacy, Numeracy, Ecolacy}

⮽ Four Laws of Ecology = {Everything is connected to something,
Everything must go somewhere, Nature knows best, No free lunch}

⮽ Negative feedback → ↑ Control → ¬{Paralysis-by-analysis, Brute-
force development}

⮽ Positive feedback → ↓ Control → {Paralysis-by-analysis, Brute-force
development}

⮽ Business Understanding Infrastructure → {↑Understanding,
↓Uncertainty, ↓Disparity, ↓Entropy}

⮽ ! ↑ Paralysis-by-analysis → Reactive Brute-force development

⮽ ! ↑ Brute-force Development → Reactive Paralysis-by-analysis

⮽ Brute-force development → ↑Disparity & ↓Agility

Entropy, order, and energy:

⮽ Entropy = {Natural Entropy, Created Entropy}

⮽ ↑ Entropy = ↓ Order, ↑Disorder

⮽ Entropy = ↑ Order, ↓Disorder

⮽ Entropy ← Energy

⮽ Dynamic business niche → ↑Created Entropy

⮽ {Effective, Efficient} => ↓Entropy

⮽ ↓Entropy => ↑Agility => ↑Quality => ↑Maturity

⮽ Business Understanding Infrastructure → ↓ Entropy

⮽ ↑Entropy → ↓Order → ↑Disparity

⮽ ↑Order → ↓Entropy → ↑Comparity

Agility and fragility:

⮽ Agility ← Business Understanding Infrastructure

⮽ Disparity → Fragility

⮽ ↑ Agility → ↓ Fragility = ↓ Entropy

⮽ ↓ Agility → ↑ Fragility = ↑ Entropy

    ▲ Disparity → ↑Entropy
    ▲ Comparity → ↓Entropy
    ▲ Comparity → Agility
    ▲ ↑Disparity → ↓Agility
    ▲ ↓ Disparity → ↑ Agility

Understanding:
    ▲ Principles of Understanding = {Resemblance, Contiguity, Cause and Effect}
    ▲ ↑Understanding → ↓Disparity
    ▲ ↓Understanding → ↑Disparity
    ▲ ↑Disparity → ↓Understanding
    ▲ ↓Disparity → ↑Understanding
    ▲ ↑Understanding → ↑Comparity → ↑Agility
    ▲ Business Understanding Infrastructure → ↑Understanding & ↓Uncertainty
    ▲ Quality = {↑Understanding, ↑Comparity, ↑Agility}

Knowledge and objectivity:
    ▲ ↑Knowledge → ↓ Objectivity
    ▲ ↓Knowledge → ↑ Objectivity

Formality and practicality:
    ▲ {Formality, Practicality} => Quality
    ▲ {Informality, Impracticality} ¬ => Quality
    ▲ ! Rampant formality → Paralysis-by-analysis
    ▲ ! Rampant practicality → Brute force development

Business change rate:
    ▲ Business Understanding Infrastructure > Business change rate => Business success
    ▲ Business Understanding Infrastructure = Business change rate => Status quo business
    ▲ Business Understanding Infrastructure < Business change rate => Business failure

Form and function
    ▲ Form = Business Understanding Infrastructure
    ▲ Function = Business operation ← Business Architecture Infrastructure
    ▲ Function = Effective & Efficient
    ▲ Form quality = How well Business Understanding Infrastructure *represents* Understanding

⏶ Function quality = How well organization *follows* Business Understanding Infrastructure

Organization entropy and organization success:

⏶ Organization entropy < Business niche entropy → Organization success

⏶ Organization entropy = Business niche entropy → Organization status quo

⏶ Organization entropy > Business Niche entropy → Organization failure

⏶ Elegance ↔ Simplicity

⏶ Semiotic Theory = {Syntax, Semantics, Pragmatics}

⏶ Three realities = {External reality, Observer reality, Internal reality}

⏶ Kinds of scientists = {Leapers, Creepers, Sleepers, Keepers, Beepers, Peepers}

⏶ Business Understanding Infrastructure ← {Leapers and Creepers}

⏶ Classes of employees = {Clueless, Business aware, Architecture aware}

⏶ Business Understanding Infrastructure ← {Business aware, Architecture aware}

GLOSSARY

The Glossary contains all formal definitions in the current book. It does not include formal definitions from any previous books. Some of the definitions may be slightly different from previous books, but that's the nature of formality. Comprehensive definitions evolve as the understanding evolves.

Several fonts and notations are used in the Glossary. Those fonts and notations are:

Italic font represents generally definitions.

Bold italic font represents formal definitions.

Bold font represents unacceptable terms.

BOLD ITALIC FONT represents formal term abbreviations.

Underscored words or terms mean that word or term is defined elsewhere in the Glossary.

See: at the end of a definition lists more appropriate words or terms.

See also: at the end of a definition lists related words and terms.

A hyphen typically sorts after a blank. However, terms are sorted alphabetically ignoring the hyphen-blank sequence for easy location

Abstract means less detail, within the same scope. See: *Detailed.*

An ***action*** is an act of will, a thing accomplished, a set of steps or tasks.

An ***actor*** is an object that plays a role or participates in events. See: *Object.*

The ***Actuality State*** represents data-in-context and processes-in-context actualities that *are of interest* to the organization. It is intermediate between the Comprehend Phase and the Chronicle Phase of the Business Niche Observation Cycle.

Agile is able to move quickly and easily, able to think and understand quickly, energetic, flexible, adaptable, iterative, and evolving.

Agile business culture is an organization mindset to achieve business agility, based on thorough business understanding, that is created and maintained in the Business Understanding Infrastructure, and leads to business success.

Agility is the quality or state of being agile.

Architecture is the art, science, or profession of designing and building structures. It is the structure or structures as a whole, such as the frame, heating, plumbing, wiring, and so on, in a building. It's the style of structures and method of design and construction, such as roman or colonial architecture. It's the design of a system perceived by people, such as the architecture of the solar system.

The *architecture component version* is a <u>chronology stamp</u> placed on each datum documenting an architecture component whenever that datum is added, changed, or deleted.

Architecture data are any data necessary to define the <u>contemporary architecture</u> for containing the business data and business processes, such as <u>data resource data</u> and <u>processes resource data</u>.

The *Architecture-Driven Model Objective* is to prepare <u>contemporary models</u> from <u>contemporary architectures</u>, for any scope of the business, at any level of detail, at any time, in any form, for any audience, so they can thoroughly understand the business and successfully operate the business.

Architecture-driven models is a technique that prepares <u>contemporary models</u> by retrieving details from a <u>contemporary architecture</u>, for any scope of the business, and presenting those details to the intended audience using appropriate model presentation techniques. See: *Model-driven architecture*.

An *architecture infrastructure* is the <u>infrastructure</u> for a set of related architectures that represent some aspect of an organization's business. It contains both intra-architecture relations and inter-architecture relations.

Architecture non-separability is a contemporary principle that the <u>architecture symmetry</u> remains intact and evolves with the organization's business niche. Multiple, often overlapping, perspectives can be taken without impacting the architecture symmetry.

Architecture processes are any processes necessary to identify and define the <u>contemporary architecture</u>, and to develop the contemporary architecture for containing the business data and business processes based on those architecture processes, such as the <u>Data Resource Cycle</u> and <u>Processes Resource Cycle</u>.

An *architecture segment* is a portion of an organization's <u>contemporary architecture</u> that represents a major segment of business understanding, such as the data resource, processes resource, <u>Business Understanding Framework</u>, and so on. Each contemporary architecture segment contains data representing that segment of business understanding.

The ***architecture segment version*** is a <u>chronology stamp</u> placed on the architecture segment whenever any component in that architecture segment has been added, changed, or deleted.

Architecture separability is a principle that parts of an object can be removed, considered on their own, and replaced without any loss of features.

Architecture super-symmetry is the <u>super-symmetry</u> across a set of related architectures.

Architecture symmetry is the <u>symmetry</u> of an architecture.

The ***Architecture Trinity*** is the three components for thoroughly understanding contemporary architectures; specifically, a descriptive component, a structural component, and an integrity component. See also: ***Trinity***

Are of interest means additional understanding of components in the organization's business niche contain data and processes that are definitely of interest to the organization. See also: *Are relevant, May be of interest, May be relevant.*

Are relevant means that data and processes have been determined to be relevant to the organization's business operation. See also: *Are of interest, May be of interest, May be of interest.*

Assisted Intelligence is the appropriate use of technology to assist human intelligence in the performance of tasks, specifically the creation and maintenance of the Business Understanding Infrastructure. It supports the shift from <u>technology-driven disparity</u> to <u>technology-assisted comparity</u>.

An ***associate contemporary interrogative*** is any of the other six contemporary interrogatives – What, How, Where, When, Who, and Why – that support or clarify the contemporary primary interrogative Which.

An ***automated process*** is a process performed by computers, or other mechanical or electronic devices, with minimal or no involvement of people.

Bad hype is hype that avoids any formality in order to achieve the results intended by the hype promoter. It usually ignores future needs in favor of current needs desired by the hype promoter. Bad hype is fueled by the lexical challenge and supports style-driven substance. See also: ***Hype, Good hype.***

A ***basic need*** is a need that when achieved resolves one or more basic problems. See also: ***Common need, Fundamental need, Specific need.***

A ***basic problem*** is an elemental problem causing one or more specific problems in one or more organizations. Resolving a basic problem, resolves associated specific problems and their associated symptomatic problems. See also: ***Common problem***, ***Fundamental problem***, ***Specific problem***, ***Symptomatic problem***.

Broken architecture symmetry is the existence of multiple, disparate, competing, conflicting, incomplete, or unclear architecture components that result in decreased understanding and increased uncertainty about the organization's business. See Also: ***Broken model perspective***.

Broken model perspective is the use of traditional models, rather than contemporary models, to build and enhance a comparate architecture, resulting in a broken architecture symmetry. See also: ***Broken architecture symmetry***.

Brute-force development is any action that bypasses or circumvents one or more phases in the formal Data Resource Cycle or Processes Resource Cycle. It's any action that jumps to a different state, or ignores the Data Resource Laws and Rules or the Processes Resource Laws and Rules.

Business replaces the term *logical* for managing data and processes.

A business activity is a set of related business processes. Business activities form a hierarchy from the entire organization to the most detailed level an organization wants to document.

The ***business activity dimension*** of the Business Understanding Framework represents a hierarchy of the organization's business activities, from the organization at large to the most detailed business activity the organization chooses to document.

Business activity process identifies the business processes used by a business activity, and the business activities that use a business process.

Business activity unit is the use of one business activity in the business activity hierarchy by one organization unit in the organization unit hierarchy.

Business agility is the state of an organization being agile in its business understanding and operation.

Business architecture is any architecture about an organization's business in the business realm.

Business climate is acceptable and goes well with business environment. See also: ***Business environment***.

The ***Business Cycle*** is an integration of the Business Niche Cycle, the Data Resource Cycle, and the Processes Resource Cycle with Organization as the focus. The organization understands its business niche, determines the data and processes needed to operate in that business niche, and operates its business according to those data and processes.

Business data are any data currently being used, will be used, or might be used that *are relevant* to the organization's business.

Business-driven means the organization's motivation drives the understanding of its business niche, which is documented in the data and processes resource. The organization's operation in its business niche is supported by the data and processes resource.

The ***Business-Driven Motto*** is the combined data and processes resource is of the business, by the business, and for the business. Development of the combined data and processes resource is driven by the business.

The ***Business-Driven Rationale*** is the degree to which an organization understands their business and develops a comparate data and processes resource equals the degree to which the organization is successful in that business.

A ***business entity*** is any person, place, thing, concept, or event that goes through a life cycle of entity states from an initiating state to a terminating state.

Business entity state identifies a specific state in the life cycle of a business entity that progresses from the initial state, through one or more interim states, to a terminal state, or references a more detailed state transition set.

Business entity state transition is the movement of a business entity from one entity state to another, or back to the same entity state, based on a business process decision.

Business entity state type identifies the entity state as an initiating state, an interim state, a terminating state, or a reference to a more detailed state transition set.

The ***business environment*** is the total of all business activities, everywhere, including commercial, industrial, scientific, environmental, education, and so on; that involves goods, services, research, and so on; conducted by large or small organizations, or individuals; whether for profit or not for profit. See also: Business climate.

Business environment architecture symmetry is the <u>architecture symmetry</u> of the <u>business environment</u> with its complex set of interacting components at a point in space-time. It has a wide scope and an organization has a limited understanding of the symmetry. See also: ***Business niche architecture symmetry***.

Business environment understanding is the organization's first level of understanding about the multitude and complexity of the interacting components in the business environment.

A *business framework* is a graphical representation of an organization's business that helps the organization thoroughly understand and manage its business activities.

Business framework data are any data necessary for thoroughly describing and understanding the construct of an organization's Business Understanding Framework.

The *business function association* is the interconnected relationship between the Understand Business Function and the Operate Business Function.

The *business information demand* is an organization's continuously increasing, constantly changing, need for current, accurate, integrated information, often on short notice or very short notice, to support its business activities.

Business information management is the formal management of general information and specific information to support an organization's business information demand.

A *business model* is a model of any architecture in the business realm. See also: *Non-business model*.

A *business moment* is a point in space-time, or the span of space-time, an organization conducts its business activities. It's a snapshot of business activities at a point in space-time or over a span of space-time.

The *business niche* is a subset of the business environment where an organization chooses to operate its business.

Business niche architecture symmetry is the architecture symmetry of the organization's business niche with its complex set of interacting components, at a point in space-time. It's a subset of the business environment architecture symmetry that *may be of interest* to the organization and the organization has a greater understanding of the symmetry. See also: *Business environment architecture symmetry*.

The *Business Niche Component State* is the set of features for a business niche component at a point in space-time or over a span of space-time.

The *business niche components* are objects, events, relationships, and rules. Business niche components are defined by a set of features.

The *Business Niche Cycle* is a cycle between the organization and its business niche. The organization understands its business niche, and operates in that business niche according to the understanding gained, and the organization's goals and objectives.

Business niche observation is the act of observing the organization's business niche, at a point in space-time or over a span of space-time, discovering components that may be of interest to the organization, understanding those components, and identifying data and processes that *may be relevant* to the organization. It's a snapshot of the business niche state during the observation moment.

The ***Business Niche Observation Cycle*** is a cycle of states and phases, where the organization's business niche is observed at a point in space-time or over a span of space-time. Possible data and processes that *may be of interest* are identified, scoped down to actual data and processes that *are of interest*, and integrated to preliminary data and processes that *may be relevant*. The preliminary data and processes feed the Data Resource Cycle and Processes Resource Cycle.

A ***business niche observer*** is one who observes the business niche to discover business niche components that may be of interest, understand those components, and identify and document data and processes that *may be relevant* to the organization.

The ***Business Niche Operate Phase*** is a phase of the Business Niche Cycle. An organization retrieves business processes, and stores and retrieves data as necessary to conduct its business activities.

Business niche reality. See: ***External reality***, ***Internal reality***.

The ***business operation architecture infrastructure*** is a set of individual business activity architectures unique to each organization's data and processes that operate their specific business.

Business niche scoping designates an organization's business niche within the business environment, consisting of components that *are of interest* to the organization based on its intended business, and that the organization can comprehend.

A ***business niche segment*** is a set of business niche components that are of interest to the organization, such as for business niche observation.

A ***business niche state*** is the set of all objects, events, relationships, rules, and features in the business niche at a point in space-time.

The ***Business Niche Understand Phase*** is a phase of the Business Niche Cycle. An organization regularly observes its business niche to gain insight about the business niche, to confirm or adjust its business niche within the overall business environment, and to adjust its business activities to successfully operate in that business niche.

Business niche understanding is the organization's second level of understanding about its business niche within the business environment, that contains a smaller set of interacting components which *may be of interest* or *are of interest* to the organization.

The ***business operation infrastructure*** is a set of individual business activity architectures unique to each organization's data and processes that operate their specific business.

The ***Business Operation Tier*** is the third tier of the contemporary business construct containing all the business activities an organization needs to successfully operate its business.

Business processes are any processes currently being used, will be used, or might be used that *are relevant* to an organization's business

Business process component identifies the <u>elemental process</u> or <u>combined process</u> that is combined with an existing elemental process or combined process to form a larger business process.

Business process connection represents the connection between two business processes.

Business process connection type identifies the type of connection between business processes, such as In-line, Called, and so on.

Business process logic connection is a connection between a business process action set and a business process decision.

Business process type identifies the level of the resulting business process in the sequence from elemental business process to the highest-level abstraction of business process.

The ***business realm*** is the sphere or extent of business activities which organizations manage. It includes all business activities, such as finance, human resource, manufacturing, medical procedures, marketing, scientific research, education, information, and so on, over which an organization has control. See also: ***Non-business realm***.

A ***business regulation*** is any law, regulation, decree, order, mandate, dictate, directive, policy, guideline, and so on, that controls, regulates, or guides an organization's business and supports a business rule. It could be internal or external to the organization, and could describe a provenance of decisions and actions leading to the business rule.

The *business resource architecture infrastructure* is a set of two architectures for the organization's data resource and processes resource.

The *Business Resource Tier* is the top tier of the contemporary business construct consisting of two segments for the data resource and the processes resource.

A *business rule* is a set of one or more conditions, criteria, requirements, restrictions, or constraints placed on an organization's business to ensure the quality and integrity of the business.

The *Business Rules Segment* is a segment of the Business Support Tier that contains the detail about business rules for data and for processes.

Business rule source identifies a single business regulation supporting a single business rule.

The *business support architecture infrastructure* is a set of individual business support architectures, connected by common data entities, that form an interconnected architecture infrastructure.

The *Business Support Tier* is the second tier of the contemporary business construct containing segments for tools and techniques that support business understanding and business operation.

The *Business Understanding and Agility Paradigm* is data and processes resource management, supported by a data and processes resource culture, to create and maintain the Business Understanding Infrastructure for an organization, so the organization can be agile and successful in its business.

Business Understanding Infrastructure Laws are laws that guide formal Business Understanding Infrastructure development, and ensure the integrity and quality of the organization's business understanding and operation.

Business Understanding Infrastructure Rules are rules that guide formal development and enhancement of the Business Understanding Infrastructure, and ensure the integrity and quality of the organization's business understanding and operation. They support the Business Understanding Infrastructure Laws.

The *Business Understanding Framework* is the construct for a complete, integrated, thorough understanding of the organization's business. It's a three-dimensional framework with dimensions for business activity, framework interrogative, and specification detail.

The *Business Understanding Framework Objective* is to provide a construct for an organization to thoroughly understand all of its business activities, to whatever level of detail desired, so it can be agile and successful in its business operation.

The ***Business Understanding Framework Segment*** is a segment of the Business Support Tier that contains the detail about the Business Understanding Framework.

The ***Business Understanding Infrastructure*** is the single, organization-wide, contemporary architecture infrastructure for an organization's business understanding, so the organization can thoroughly understand its business, be agile, and successfully operate its business.

The ***Business Understanding Infrastructure Objective*** is to provide an overarching architectural construct that supports the two major business functions to understand the business and to operate the business. It leads to a common understanding context that anyone in any public or private sector organization can use to carry out their business activities.

The ***Business Understanding Sequence*** is a series of five levels of an organization's understanding from business environment understanding, to business niche understanding, to preliminary data and processes understanding, to data and processes architecture understanding, to data and processes understanding.

The ***Business Understanding Vision*** is an overarching construct for business understanding and agility, supported by an underlying foundation of theories, concepts, principles, and techniques to create and maintain that overarching construct.

The ***Business Understanding Workflow*** is a seamless business workflow to create and maintain the Business Understanding Infrastructure. It includes all NeedSpec and ConOps activities from observing the business niche, the entire sequence of activities for observing the organization's business niche, identifying business needs, design specifications to meet those business needs, constructing a solution according to the design specifications, deploying that solution, and operating that solution to support the organization's business operation.

Business universe should be avoided, because it is oriented to space and astronomy. See: ***Business environment***.

A ***business workflow*** is a flow of work through a set of subordinate business processes for a parent business process which are initiated or performed by an organization unit. A preceding business process triggers a subsequent business process in the workflow.

292

Business workflow process is the use of a business process in the workflow of a business workflow set.

Business workflow process connection is the connection between two business processes in a business workflow set.

The *Business Workflow Segment* is a segment of the <u>Business Support Tier</u> that contains detail about the flow of business, through business processes, that are performed by organization units.

A *Business workflow set* represents a parent business process and shows the business workflow through the subordinate business processes in that parent business process.

Business world should be avoided, because it is restrictive to the earth. See: *Business environment*.

Cause-effect designation identifies the event-state that is the cause, and the event-state that is the effect.

The *Chronicle Phase* is the third phase of the <u>Business Niche Observation Cycle</u>. Observers document their mental visions of data and processes actualities as a mental model. The Chronicle Phase leads to the <u>Mental Model State</u>.

A *chronology stamp* is a date-time stamp, with a level of accuracy acceptable to an organization, that is placed on architecture data and business data contained in the contemporary architecture any time those data are added, changed, or deleted.

A *citizen* is a person that develops a relationship with a public-sector organization. See also: *Customer*.

Citizen relationship management is the relationship between citizens and public-sector organizations. See: Customer relationship management. See also: *Customer relationship management*.

A *code table* is a data entity that contains a set of coded data values. A code table typically has data attributes for the coded data value, the name of the coded data value, and possibly other data related to the code table, such as a description, begin date, and so on.

A *code table item* is a specific coded data value, or logical record, in a code table. Examples of code table items are *M* for *Male*, *F* for *Female*, and *U* for *Unknown*.

A *combined process* is the combination of two or more elemental processes, or combined processes, to form a larger process. The combination of processes is dependent on the organization's business needs.

A *common need* is a need that when achieved resolves one or more associated common problems. See also: *Basic need, Fundamental need, Specific need*.

A *common problem* is a specific problem that is widespread across many organizations. See also: *Basic problem, Fundamental problem, Specific problem, Symptomatic problem*.

Comparate means fundamentally similar in kind, quality, and character; without defect; concordant; homogeneous; nearly flawless; nearly perfect; high quality, easily understood, and readily integrated to support the organization's activities. See also: *Disparate*.

A *comparate data resource* is composed of comparate data that adequately support the current and future business information demand. The data are easily identified and understood, readily accessed and shared, and utilized to their fullest potential. It is an integrated, subject oriented, business-driven resource that is the official record of reference for the organization's business. See also: *Disparate data resource*.

A *comparate processes resource* is composed of comparate processes that adequately support the current and future business information demand. The processes are easily identified and understood, readily accessed and shared, and utilized to their fullest potential. It's is an integrated, business driven resource that is the official record of reference for the organization's business. See also: *Disparate processes resource*.

Comparity is the noun form of *comparate*. See also: *Disparity*.

Complementarity means many different perspectives of an object are equally valid, and a person must choose one perspective that is valid and meaningful for that person at that point in time. Multiple perspectives define the whole object.

Complex is very intricate. See also: *Overly complex, Simple*.

Complicated refers to the difficulty of understanding, not to degrees of intricacy. See also: *Less complicated, More complicated, Overly complicated*.

ConOps is an acronym for the construction and operation of systems to support business operation. ConOps includes activities to construct a solution according to the design specifications, deploy the solution ready for operation, and operate that solution to support the business.

The *Comprehend Phase* is the second phase of the Business Niche Observation Cycle. Observers gain understanding, add meaning to data and processes possibilities, and identify data and processes actualities that *are of interest* to the organization. Raw data and processes become data-in-context and processes-in-context, and the observer's initial perceptions become mental visions. The Comprehend Phase leads to the Actuality State.

The term *conceptual* is a greatly misused and abused term that has no denotative meaning, and likely never will.

The **Consensus Phase** is the fourth phase of the Business Niche Observation Cycle. Observers integrate the data and processes actualities in multiple mental models and identify preliminary data and processes that *may be relevant* to the organization. The Comprehend Phase leads to the Data Resource Initial State and the Processes Resource Initial State.

Contemporary typically means modern, state of the art, cutting edge, leading edge, innovative, and so on.

A **contemporary architecture** is a proper architecture that contains a thorough understanding about an organization's unique business in a manner that the organization can easily store and retrieve.

The **Contemporary Architecture Objective** is to develop an organization-wide, contemporary architecture that contains a thorough understanding about an organization's business and fully supports its business operation.

The **contemporary architecture symmetry** is the symmetry of the organization's contemporary architecture at a point in space-time. It's a subset of the business niche architecture symmetry that *is relevant* to understanding and operating the organization's business.

The **contemporary business construct** is an overarching construct, composed of contemporary architectures, for an organization to thoroughly understand and successfully operate its business. The construct consists of three tiers for business understanding, business support, and business operation, and is supported by an underlying foundation of theories, concepts, principles, and techniques.

The **contemporary interrogatives** are Which, What, How, Where, When, Who, and Why.

A **contemporary model** is a model of a contemporary architecture, either for building and enhancing that contemporary architecture or for portraying that contemporary architecture.

The **Contemporary Model Objective** is to develop contemporary models that contribute to building and enhancing a contemporary architecture with model-driven architecture techniques, and to portray portions of a contemporary architecture to a recipient with architecture-driven model techniques.

Contemporary model perspective is a perception of a <u>contemporary architecture symmetry</u> represented by a <u>contemporary model</u>, either for enhancing a contemporary architecture or for portraying a contemporary architecture. Each contemporary model perspective is different, depending on the purpose of the model and the intended audience.

The *contemporary model version* is a <u>chronology stamp</u> that indicates the point in time when the contemporary model was prepared to enhance a contemporary architecture, or prepared to portray a contemporary architecture.

Create is generally defined as to cause something to happen; to invent something; to bring something into existence; to invest with a new form; to produce or bring about by a course of action or behavior.

Created entropy is the <u>entropy</u> an organization creates by not using contemporary models or formally developing a contemporary architecture. See also: *Natural entropy*.

Culture has many very broad and lengthy definitions. Sociologists generally define culture as consisting of values, beliefs, languages, communications, and practices that people share and that define them as a group.

A *customer* is a person that develops a relationship with a private sector organization. See also: *Citizen*.

Customer relationship management is the relationship between customers and private sector organizations. See: *Citizen relationship management*.

Data are individual facts, combined facts, or calculated facts that are out of context, have no meaning, and are difficult to understand. The term *data* is plural.

Data and processes architecture understanding is the organization's fourth level of understanding about the data and processes that *are relevant* to the organization.

The *data and processes resource* is a combined data resource and processes resource that is an interdependent, critical resource of the organization. It is the combined record of reference for the organization. It provides an interdependent business understanding resource that is greater than the sum of the separate resources.

Data and processes resource culture is an organizational culture that supports formal data and processes resource management. It includes lexical richness, good hype, substance-driven style, and technology-assisted comparity, as well as other cultural aspects that promote thorough business understanding and successful business operation.

Data and processes resource management is the formal management of all data and processes the organization has available, as a critical resource, based on established theories, concepts, principles, and techniques, leading to a comparate resource that fully supports the current and future business information demand.

Data and processes scoping reduces the scope of data and processes from those that *may be of interest*, to those that *are of interest*, to those that *may be relevant*, to those that *are relevant*, which are incorporated into the organization's data and processes resource.

Data and processes understanding is the organization's fifth level of understanding about the data that populate the data resource architecture and the processes that populate the processes resource architecture to operate the business.

Data architecture is the method of the design and construction of an integrated data resource, within a single organization-wide data architecture, that is business driven, based on business niche components as perceived by the organization, and implemented into appropriate operating environments. It consists of component descriptions, structures and relations, and integrity rules that provide a consistent foundation across organizational boundaries for easily identifiable, readily available, high-quality data that support the current and future business information demand.

A ***data architecture model*** is a model of a data architecture that either represents a portion of an existing data architecture, or represents the development of, or enhancements to, a data architecture.

A ***data attribute*** represents a specific feature – a fact – that describes or characterizes a data entity. Examples of data attributes are Student. Name, Student. Birth Date, Vehicle. Color, and Vehicle. Weight.

A ***data characteristic*** is an individual fact that describes or characterizes a data subject. It represents a business feature and contains a single fact, or closely related facts, about a data subject.

A ***data characteristic variation*** is a variation in the content or format of a data characteristic. It represents a variant of a data characteristic, such as different measurement units, different monetary units, different sequences of a person's name, and so on.

Data denormalization takes data out of their normal form in the single organization-wide data architecture for a special purpose. The normalized form in the single organization-wide data architecture is not altered in any way.

Data-driven means the data drive the organization's business. Many business decisions and actions are based on data values. A comparate data resource provides the quality data for making decisions and taking actions.

A *data entity* is a person, place, thing, event, or concept that is relevant to the organization. Examples of a data entity are Student and Vehicle.

A *data flow* is a data set moving into a business process, an internal data set within a business process, or a data set moving out of a business process.

Data Flow Characteristic Variation identifies a single data characteristic variation contained in a single data flow.

The *Data Flow Segment* is a segment of the Business Support Tier that contains the detail about data flows into, within, and out of business processes.

Data Flow Type identifies whether the data flow is an input to a business process, internal data within a business process, or an output from a business process.

Data in context are data that have meaning and can be readily understood. They are raw data wrapped with meaning.

The *Data–Information–Knowledge Cycle* is a cycle from data, to data in context, to relevant information (specific or general), to knowledge, and back to data when that information or knowledge is stored.

A *data keep* is any location, real or virtual, within or without the organization, where data in any form, electronic or manual, are stored and can be retrieved. Design of the data keep is usually based on the implement data.

Data management is a traditional term representing the management of data, usually not as a critical resource and not formal. See: *Traditional data management*.

Data normalization normalizes data into a single organization-wide data architecture, to achieve and maintain data resource comparity and understanding, with minimum energy.

A *data occurrence* is a logical data record that represents the existence of an object or event.

Data–processes interdependence is the situation in which data are dependent on processes, and processes are dependent on data, but the architecture of one resource does not drive the architecture of the other resource.

A *data property* is a single feature, trait, or quality within a grouping or classification of features, traits, or qualities belonging to a data characteristic.

A *data reference item* is a single set of data values, data names, and data definitions representing a single data property in a data reference set.

A *data reference set* is a set of data items for a general topic, such as gender or education level.

A *data reference set variation* is a variation of a data reference set that has a different domain of data reference items, their coded data values, their names, or substantial difference in the data definitions.

Data resource is the total collection of all data available to the organization, from within or without the organization, however, whenever, and wherever those data are stored and retrieved.

The *Data Resource Business State* represents business data that *are relevant* to the organization. It is intermediate between the Data Resource Realize Phase and the Data Resource Formalize Phase.

Data resource component is any component of the organization's data resource. It can be a single datum or a set of datum.

The *Data Resource Customize Phase* is the third phase of the Data Resource Cycle. Proper data are formally denormalized to implement data, without compromising those proper data, so the operating environment operates efficiently. The Data Resource Customize Phase lads to the Data Resource Implement State.

The *Data Resource Cycle* is a cycle of data resource design, development, and management that begins with an organization's understanding of the business niche where it operates, progresses through formal design and development of a comparate data resource based on that understanding, and to use of the data resource to support the organization's agility and successful operation in their business niche.

Data resource data are any data necessary for thoroughly understanding, formally managing, and fully utilizing the organization's data resource to the support the organization's current and future business information demand. Data resource data include formal data names, denotative data definitions, proper data structures, and precise data integrity rules.

The *Data Resource Formalize Phase* is the second phase of the Data Resource Cycle. Business data are formally normalized to proper data within the single organization-wide data architecture for a common and thorough understanding of the data resource. The Data Resource Realize Phase leads to the <u>Data Resource Proper State</u>.

The **Data Resource Implement State** represents implement data that have been formally denormalized from proper data.

The **Data Resource Initial State** represents the preliminary data that *may be relevant* to the organization. It is intermediate between the <u>Consensus Phase</u> of the Business Niche Observation Cycle and the <u>Data Resource Realize</u> Phase.

Data Resource Laws are laws that guide formal data resource management, and ensure integrity and quality of the organization's data resource.

Data resource management is the formal management of all data at organization's disposal, including both manual and automated data, as a critical resource of the organization, based on established theories, concepts, principles, and techniques, leading to a comparate data resource, that fully supports the organization's current and future business information demand. See also: **Traditional data management**.

The **Data Resource Method** is the formal discipline for managing data as a critical resource of the organization. It's the study of objects, events, rules, relationships, and empirical values in the business niche where an organization operates, within a single organization-wide data architecture, expressed in a variety of different models depending on the scope, audience, and the understanding needed to reduce uncertainty, increase agility, and successfully operate the business. It's the discovery, understanding, and documentation of an organization's internal perception of the external business niche that is pervasive in all disciplines.

The **Data Resource Method Objective** is to get the right data, to the right people, in the right place, at the right time, in the right form, at the right cost, so they can make the right decisions, and take the right actions.

Data resource normalization puts data into a single organization-wide data architecture, to achieve and maintain data resource comparity and understanding, with minimum energy.

The **Data Resource Proper State** represents proper data within the single organization-wide data architecture. It is intermediate between the <u>Data Resource Formalize Phase</u> and the <u>Data Resource Customize Phase</u>.

The **Data Resource Realize Phase** is the first phase of the <u>Data Resource Cycle</u>. <u>Preliminary data</u> that *may be relevant* to the organization are reviewed and business data that *are relevant* to the organization are identified. The Data Resource Realize Phase leads to the <u>Data Resource Business State</u>.

Data Resource Rules are rules that guide formal data resource management, and ensure the integrity and quality of the organization's data resource. They support the Data Resource Laws.

A ***Data Resource Segment*** is a segment of the <u>Business Resource Tier</u> that contains the facts about an organization's business.

The ***Data Resource Utilize Phase*** is the fourth phase of the <u>Data Resource Cycle</u>. <u>Operational data</u> are stored in a data keep, and retrieved to support the organization's business.

A ***data rule*** is a business rule pertaining to the quality and integrity of data in the data resource.

A ***data set*** is a grouping of one or more data characteristic variations.

A ***data subject*** is a person, place, thing, event, or concept that is relevant to the organization. Examples of a data subject are Student and Vehicle.

A ***data value model*** is a model of a set of data values.

Datum is the singular form of data representing one fact.

Datum architecture is meaningless, because an architecture can't represent a single item of data.

Datum in context is an individual <u>datum</u> that has meaning and can be readily understood. It is a raw datum wrapped with meaning.

A **datum model** is meaningless, because a datum is a single data item and can't be modeled.

Datum resource is not a valid term. It would be a resource of only one datum.

A ***decision*** is a conclusion, determination, or resolution reached after consideration; the process of deciding something; the resolution of a question.

Denormalize is taking something out of normal or standard form for a specific purpose.

Detailed means more detail, within the same scope. See also: *Abstract*.

Develop is generally defined as to grow or cause to grow; to become mature, advanced, or elaborate; to come into existence or operation; to bring into being or activity; to grow to a more mature or advanced state.

The ***Discover Phase*** is the first phase of the <u>Business Niche Observation Cycle</u>. Observers observe the business niche and form initial perceptions of raw data and processes possibilities that *may be of interest* to the organization. The Discover Phase leads to the <u>Possibility State</u>.

Disparate means essentially not alike; fundamentally distinct or different in kind, quality, or character; low quality, defective, discordant, ambiguous, and heterogenous; poorly understood, and cannot be readily integrated to support an organization's activities. See also: ***Comparate***.

A ***disparate data resource*** is substantially composed of disparate data that are dis-integrated and not subject-oriented. It is a state of disarray, in which the low quality does not, and cannot, adequately support an organization's business information demand. See also: ***Comparate data resource***.

A ***disparate processes resource*** is substantially composed of disparate processes that that are dis-integrated. It is a state of disarray, in which the low quality does not, and cannot, adequately support an organization's business information demand. See also: ***Comparate processes resource***.

Disparity is the noun form of disparate.

DPR is the abbreviation for *Data and Processes Resource*.

DPRC is the abbreviation for *Data and Processes Resource Culture*.

DPRM is the abbreviation for *Data and Processes Resource Management*.

DRM is the abbreviation for *Data Resource Management*.

Effective is doing the right thing.

Efficient is doing the thing right.

Elegance is the quality of neatness; pleasingly ingenious; dignified propriety; exhibiting refined form or style.

An ***elemental process*** is a set of logic consisting of one or more closely related sets of actions and decisions that can't be further divided and retain any meaning to business professionals. It's the lowest level of detail that business professionals perceive for managing their business.

Emergence is the act of emerging; to become manifest; to come into view; to rise from obscurity.

Endurance is the ability to withstand hardship or adversity; to remain active over a long period of time; to resist adversity.

Energy is generally defined as the capacity for doing work; effort.

An ***enhance model perspective*** is a contemporary model perspective that enhances the contemporary architecture symmetry using model-driven architecture techniques. See also: ***Portray model perspective.***

Entropy is the state or degree of disorderliness. It's a loss of order, which is increasing disorderliness. Entropy steadily increases over time, meaning that things become more disorderly over time.

An ***event*** is a single happening or interaction between two or more objects at a <u>point in space-time</u> or over a <u>span of space-time</u>. An event cannot happen without objects. An event has a unique set of features, and a unique set of features define an event.

An ***Event-state*** can be both a cause – the event – resulting in one or more effects – the states. The resulting state could become an event with a resulting state.

The ***Event-State Segment*** is a segment of the <u>Business Support Tier</u> that identifies events and the states resulting from those events.

Explicit knowledge, also known as *formal knowledge,* is knowledge that has been codified and stored in various media, and is held for mankind. It is readily transferable to other media and capable of being disseminated. See also: ***Tacit knowledge.***

External reality is the reality contained in the business niche that is external to the organization. The business niche state at a point in space-time or over a period of space-time is the external reality. External reality is sometimes referred to as *business niche reality.* See also: ***Internal reality.***

Faith is the belief that the Business Understanding and Agility Paradigm will help an organization evolve to a future environment of comparity, low entropy, and business understanding, agility, and success.

The *familiarity syndrome* is generally defined as the more a person knows about a topic, the less objective that person becomes about that topic.

Fantasy is the belief that something miraculous and fantastical can happen for an organization can understand its business, achieve agile, and become successful in its business endeavor.

Fashion is the current mode of understanding an organizations business and managing its data and processes that lead to disparity, high entropy, limited agility, and limited success.

A *feature* is a fact about an object, event, relationship, or rule.

The ***first interrogative role*** is an ongoing cycle of queries where the interrogatives are asked and answered as needed until a thorough understanding of the organization's business is achieved. See also: ***Second*** *interrogative role, Third interrogative role.*

Form is the Business Understanding Infrastructure. It's the architecture super-symmetry that contains the business understanding. See also: ***Function***.

Formal is relating to or involving the outward form, structure, and relationship of elements; according to established form.

Formal knowledge – See: ***Explicit knowledge***.

Formality is the quality or state of being formal.

Formality-practicality balance is a point in the formality-practicality continuum that is that is optimal for the organization's business.

The ***formality-practicality continuum*** is a range from total formality without practicality, to total practicality without formality.

A ***framework*** is a graphical representation of a topic that helps people understand that topic.

Framework cells form the matrix of the <u>Business Understanding Framework</u>. Each framework cell is qualified by business activity, framework interrogative, and specification level.

Framework Interrogatives are the six associate contemporary interrogatives that qualify a Framework Cell: What, How, Where, When, Why, and Who.

Function is business operation according to that Business Understanding Infrastructure. It's implementation of the architecture super-symmetry to operate the business. See also: ***Form***.

A ***fundamental need*** is a need that when achieved resolves one or more fundamental problems. See also: ***Basic need, Common need, Specific Need***.

A ***fundamental problem*** is a major problem that is the origination or generation of one or more basic problems. It's the root cause of basic problems. See also: ***Basic problem, Common problem, Specific problem, Symptomatic problem***.

General means a broader scope. See also: *Specific*.

General information is a set of data in context that *could be* relevant to one or more people at a point in time or for a period of time.

Generic means relating to, or characteristic of, a whole group or class; being or having a nonproprietary name. Synonyms for *generic* are *broad, common, universal, basic,* and *widespread.*

A *generic architecture* is an architecture that is intended to have widespread use across many different public and private sector organizations for quickly developing an architecture. See also: *Unique architecture*.

Good hype is hype that supports formality to achieve the results intended by the promoter. It does not compromise formality for quick results. It recognizes future needs as well as current needs. Good hype is supported by lexical richness and supports substance-driven style. See also: *Bad hype*, *Hype*.

A *hallucination* is a perception of something not in the business niche. It's something that does not exist in business niche, but was perceived by the observer.

Hidden disparity is the disparity in data and processes that is not readily visible or obvious to the organization. See also: *Visible disparity*.

The *How Dilemma* is an uncertainty about whether How on a traditional business framework represents only processes related to the data What, or all processes for an organization. See also: *Topic Dilemma*, *What Dilemma*.

Hype is to promote or publicize extravagantly, to put on or to deceive, to inspire people for or against some purpose. Hype is driven by personal and organizational agendas, which can be good or bad, depending on a person's perspective. Hype seldom provides comprehensive definitions that provide any thorough understanding of the purpose. See also: *Bad hype*, *Good hype*.

An *illusion* is an incorrect perception about something in business niche. It's something that exists in business niche, but was incorrectly perceived by the observer.

Implement data are proper data that have been formally denormalized for optimum operational performance, without compromising the proper data. They are the design for a data keep.

Implementation replaces the term *physical* for managing data and processes.

Implicit knowledge – See: *Tacit knowledge*.

Impractical is not practical; incapable of dealing sensibly or prudently with practical matters.

Improper means not proper; not in accord with fact, truth, or right procedure; incomplete or incorrect; not suited to the circumstances, design, or end.

Informal is the lack of formality.

Information is a set of data in context, with relevance to one or more people at a point in time or for a period of time. Information is more than data in context – it must have relevance and a time frame.

Information management is coordinating the need for information across the organization to ensure adequate support for the current and future business information demand. It should not be confused with data resource management that provides the raw material to produce information.

Information resource is not a valid term, because the timeliness and relevance of an individual or group of individuals cannot be managed as a resource.

Information resource management is not a valid term, because the timeliness and relevance of an individual or group of individuals cannot be managed as a resource.

Information technology is generally defined as the study or use of systems, especially computers and telecommunications, for storing, retrieving, and sending information; the use of any computers, storage, networking, or other physical devises, infrastructure, and processes to create, process, store, secure, and exchange all forms of electronic data, typically for enterprise operations.

Infrastructure is the resources required for an activity; the underlying foundation or basic construct of something; the organizational structure needed for some activity.

Intelligence is broadly defined as the ability to acquire and apply knowledge and skills; the ability to accomplish complex goals; the ability to learn or understand, or to deal with new or trying situations; the skilled use of reason; the ability to apply knowledge to manipulate one's environment, or to think abstractly as measured by objective criteria; the capability for learning, reasoning, understanding, and similar forms of mental activity; the aptitude for grasping truths, relationships, facts, meanings, and so on.

Internal reality is the reality an organization has about its business that is internal to the organization. The internal reality is contained in the organization's combined data and processes resource. Internal reality is sometimes referred to as *organization reality*. See also: ***External reality***.

An ***interrogative*** is a word used to pose a question or a hypothesis, and seek an answer to the question, or a confirmation or refutation of the hypothesis.

The ***interrogative dimension*** of the Business Understanding Framework represents the six contemporary associate interrogatives for understanding the organization's business.

Invariance means an object appears different when the perspective changes. The features of the object are common to all perspectives and are valid from all perspectives.

Knowledge is cognizance, cognition, the fact or condition of knowing something with familiarity gained through experience or association. It is information that has been retained with an understanding about the significance of that information.

Knowledge-objectivity reciprocity is the reciprocal relationship between knowledge and objectivity. When knowledge goes up, objectivity goes down, and when knowledge goes down, objectivity goes up.

Knowledge management is the management of an environment that encourages people to generate tacit knowledge, render it into explicit knowledge, and feed it back to the organization.

A ***law*** is a binding custom or practice, a rule of conduct or action prescribed or commonly recognized as formally binding or enforced.

Less complicated means less difficult to understand. See also: *Complicated, More complicated, Overly complicated.*

The ***lexical challenge*** is the creation of words and terms, often with no definitions, minimal definitions, unclear definitions, incorrect definitions, multiple definitions, and conflicting definitions; which have a non-denotative meaning, with many connotative meanings that fit a wide variety of situations; are often used interchangeably and inappropriately; often create confusing synonyms and homonyms; are misused, abused, and corrupted; and are defined and redefined to the point they are worn out and meaningless, then are discarded without regard for their real meaning or impact on an organization's activities. New words and terms are created, and the cycle continues. See also: ***Lexical richness.***

Lexical richness is the creation of words and terms, with comprehensive, denotative definitions that have no connotative meanings; that are complete, clear, correct, meaningful, and consistently used; and are persistent over time. See also: ***Lexical challenge.***

Logical is no longer used for managing data and processes. *Business* is used to replace *logical.*

Loss of architecture symmetry is a loss of proper architecture symmetry that has been achieved by failing to rigorously maintain that proper architecture symmetry.

Maintain is generally defined as to cause or enable to continue; to keep in existence; to keep in good condition and working order; to preserve from failure or decline; to sustain against opposition or danger.

A *manifestation* is the act, process, or instance of making evident or certain by showing or displaying.

A *manual process* is a process performed manually by people, such as employees of an organization, or citizens or customers of the organization.

Mathematics is the science of numbers and their operations, interrelations, combinations, generalizations, abstractions, configurations, and so on. It includes mathematical structures, empirical domains, and any correspondence linking those structures and domains. The correspondence is relationships and rules.

Maturity is the state of being mature; being fully developed; having reached the most advanced stage of development.

May be of interest means the initial identification of components in the organization's business niche contain data and processes that could possibly be of interest to the organization. See also: *Are of interest, Are relevant, May be relevant.*

May be relevant means that data and processes identified in the organization's business niche could possibly be relevant to the organization's business operation. See also: *Are of interest, Are relevant, May be of interest.*

A *mental model* is the documentation of an observer's mental vision that evolves during the <u>Comprehend Phase</u> of the <u>Business Niche Observation Cycle</u>. It clarifies the observer's understanding, and uncertainty, about the data and processes identified during observation.

The *Mental Model State* represents the documented mental visions of data and processes actualities as a mental model. It is intermediate between the <u>Chronicle Phase</u> and the <u>Consensus Phase</u> of the <u>Business Niche Observation Cycle</u>.

A *mental vision* is a set of refined initial perceptions of data-in-context and processes-in-context based on additional understanding gained by the observer.

Method is a procedure or process for attaining a goal; a way, technique, or process for doing something; a body of skills or techniques; a discipline that deals with principles and techniques.

Methodology is derived from *methodo* and *ology* meaning 'method study' or the 'study of methods.'

A *model* is a set of plans, a structural design, a miniature representation or manifestation of something, or a pattern of something to be made.

Model-driven architectures is a technique that develops contemporary models from an analysis of business needs and uses those models to build or enhance contemporary architectures. See also: *Architecture-driven models*.

The *Model-Driven Architecture Objective* is to develop and enhance contemporary architectures, for the entire scope of the organization's business, from multiple contributing contemporary models, that include all the detail necessary to thoroughly understand and successfully operate the organization's business.

A *model perspective* is a model of perspective of an architecture symmetry.

A *model super-perspective* is a model of a super-perspective.

Model reengineering is the process of taking a model prepared using one format and set of notations and converting it to a model with another format and set of notations.

More complicated means more difficult to understand. See also: Complicated, Less complicated, Overly complicated.

Natural entropy is the entropy the occurs naturally as the business environment, business niche, and organization continually evolve over time. See also: *Created entropy*.

A *need* is something requisite, desirable, or useful; something wanted or necessary for well-being of the business. When achieved, it will resolve one or more associated problems.

NeedSpec is an acronym for identifying business needs and designing the specifications to meet those business needs. It includes activities to observe the business niche, identify business needs, and design specifications to support those business needs.

A *negative feedback loop* gains control. See also: *Positive feedback loop*.

Non-business architecture is any architecture about the non-business realm.

Non-business data are any data used, created, or managed by non-business processes.

A *non-business model* is a model of any architecture in the non-business realm. See also: *Business model*.

Non-business processes are any processes in the non-business realm.

The *non-business realm* is the sphere or extent of activities which organizations cannot manage. It includes physical, chemical, biological, and radiological activities, and the combinations of those activities, over which an organization has no control. See also: ***Business Realm.***

Non-information is a set of data in context that is not relevant or timely to the recipient. It is often called out-formation, because it is out of relevance and the time frame for a recipient.

Normalize is to put something into a normal or standard form for an intended purpose.

An ***object*** is a person, place, thing, or concept.

An *objective* is something toward which effort is directed; an aim or end of an action; a goal.

Objectivity is generally defined as the quality or character of being objective; lack of favoritism; freedom from bias; judgement based on observable phenomena and uninfluenced by emotions or persona prejudices; the capacity to assess situations or circumstances and draw sound conclusions.

Observation is the act of observing; an act of recognizing and noting a fact or occurrence; a judgement on or influence from what one has observed.

An ***observation moment*** is the point in space-time, or the span of space-time, that an observer is observing the business niche and forming perceptions about that business niche. It's a snapshot of the business niche state by an observer based on their observer state.

Observation scoping identifies the segment of the organization's business niche that will be observed during an observation or set of observations. It designates the segment of the business niche that is of interest to the organization for an observation or a set of observations.

Observe is to inspect or take note; to watch carefully, especially with attention to details or behavior; to come to realize or know; to take notice.

Observer reality is the perceptions gained by an observer during business niche observation that are intermediate between the external reality in the business niche and the internal reality of the organization.

The ***observer state*** is the total makeup of the observer during the observation moment. It includes the observer's perspective, the observer's experience, the observer's physical and mental state, and all aspects of the observer during the observation moment.

Occam's razor states that the simplest theory is likely to be the correct theory, and the more complex theory is likely to be falsifiable. The simplest actuality is likely to be the correct actuality, and the more complex actuality is likely to be falsifiable.

An *omission* is a non-perception of something in the business niche. It's something that exists in business niche, but was not perceived by the observer.

The *Operate Business Function* is oriented toward successfully operating the organization's agile business during the Business Niche Operate Phase.

Operational data provide an understanding of the organization's business that supports day-to-day business operations and operational decision making. They are the contents of a data keep according to the implement data.

Operational processes are proper processes that have been formally denormalized for optimum operational performance, without compromising the proper processes. They provide an understanding of the organization's business that supports day-to-day business operations.

Organization includes any public sector, quasi-public sector, or private sector group, conducting some form of activity, whether for profit or not for profit, regardless of size, for however long it has operated or intends to operate.

Organization reality. See also: *Internal reality*.

Organization unit involvement is any involvement of an organization in an Event-State.

Organization unit involvement type is how or why an organization unit is involved in an event-state, such as Responsibility, Investigation, Interest, and so on.

Organizational knowledge is information that is of significance to the organization, is combined with experience and understanding, and is retained. It is information in context with respect to understanding that is meaningful to the business.

Overly complicated refers to something that is more difficult to understand than necessary. See also: *Complicated, Less complicated, More complicated.*

Overly complex is more intricate than necessary for understanding. See also: *Complex.*

Overly simple is less intricate than necessary for understanding. See also: *Simple.*

An *organization unit* is a set of related responsibilities and reporting relationships in an organization. Organization units form a hierarchy from the entire organization to the most detailed level an organization wants to document.

Organization unit involvement is the involvement of an organization in an Event-State.

Organization unit involvement type is how or why an organization unit is involved in an event-state, such as Responsibility, Investigation, Interest, and so on.

Paralysis-by-analysis is an on-going, ad nauseum, over-analysis of business data and processes, that unnecessarily delays development and implementation of the data and/or processes needed to support the business.

A *perception* is a mental image; an awareness of elements gained through sensations; an interpretation in light of experience; it's intuitive, and involves cognition and comprehension.

Persistence is a firm course of action; the ability to stay the course; continuing to exist or endure over a prolonged period in spite of opposition, obstacles, or discouragement.

Perspective is a specific perception of an object. When an object is perceived from different directions, it may appear different. The perspective of the object is different, but the symmetry of the object is the same. All perspectives are correct, even though each perspective is different.

Physical is no longer used for managing data and processes. *Implementation* is used to replace *physical*.

Plausible means it's probable, reasonable, valuable, credible, believable, and worthy of approval and acceptance.

A *point in space-time* is a single location in space and a single point in time. See also: *Space-time*, *Span of space time*.

A *portray model perspective* is a contemporary model perspective that portrays the contemporary architecture symmetry using architecture-driven model techniques. See: Enhance model perspective. See also: *Enhance model perspective*.

A *positive feedback loop* loses control. See also: *Negative feedback loop*.

The *Possibility State* represents raw the data and processes possibilities that *may be of interest* to the organization. It is intermediate between the Discover Phase and the Comprehend Phase of the Business Niche Observation Cycle.

Practical is of, relating to, or manifested in practice or action; capable of being put to good use.

Preliminary data are any data the organization identifies during observation of its business niche that *may be relevant* to the organization's business.

Preliminary data and processes understanding is the organization's third level of understanding about the preliminary data and processes that *may be relevant* to the organization.

Preliminary processes are any processes the organization identifies during observation of its business niche that *may be relevant* to the organization's business.

The ***primary contemporary interrogative*** is the interrogative Which that identifies the business activity and sets the scope for achieving a thorough understanding.

PRM is the abbreviation for *Processes Resource Management*.

A ***problem*** is a source of perplexity, distress, or vexation; a difficult situation disrupting or impacting the organization's business.

A ***process*** is a specific grouping of one or more sets of actions and decisions defining the logic that responds to an event. Conversely, a specific grouping of one or more sets of actions and decisions uniquely defines a process. Two or more processes cannot have the same specific grouping of sets of actions and decisions.

A ***process action set*** is a grouping of closely related actions representing the flow of process logic without a decision. It may end with a decision, or with termination of a process.

Process architecture is the architecture of a single process.

A ***process decision*** is a decision that results in a branch in the logic. Each decision follows the form of *When (condition) Then (action set).*

Process in context is an individual process that has meaning and can be readily understood. A raw process wrapped with meaning.

Process logic is the combination of process action sets and process decisions in a process, including comments, with the possible routes through those action sets and decisions.

Process management is the management of a single business process the organization uses to support its business activities.

A ***process model*** is a model of a single process.

Process resource is not a valid term. It would be a resource of only one process.

Processes is the plural form of process.

Processes architecture is the method of design and construction of an integrated processes resource, within a single organization-wide processes architecture, that is business driven, based on business niche components as perceived by the organization, and implemented into appropriate operating environments. It consists of component descriptions, structures and relations, and integrity rules that provide a consistent foundation across organizational boundaries, for easily identifiable, readily available, high-quality processes that support the current and future business operations.

A *processes architecture model* is a model of the processes architecture. that either represents a portion of an existing processes architecture, or represents the development of, or enhancements to, a processes architecture.

Processes denormalization takes processes out of their normal form in the single organization-wide processes architecture for a special purpose. The normalized form in the single organization wide processes architecture is not altered in any way.

Processes disparity is the disparity across all the processes that an organization uses to manage its business activities.

Processes-driven means processes drive the organization's business. A process makes decisions and takes actions, which often trigger other processes. A comparate processes resource provides the quality decisions and actions.

Processes in context are processes that have meaning and can be readily understood. They are raw processes wrapped with meaning.

The *processes keep* is any location, real or virtual, within or without the organization, where operational processes in any form, electronic or manual, are stored and can be retrieved.

Processes management is a traditional term representing the management of processes, usually not as a critical resource and not formal. See also: *Processes resource management, Traditional processes management*.

Processes normalization normalizes processes into a single organization-wide processes architecture, to achieve and maintain processes resource comparity and understanding, with minimum energy.

Processes resource is the total collection of all processes available to the organization, from within or without the organization, however, whenever, and wherever those processes are stored and retrieved.

The *Processes Resource Business State* represents business processes that *are relevant* to the organization. It is intermediate between the ~~Processes Resource Realize Phase~~ and the <u>Processes Resource Formalize Phase</u>.

Processes resource component is any component of the organization's processes resource. It can be anywhere in the structure of business processes.

The *Processes Resource Customize Phase* is the third phase of the <u>Processes Resource Cycle</u>. Proper processes are formally denormalized to implement processes, without compromising those proper processes, so the operating environment operates efficiently. The Processes Resource Customize Phase lads to the <u>Processes Resource Implement State</u>.

The *Processes Resource Cycle* is a cycle of processes resource design, development, and management that begins with an organization's understanding of the business niche where it operates, progresses through formal design and development of a processes resource based on that understanding, to use of the processes resource to support the organization's agility and successful operation in their business niche.

Processes resource data are any data necessary for thoroughly understanding, formally managing, and fully utilizing the organization's processes to fully support the organization's current and future business information demand.

The *Processes Resource Formalize Phase* is the second phase of the <u>Processes Resource Cycle</u>. Business Processes are formally normalized to proper processes within the single organization-wide processes architecture for a common and thorough understanding of the processes resource. The Processes Resource Realize Phase leads to the <u>Processes Resource Proper State</u>.

The *Processes Resource Implement State* represents implement processes that have been formally denormalized from proper processes.

The *Processes Resource Initial State* represents the preliminary processes that *may be relevant* to the organization. It is intermediate between the <u>Consensus Phase</u> of the <u>Business Niche Observation Cycle</u> and the <u>Processes Resource Realize Phase</u>.

Processes Resource Laws are laws that guide formal processes resource management, and ensure integrity and quality of the organization's processes resource.

Processes resource management is the formal management of all processes at the organization's disposal, including both manual and automated processes, as a critical resource of the organization, based on established theories, concepts, principles, and techniques, leading to a comparate processes resource that fully supports the organization's current and future business information demand. See also: *Traditional processes management*.

The *Processes Resource Method* is the formal discipline for managing processes as a critical resource of the organization. It's the study of the objects, events, rules, relationships, and processes in the business niche where an organization operates, within a single organization-wide processes architecture, expressed in a variety of different models, depending on the scope, audience, and understanding needed to reduce uncertainty, and successfully operate the business. It's the discovery, understanding, and documentation of an organization's internal perception of the external business niche that is pervasive in all disciplines.

The *Processes Resource Method Objective* is the right processes, used by the right people, in the right place, at the right time, in the right form, at the right cost, so they can make the right decisions, and take the right actions.

Processes resource normalization puts processes into a single organization-wide processes architecture, to achieve and maintain processes resource comparity and understanding, with minimum energy.

The *Processes Resource Proper State* represents proper processes within the single organization-wide processes architecture. It is intermediate between the Processes Resource Formalize Phase and the Processes Resource Customize Phase.

The *Processes Resource Realize Phase* is the first phase of the Processes Resource Cycle. Preliminary processes that *may be relevant* to the organization are reviewed and business processes that *are relevant* to the organization are identified. The Processes Resource Realize Phase leads to the Processes Resource Business State.

Processes resource rules are rules that guide formal processes resource management, and ensure the integrity and quality of the organization's processes resource. They support the Processes Resource Laws.

The *Processes Resource Segment* is a segment of the Business Resource Tier that contains the sets of actions and decisions for operating the organization's business.

The *Processes Resource Utilize Phase* is the fourth phase of the Processes Resource Cycle. Operational Processes are retrieved from the processes keep and initiated to support the organization's business.

A *processes rule* is a business rule pertaining to the quality and integrity of processes in the processes resource.

A *Production Business Understanding Workflow* is a Specific Business Understanding Workflow that has been adapted for production operation of a business activity. It follows the Specific Business Understanding Workflow, but is unique to production operation.

A *Project Business Understanding Workflow* is a Specific Business Understanding Workflow for building or maintaining a business activity, that has been adapted to a specific project. It follows the Specific Business Understanding Workflow formality, but is unique to a project.

Proper means marked by suitability, rightness, or appropriateness; in a thorough manner; complete and correct; organized, coordinated, and appropriate.

Proper architecture is an architecture that is complete, correct, organized, coordinated, and appropriate for fully supporting the organization's business. It minimizes disparity, maximizes understanding, and promotes comparity. It's the result of the formal development of organization-wide architectures.

Proper architecture symmetry is the existence of a contemporary architecture, consisting of comparate, single, organization-wide data and processes architectures that result in increased understanding and decreased uncertainty about the organization's business.

Proper data are business data that have been formally normalized within the single organization-wide data architecture.

A *proper model* is a model that is complete, correct, organized, coordinated, and appropriate for developing or enhancing a proper architecture, or for portraying a portion of a proper architecture.

Proper model perspective is the consistent use of contemporary models to build and enhance the organization's proper architecture symmetry, and to portray perspectives of a proper architecture symmetry. It avoids the use of traditional models and brute-force approaches to build and maintain a contemporary architecture, and to portray a contemporary architecture.

Proper processes are business processes that have been formally normalized within the single organization-wide processes architecture.

The *prospective query mode* is the use of queries before the fact to understand and plan what should happen in response to an input from an event.

Quality is the degree of excellence; fit for a purpose; meets a high standard.

Quality of form is how well the Business Understanding Infrastructure represents the organization understanding of its business niche.

Quality of function is how well the organization follows the Business Understanding Infrastructure to operate the business.

Raw data are data that are out of context, have no meaning, and are difficult

317

to understand.

Raw datum is an individual datum that is out of context, has no meaning, and is difficult to understand.

Raw process is a process that is out of context, has no meaning, and is difficult to understand.

Raw processes are processes that are out of context, have no meaning, and are difficult to understand.

A ***relationship*** is an association, connection, bond, or tie between objects, between objects and events, between events, between features and the components they define, and between rules and the components they qualify.

Relativity means the same object can be represented in many different ways without loss of meaning.

Relevant means it's appropriate for the current situation, and has significant and demonstrable benefits.

Resistance to change is generally defined as the situation in which the more a person knows about a topic, and the more a person has been involved with a topic, the less likely that person is to accept change related to that topic.

A *response* is generally defined as the act of responding; a reply or action; an activity; an answer; or an act. A response is more specifically defined for the organization's business.

A ***response*** is the act of responding; a reply, answer, action, reaction, or other act triggered by an input. It's an event responding to a trigger. A response cannot begin without an input, meaning it cannot self-start.

The ***retrospective query mode*** is the use of queries after the fact to investigate what actually happened during an event.

A ***rule*** is an authoritative, prescribed direction for conduct, or a usual, customary, or generalized course of action or behavior; a statement that describes what is true in most or all cases; a standard method or procedure for solving problems.

The ***second interrogative role*** is identifying specific data and processes needed to support an organization's business activities in its business niche, including detailed description, structure, and integrity. See also: ***First interrogative role***, ***Third interrogative role***.

The ***self-fulfilling prophecy*** states that a preconceived perception will become the verified perception, which may not be true.

Simple is less intricate. See also: *Overly Simple*, *Complex*.

Simplicity is easy to understand or do; uncomplicated.

Single organization-wide architecture is a formally developed proper architecture, spanning the entire organization, which includes all related components, either data components or processes components, available to the organization, from within or without, in any form, that the organization needs to conduct business.

The **single organization-wide data architecture** is one, formally developed, proper data architecture, spanning the entire organization, which includes all data available to an organization, from within or without, in any form, that the organization needs to conduct business.

The **single organization-wide processes architecture** is one, formally developed, proper processes architecture, spanning the entire organization, which includes all processes available to the organization, from within or without, in any form, that the organization needs to conduct business.

Space-time is combined location and time. Location is useless without time, and time is useless without location. Space-time must include both location and time.

A **span of space-time** is either an area of space at a point in time, a period of time at a point in space, or both an area of space and a period of time. See also: **Point in space time**, **Space time**.

Specific means a narrower scope. See also: *General*.

A **Specific Business Understanding Workflow** is a <u>Business Understanding Workflow</u>, developed by an organization, based on how that organization desires to thoroughly understand and successfully operate its business. It's follows the Business Understanding Workflow formality, but is specific to a particular organization.

Specific information is a set of data in context that *is* relevant to one or more people at a point in time or for a period of time.

A **specific need** is a need that when achieved resolves one or more specific problems. See also: **Basic need**, **Common need**, **Fundamental need**

A **specific problem** is a situation identified within an organization resulting in one or more symptomatic problems that impact the organization's business. It's an indication of a deeper basic problem. Resolving a specific problem only allows other specific problems to surface. See also: **Basic problem**, **Common problem**, **Fundamental problem**, **Symptomatic problem**.

319

Specification Level is the level of detail for the <u>Business Understanding Framework</u> from abstract to detailed that qualifies each <u>Framework Cell</u>.

The *specification level dimension* of the <u>Business Understanding Framework</u> represents the levels of specification detail from the highest abstraction to the most detailed specification.

State is the condition or stage of physical being characterized by definite properties or features.

The *State Transition Segment* is a segment of the <u>Business Support Tier</u> that contains the detail about the state transitions for business entities.

State transition set is a set of related state transitions for a business entity during that business entity's life cycle.

Style is the manner of accomplishment, the way that something is performed or accomplished; the action, method, or technique to accomplish an end result.

Style-driven substance is a traditional management situation, characterized by a lexical challenge, bad hype, and technology-driven disparity, leading to a disparate data resource and a disparate processes resource that are poorly understood and fail to fully support an organization's activities.

Substance is the end result; the product; the essence of some action, method, or technique.

A *subject area* is a portion of the organization's contemporary architecture that represents an area of interest to the organization. It may represent the five critical resources, business activities, or other areas of interest to the organization. Subject areas could be numerous and may overlap.

Substance-driven style is a formal management situation, characterized by lexical richness, good hype, and technology-assisted comparity, leading to a comparate data resource and comparate processes resource that are thoroughly understood and fully support an organization's activities.

A *super-perspective* is a perspective across multiple architectures symmetries in an <u>architecture super-symmetry</u>.

Super-symmetry is the symmetry across multiple objects in a set of related objects, including relationships within and between the individual symmetries of those objects.

Symmetry is the shape, form, and makeup of an object, such as a cube, sphere, or blob.

A *symptom* is subjective evidence of a disturbance or disorder; something that indicates the existence of something else.

A *symptomatic problem* is a symptom or manifestation of a deeper problem, at a point in time or over a period of time, and may be persistent or sporadic. Resolving a symptomatic problem only allows other symptomatic problems to surface. See also: *Basic problem*, *Common problem*, *Fundamental problem*, *Specific problem*.

Tacit knowledge, also known as *implicit knowledge*, is the knowledge that a person retains in their mind. It's relatively hard to transfer to others and to disseminate widely. See also: *Explicit knowledge*.

TDM is the abbreviation for *Traditional Data Management*.

Technology is widely defined as the application of scientific knowledge for practical purposes; machinery and equipment developed from the application of scientific knowledge; the knowledge of techniques and processes embedded in machines; the branch of knowledge dealing with the creation and use of technical means; the study and transformation of techniques, tools, and machines created by humans; the branch of knowledge dealing with engineering or applied sciences; the sum of techniques, skills, methods, and processes for the production of goods and services, or in accomplishing objectives.

Technology-assisted comparity is the use of technology to assist the formal development of comparate data and processes resources, rather than drive the development of disparate data and disparate processes resources. It's a major feature of substance-driven style that directly supports the cognitive processes of data and processes resource management. See also: *Technology-driven disparity*.

Technology-driven disparity is the use of technology to drive the development of disparate data or disparate processes without any regard for formal theories, concepts, principles, or techniques, or any formal data resource or processes resource development. It usually considers current needs without any consideration for future needs. See also: *Technology-assisted comparity*.

Testing is broadly defined as the action or process of checking someone or something; inquiring into something thoroughly and systematically; the means by which the presence, quality, or genuineness of something is determined; the procedure leading to proof or disproof, or to acceptance or rejection; the actual testing of a product to meet quality control standards; stress testing a product to see if the actual results match the expected results; a process to evaluate the functionality of a product with an intent to find whether the product met the specified requirements or not, and to identify the defects to ensure that the product is defect-free; quality assurance.

The ***third interrogative role*** is the primary contemporary interrogative identifying business activities, and the associate contemporary interrogatives identifying columns in the Business Understanding Framework. See also: ***First interrogative role***, ***Second interrogative role***.

The ***Topic Dilemma*** is an uncertainty about how both data and processes are understood in a traditional business framework. See also: ***How Dilemma***, ***What Dilemma***,

Thorough means detailed, exhaustive, meticulous, comprehensive, and complete.

TPM is the abbreviation for *traditional processes management*.

Traditional typically means an established or customary pattern of thought, action, or behavior.

A ***traditional associate interrogative*** is any of the other five traditional interrogatives–How, Where, When, Who, and Why—that support or clarify the traditional primary interrogative.

Traditional data management is the way data are typically managed in most organizations today. It is seldom based on established theories, concepts, principles, and techniques, and leads to a disparate data resource that does not support the organization's current or future business information demand. See also: ***Data resource management***.

The ***traditional interrogatives*** are What, How, Where, When, Who, and Why.

The ***traditional primary interrogative*** is What that sets the focus or scope for achieving understanding.

Traditional processes management is the way processes are typically managed in most organizations today. It is seldom based on established theories, concepts, principles, and techniques, and leads to a disparate processes resource that does not support the organization's current or future business information demand. See also: ***Processes resource management***.

A *trigger* is generally defined as a stimulus to initiate a process; to initiate, actuate, or set off a process. A trigger is more specifically defined for the organization's business.

A ***trigger*** is the arrival of a stimulus to initiate, actuate, or set off a process. It's the arrival of an input, in any form, that initiates or could initiate a response to handle that input.

Trinity is the state of being threefold; a group of three closely related persons or things. See also: ***Architecture trinity***.

Uncertain is indefinite; indeterminate; not certain to occur; not reliable; not known beyond doubt; not having certain knowledge; not clearly identified or defined; not constant.

Uncertainty is the quality or state of being uncertain; something that is uncertain.

Understand is to grasp the reasonableness of something; to grasp the meaning of; to have thorough or technical acquaintance with or expertness in the practice of; to be thoroughly familiar with the character and propensities of to accept as fact or truth or regard as plausible, to interpret in one of a number of possible ways; to achieve a grasp of the nature, significance, or explanation of something; to believe or infer something to be the case.

The *Understand Business Function* is oriented toward thoroughly understanding the organization's business during the Business Niche Understand Phase.

Understanding is a mental grasp; comprehension; the power of comprehending; the capacity to apprehend general relations of particulars; the power to make experience intelligible by applying concepts and categories.

Understanding-uncertainty reciprocity is the reciprocal relation between understanding and uncertainty. As understanding goes up, uncertainty goes down, and as understanding goes down, uncertainty goes up.

A *unique architecture* is an architecture that an organization develops based on its understanding of the business niche where it operates, and how it chooses to do business in that business niche. See also: *Generic architecture*.

Visible disparity is the disparity in data and processes that is readily visible and obvious to the organization. See also: *Hidden disparity*.

The *What Dilemma* is an uncertainty about whether What on a traditional business framework represents data or processes. See also: *How Dilemma*, *Topic Dilemma*.

BIBLIOGRAPHY

Brackett, Michael H. *Developing Data Structured Information Systems.* Topeka, KS: Ken Orr and Associates, Inc., 1983.

_____. *Developing Data Structured Databases.* Englewood Cliffs, NJ: Prentice Hall, 1987.

_____. *Practical Data Design.* Englewood Cliffs, NJ: Prentice Hall, 1990.

_____. *Data Sharing Using a Common Data Architecture.* New York: John Wiley & Sons, Inc., 1994.

_____. *The Data Warehouse Challenge: Taming Data Chaos.* New York: John Wiley & Sons, Inc., 1996.

_____. *Data Resource Quality: Turning Bad Habits Into Good Practices.* New York: Addison-Wesley, 2000.

Data Resource Simplexity Series:
Brackett, Michael. *Data Resource Simplexity: How Organizations Choose Data Resource Success or Failure.* New Jersey: Technics Publications, LLC, 2011.

_____. *Data Resource Integration: Understanding and Resolving a Disparate Data Resource.* New Jersey: Technics Publications, LLC, 2012.

_____. *Data Resource Design: Reality Beyond Illusion.* New Jersey: Technics Publications, LLC, 2012.

_____. *Data Resource Data: A Comprehensive Data Resource Understanding.* New Jersey: Technics Publications, LLC, 2014.

_____. *Data Resource Understanding: Utilizing the Data Resource.* New Jersey: Technics Publications, LLC, 2015.

_____. *Data Resource Guide: Managing the Data Resource.* New Jersey: Technics Publications, LLC, 2016.

Speculative Business Fiction Series:
Brackett, Michael. *The Datamatic Cycle: A Novel.* South Carolina: CreateSpace Independent Publishing Platform, 2016.

_____. *The Processmatic Cycle: A Perspective.* South Carolina: CreateSpace Independent Publishing Platform, 2017.

_____. *The Businessmatic Architecture: A Unified Symmetry.* South Carolina: CreateSpace Independent Publishing Platform, 2018.

INDEX